Media Policy and Globalization

Media Policy and Globalization

Paula Chakravartty and Katharine Sarikakis

RAWAT PUBLICATIONS
Jaipur • New Delhi • Bangalore • Mumbai • Hyderabad • Guwahati

ISBN 81-316-0099-8

Indian Reprint, 2007

This edition published by arrangement with
Edinburgh University Press Ltd
22 George Square, Edinburgh.

For sale in South Asia (India, Nepal, Sri Lanka, Maldives, Pakistan, Bhutan, Bangladesh) only.

Published by
Prem Rawat for **Rawat Publications**
Satyam Apts., Sector 3, Jawahar Nagar, Jaipur - 302 004 (India)
Phone: 0141 265 1748 / 7006 Fax: 0141 265 1748
E-mail : info@rawatbooks.com
Website: rawatbooks.com

New Delhi Office
4858/24, Ansari Road, Daryaganj, New Delhi 110 002
Phone: 011-23263290

Also at Bangalore, Mumbai, Hyderabad and Guwahati

Printed at Chaman Enterprises, New Delhi

Contents

Tables and figures

Tables

Figures

Preface

As you set out for Ithaca
hope your road is a long one,
full of adventure, full of discovery.
(K. Kavafis 1911)

From the conception to its publication, this book has been a rich, enjoyable and, at times, frustrating transnational journey where we both learned a great deal, not only about our subject matter but also about ourselves. The road was longer than we anticipated, but only because life is unstoppable and all present: the book apart from the standard daily routines of leading full academic lives, the winter flues included, witnessed a research leave and multiple stays abroad, four house moves, the birth of a baby girl (Aisha), two job moves and a wedding, and throughout these life experiences our families and friends made the process more enjoyable. Our journey to this 'Ithaca' has made us richer in knowledge and friendship, collegiality and confidence.

This book explores the conditions and ideas behind global communications policies; our writing travels back and forth, across continents and socioeconomic realities to identify and analyze common policy concerns, conflicting interests, and the place and voice of publics. Throughout the writing process, we relied heavily on electronic communications to update information, track down electronic archives and conduct basic literature searches. We conceived and discussed the ideas in this book first online and then by telephone and continued developing the book in the same way, with only one brief off-line meeting. We have used six different computers between us (two of which crashed) and have been dependent on Internet access with speedy connections (broadband). These tools were available to us as researchers based in academic institutions, in our homes and hotels and Internet cafes located in the connected parts of the world where we wrote this book – Amherst, Athens, Coventry, Kolkata, London, Montreal, Pittsburgh and Salvador – enabling us to communicate with colleagues across the world instantly. Access to technology and skills are important material and cultural capital not fairly shared, between the North and South but also *within* the locales where we wrote. We recognize our privileged position as observers and critics and hope that we have been responsible in our use of these means to bring attention to some of the most urgent questions surrounding global communications and media policy.

We are thankful to Sarah Edwards for her prompting Katharine to write a book on media policy, and for her continued patience and support. Without John Downing's introducing us to each other, we would probably have not met just yet and this would have been a different book or would not have been written at all. Our colleagues Andrew Calabrese (University of Colorado, Boulder), Cynthia Chris (City University of New York-Staten Island), Myria Georgiou (University of Leeds), David Hutchison (Glasgow Caledonian University, Scotland), Vincent Mosco (Queens University), Srirupa Roy (University of Massachusetts, Amherst), Leslie Shade (Concordia University), and Yuezhi Zhao (Simon Fraser University) have given us insightful comments on earlier drafts.

Katharine has benefited from a British Academy Research Grant in 2004 and from a McGill Centre of Research and Training on Women visiting fellowship the same year, during which period research into Canadian communications policies was conducted. She would also like to thank Ms Mary Damianakis (International Mediation, Canada) for support throughout the research leave. Paula is grateful for the support of Dean Janet Rifkin and her Chair Michael Morgan, as well as for research grants from the Centre for Public Policy and Administration (CPPA) and the College of Social and Behavioural Sciences (CSBS) at the University of Massachusetts, Amherst. The Healy Faculty Research Grant also allowed Paula to attend the World Summit on the Information Society in Tunis. Sumati Nagrath (University of Northampton) provided enormous help indexing the book. Daniel Kim and Elizabeth Gonzalez (both from the University of Massachusetts, Amherst) were helpful in providing research assistance for the completion of the manuscript. We also thank our friends and family who provided support and sanity through this long process, especially Nerissa Balce, Dolon Chakravartty, Stephanie Luce and Mary and George Sarikakis. Last but never least, we extend our warmest thanks to our life companions Gianpaolo Baiocchi and Alexander Bismarck for without their faith in us a great deal of our achievements would have not tasted as good!

Paula Chakravartty and Katharine Sarikakis
October 2005

The ideas and explanation in this book are a very welcome antidote to the dominant discourse of the virtues of the market, new technologies and competition. The proponents of technological determinism have for the past ten years asserted that greater audiovisual delivery capacity will automatically deliver diversity and pluralism and have sought to roll back virtually all audiovisual regulation. The authors describe well the valid political, social, economic and particularly cultural questions which demand an answer if the public interest is to be served in communications policy and the regulation which should flow from it.

The authors rightly underline that the screen, large or small, is central to our democratic, creative, cultural and social life and that policy-makers should give greater space to the views of civil society and parliamentarians interested in advancing the public interest. Rare is the attention paid to the realities of the digital divide as played out across the globe which provides important information for campaigners for greater technological redistribution and cultural diversity worldwide.

Carole Tongue
Visiting Professor, University of the Arts, London
Former MEP spokesperson on public service broadcasting

Premised on the fact that there are different globalizations going on today, this comprehensive study successfully integrates structural and symbolic analyses of communications and media policy in the conflicted spaces of the nation-state, trans-nation, and sub-nation. Chakravartty and Sarikakis's remarkably systematic approach to media policy, technology, content, and civil society formation fills in crucial details left behind by grand theory, including progressive postcolonial theories of global communication. In doing so, the book re-energizes the hackneyed field of international media studies and transforms it.

John Nguyet Erni
City University of Hong Kong

Abbreviations

ABT	Agreement on Basic Telecommunications
AFL-CIO	American Federation of Labor and Congress of Industrial Organizations
AISI	African Information Society Initiative
Anatel	National Agency of Telecommunications (Brazil)
APEC	Asian Pacific Economic Community
BJP	Bharatiya Janata Party
CBC	Canadian Broadcasting Corporation
CRTC	Canadian Radio-television and Telecommunications Commission
DOT	Digital Opportunity Task Force
ECA	United Nations' Economic Commission for Africa
ECOSOC	UN Economic and Social Council
FCC	Federal Communications Commission
FDI	Foreign Direct Investment
G7	Group of Seven
G8	Group of Eight
GATS	General Agreement on Trade in Services
GATT	General Agreement on Trade and Tariffs
GBD	Global Business Dialogue on Electronic Commerce
GIIC	Global Information Infrastructure Commission
GIS	Global Information Society
HDTV	High Definition Television
ICANN	Internet Corporation for Assigned Names and Numbers
ICT	Information and Communication Technology
IMF	International Monetary Fund
INSTRAW	Institute for the Advancement of Women
IT	Information Technology
ITU	International Telecommunications Union
NAFTA	North American Free Trade Agreement
NAM	Non-aligned Movement
NASA	National Aeronautics and Space Administration
NGO	Non-Government Organization

NICS	Newly Industrialized Countries
NIEO	New International Economic Order
NTP	National Telecom Policy (India)
NWICO	New World Information and Communication Order
OECD	Organization for Economic Co-operation and Development
PSB	Public Service Broadcasting
PTO	Post and Telecommunications Operator
SAP	Structural Adjustment Policy
SAPT	South African Posts and Telecommunication
TRAI	Telecom Regulatory Authority of India
TRIMS	Trade-Related Aspect of Investment Measures
TRIPs	Trade-Related Aspects of Intellectual Property Rights
TVWF	Television Without Frontiers
UN	United Nations
UNESCO	United Nations Educational Scientific and Cultural Organization
USAID	United States Agency for International Development
WB	World Bank
WEF	World Economic Forum
WIPO	World Intellectual Property Organization
WSF	World Social Forum
WSIS	World Summit on the Information Society
WTO	World Trade Organization

Part One

Policy contexts

1 Capitalism, technology, institutions and the study of communications and media policy

This book is about communication and media policies in the context of globalization. Its central focus is the analysis of the conditions and the nature of the policies that have shaped and are actively structuring the world's communication infrastructure. In this book we argue that the processes of globalization have been accompanied by a continuous transformation of the communication and media landscapes around the world sustained by a complex net of interdependent factors. The changes experienced in media landscapes are facilitated by de facto structural changes in the mode of production and terms of international trade. These changes are also 'normalized' through a set of policy-making processes that increasingly involves new regulatory processes and institutional actors, signalling a profound shift in the role of nation-states in the policy-making process. We argue that these changes are not experienced as homogenous processes across the globe and draw attention to the cultural, social and political contexts that render such transformations distinct. However, we also stress, and indeed turn our attention to the fact that, there are overarching questions that cut across the specific positions of groups of societies, countries, cultures and even economies. We further argue that the study of communications and media policy needs to develop tools for making macro-level observations of patterns without losing sight of the micro-level of realities of experience.

In this chapter, we begin by examining the nature and conditions of global communication and media policy analysis. We first address the common assumption that policy-making is an apolitical processes based on value-free principles, and trace how these assumptions are rooted in similar claims about the supposed neutrality of communications technologies. Our study of communication and media policy draws from a multidisciplinary approach, incorporating perspectives from political economy, political theory, as well as postcolonial and feminist studies. In this chapter, we explore the most significant, visible parameters in the shaping of policy, technology and the state, and situate them within the macro-level of increased market integration and trends in the globalization of capital. We define the political contexts that will shape our study in the following pages. Finally, we discuss the communication and media policy areas that have attracted most attention from scholars in communication studies.

'People who demand neutrality in any situation are usually not neutral but in favor of the status quo.' (Max Eastman)

In *Selling the Air: A Critique of Commercial Broadcasting in the United States*, Thomas Streeter points out that it is only in the English language, that there is a distinction between the words 'policy' and 'politics' (1996: 125). Whether this is strictly the case, as none of us can claim knowledge of more than a few world languages, it is certainly true that most European languages, such as French, German, Greek, Italian, Spanish, Portuguese and Russian, use the same word, variations of the Greek πολιτική (politike) to express decisions and the decision-making process as inseparable from politics. The implicit ideological assumption of the neutrality of the policy-making process is expressed perhaps most clearly in the words of a pioneer of Media Studies in the US, Harold Lasswell, who wrote in 1951: ' "Policy" is free of many of the undesirable connotations clustered about the world political, which is often believed to imply "partisanship" or "corruption" ' (1951: 5). Lasswell spells out the moral superiority of an *apolitical* bureaucratic, administrative process – the policy-making process – separated from the tainted world of politics in a fashion that is a peculiar and resonant feature of Anglo-American political culture. In the contemporary arena of US broadcasting, for instance, conservative Republicans have been successful in dominating public discourse about liberal bias as a pernicious legacy of the 1960s 'politicization' of regulatory bodies such as the Federal Communications Commission (FCC). In the UK, the renaissance of 'evidence-based' policy bears the assumptions of a modernist 'scientific' approach that holds the 'truth' irrespective of interests and persuasion. Meanwhile, these same politicians who claim neutrality promote *apolitical* remedies for market expansion through the deregulation and intensified privatization of broadcasting policy.

Removing politics from the policy-making process in areas ranging from basic telecommunications services and the broadcasting and cultural content to the trade in digital media content is one of the most significant

American successes in shifting the discourse of policy, which ultimately shapes its outcome. We cannot but point to the writings of Kathy Ferguson, who, referring to the similar case of the sterilized ('neutral') field of public administration studies, argues that bureaucratic discourse 'rebuffs the project of social criticism and political change' (1984: 82). We also assert that a separation of politics from policy (Bobrow et al. 1977), apart from being an artificial, ideologically loaded position that falsely claims neutrality, is neither possible nor desirable nor purposeful for the project of critical analysis of and reflection upon the contexts that determine the availability of communication channels and conditions for personal and cultural, social and political expression. Feminists across a variety of disciplines have historically focused on the politics of practice, whether writing about the realm of elite politics and political decision-making or 'personal' politics. Policy, in its form of governmental or other state-like authority-derived assertions, and lack thereof, has never been considered irrelevant to or unwanted from political analysis in the writings of Staudt (1998), which address development and international policy-making, or by feminists in the field of ICTs, technology and media (Cockburn 1998; Cockburn and Ormrod 1993; Crow and Longford 2004; Huws 2003; Wajcman 2005).

In the era of globalization, or more precisely of market and finance integration, the actors involved in decision-making are located not only at the national level but also at the supranational, regional and local, transnational (institutional bases spanning more than one nation) and translocal (institutional bases spanning more than one city across nations) levels. This means that influential policy actors are based not only in national governments but also in supranational bodies, regional and local administrations as well as transnational and translocal networks and corporations. Concentrated in the terrain of 'elite' politics these institutions can be formally organized or loosely affiliated to the state, through such things as subcontracted organizations or think tanks. Policy actors participate in policy-making processes that often take place in informal settings that are difficult to document and map. Alongside the official, documented and institutionalized realm of policy-making, we recognize that there is also the ground of politics occupied by publics that engage in more informal ways with the social outcomes of policy shifts whether as audiences, consumers, citizens or merely by exclusion. The politics of everyday life, cultural expression and intentional as well as informal dissent is for this study a structuring component of the field of global communications policy. Although these publics are not the central object of analysis in this book, the underlying assumption of our work is that critique and social change is inseparable from practice and agency. Our approach to the analysis of communications policy takes as its 'measuring standard' not the outcomes for media industries or transnational actors but the interest of the publics, in terms of recognition as political subjects, democratic participation in policy processes and equality of social outcome. Therefore, throughout this work, we take into account the hegemonic constructions of meanings surrounding major policy directions and we juxtapose them to the realities of material and symbolic experience of the minoritized majorities. In this process, two factors central to the contextualization and affirmation of communication policy occupy a prominent position in our study: technology and the state. Their role within the context of capitalism (and its ideologue of 'free market') in serving as and constructing hegemonic discourses about the drives and necessity for policy will be systematically investigated in the following pages.

Making sense of global markets, the state and communications

Early analysts of globalizing trends in communications argued that we were witnessing a significant change in the role and power of the nation-state to govern in matters of national interest. For proponents of globalization, new 'technologies of freedom' allowed citizens to subvert government control (Pool 1983) enhanced by a 'borderless world' where nation-states were rendered powerless over market forces that they could no longer control (Ohmae 1990: 80). They argued that the rapid proliferation of new technologies coupled with the decline of the role of governments in regulating national broadcasting and telecommunications would expand the range of choices for consumers. The expansion of private communication networks across national boundaries and the rapid circulation of information through new media – threatened the notion of state sovereignty and promised greater accountability and overall efficiency of communications services. For critics, the perceived, diminishing power of nation-state has to be understood in the context of the growing influence of transnational corporations (TNCs) to override national sovereignty and undermine democratic accountability. Political economists of communication asserted that the freedom of the market celebrated by critics of government intervention failed to account for the anti-democratic tendencies associated with the shrinking of public debate resulting from global media conglomeration and the information disparities between the wealthy and poor, a consequence of privatization and deregulation (Herman and McChesney 1997; Schiller 1996).

Social scientists today are generally more circumspect about the 'withering away of the state' and the emergence of a 'borderless world'. While some question the very idea that any kind of historical transformation has actually occurred in altering state–market dynamics in the longer history of the modern market economy (Hirst and Thompson 1995), most argue that we need to examine how the role of the state has changed, while recognizing that nation-states remain integral in global governance (Held 1997). Historically, national governments have regulated communication and media industries, assuming that communication goods represent some kind of 'public good' both as a technological resource and as culture. Recently, scholars have turned their attention to how specific states have responded to global pressures from TNCs and multilateral bodies such as the World Trade Organization (WTO) precisely because communications as an object of public policy remains vital to both economic and political national interest. For many critics of rampant liberalization, the nation-state remains the most effective institutional actor capable of public accountability. Drawing on the legacies of public service and public interest in Western democracies, these scholars point to the affirmative role of nation-states in ensuring equity, access and diversity (Beale 1999; Winseck 1998).

As political economic and technological changes transform the traditional bounds of state intervention in matters of policy-making, it is important to recognize that control over communications industries is directly related to the economic well-being of any modern nation-state in the form of foreign investment, export and taxable revenues and the generation of employment, among other factors. Thus governments increasingly link communication policy to economic interests – from enforcing intellectual property rights to ensuring that private firms have access to the latest telecom infrastructure, to promoting information and communications technology (ICT)-based exports, to subsidizing foreign investment in communications-related industries as a development strategy. Beyond economic interests, 'governments retain the capacity to control the media to reinforce legitimacy or fortify a regime's hold on power' (Waisbord and Morris 2001: xi–xii). The latter form of state control over communications should not be seen as a feature restricted to 'backward' authoritarian regimes in the Third World, but rather a growing feature of contemporary debates about communication and media policy in the 'developed world', especially in light of the 'War on Terror'. Today, the US government marshals new restrictions over freedom of information and media content domestically through the Patriot Act while simultaneously policing and silencing foreign commercial media content that is seen to 'promote terrorism' – the controversial case of Al Jazeera is only one example of this trend (Miles 2005).

According to the Privacy and Human Rights Report (PHR) 2004 (Privacy International & ERIC), in the aftermath of 11 September 2001 governments have used the pretext of terrorism to introduce illegal laws of spying and surveillance. The PHR report emphasizes the increased volume of invasion of privacy and warns that the effects of these laws on civil liberties will be only fully understood after many years. The report identifies some major tendencies in countries across the world:

- New identification measures and new traveller pre-screening and profiling systems
- New anti-terrorism laws and governmental measures provide for increased search capabilities and sharing of information among law-enforcement authorities
- Increased video surveillance
- DNA and health information databases
- Censorship measures
- Radio frequency identification technologies
- New electronic voting technologies
- Mismanagement of personal data and major data leaks

In this moment when the US government exerts the moral superiority of freedom and democracy to impose a very specific juridical system to guide 'free trade' and 'freedom of expression', it is imperative to critically consider the broader context of policy-making.

In this quest, understanding the historical change of capitalism and its variations depending on local and regional conditions and the role of regions (whether core or semi-peripheral) in the international regimes is of primary importance. What globalization has achieved is not the unified leap to higher profitability for all national industries or to wealth for all parts of the world. Gordon, for example, explains that it is short-term financial capital that rapidly moves across borders while at the same time foreign direct investment has become increasingly selective (1994: 295). Park (2000) also points to the varying degree of state presence for the shaping of economies in the North and Southeast Asian countries, concluding that the role of the state in protecting local economies from financial crises has been more effective than in those countries that depended totally on market forces. According to Gordon, the era of globalization has been characterized by a process whereby TNCs have sought 'stable and insulated political and institutional protection against the increasing volatility of international trade and the collapse of the dollar-based 'free market' expansion of international trade growth' (1994: 295). Hay (2004), examining the EU model, argues that market integration forges divergent rather than convergent economies. Our understanding of the symbiotic relationship between states, markets and society is influenced not only by the French Régulation School, but also from an earlier and prescient analyst of capitalist transformation, Karl Polanyi. Polanyi wrote that capitalism, or the market economy, was determined by both the material forces of production and distribution, as well as by social practices that legitimated the market system. Thus in addition to the state's integral role in (often violently) introducing 'market organization on society for non-economic ends', Polanyi was also concerned with the type of society and economic subject that the market needs in order to function. In his famous historical overview of the development of the welfare state, the 'double movement' of capitalism showed that the expansion of market mentality to all areas of social life was met by state-sanctioned social protections that inadvertently allowed the market to function by insulating society from the 'dislocating effects' of the self-regulating market (Polanyi 1957: 76).

Today, we see institutional change in various parts of the world, such as the EU and other regional and supranational bodies of governance that serve as the means to control financial uncertainty on behalf of 'free markets'. Foreign Direct Investment (FDI) is highly selective – much of new FDI associated with globalization in the last decade is concentrated in strategic sites within Asia, where rising rates of inequality and financial instability threaten gains from higher wages in fast-growing sectors (Hanson 2001). TNCs seek entry into developing markets in search of lower relative wages but also stable markets and specialized infrastructure.[1] Gordon argues that the construction of 'highly specialised and institutionally particular economic sites' has resulted not in an increasingly more 'open' international economy but in an increasingly closed economy for productive investment if we consider the relationship between FDI and larger economic development goals. This analysis is applicable to modern labour relations, only too visible in the organization of transnational production-accumulation regimes, characterized by First World sweatshops for the production of microchips for the 'information revolution' and the environmental racism apparent in the global city centres of the 'knowledge economies'. It also points to the high rates of exploitation across the First and Third world economies that becomes painfully visible through renewed attack against unions and welfare and civil rights.[2] There is not much new about the low wages across the newly industrialized countries: however, what is now distinctive is the fact that TNCs 'negotiate with *each other* and host countries for joint production agreements, licensing and joint R&D contracts. They search among potential investment sites for institutional harbours promising the greatest *protection against an increasingly turbulent world*' (Gordon 1994: 295, our emphasis).

The dynamics of international trade and the dialectics of market and state cannot be excluded from the study of communications policy. In the following chapters we make sense of globalization by following the evolving relationship between the mode of accumulation and the mode of regulation, 'the ensemble of rules, norms, conventions, patterns of conduct, social networks, organizational forms and institutions which can stabilize an accumulation regime' (Jessop 1997: 291). The role of the nation-state has been transformed. But it is not necessarily diminished in the face of globalization. Gordon argues that state policies have actually become 'increasingly decisive on the institutional fronts, not more futile' (1994: 301). Mistral before him, also from the French Régulation School, argues that the forms of international régulation do not suppress national differences in the form of internal policy and regulation but reduce divergences (Robles 1994).

So, is globalization a state of affairs, a fixed process of international entropy, a highly specific and catholic-experienced condition? Does it mean the end of history and therefore of the political? Our discussion on the role of the state and the international trade and policy regimes shows that, if anything, this is a period when different levels of globalization exist simultaneously according to conditions and context, whereby different faces of capitalism are experienced across the world. The relations between capital and labour and their relation to culture and state are experienced through the filters and conditions of class, but also gender, race, nationality and religious difference. These mediating factors matter in the 'configuration of political struggle' and to the social regime of accumulation (Albelda and Tilly 1994: 228).

Beyond establishing the importance of historical specificity lies for us the larger conceptual goal of examining the symbolic as well as material dimension of state power in shaping public policy. While there is a range of perspectives on the cultural analyses of the state, it is helpful to consider the work of French Sociologist Pierre Bourdieu. Bourdieu expands on Max Weber's famous formula that the state 'successfully claims the monopoly of the legitimate use of physical and *symbolic* violence over a definite territory and over the totality of the corresponding population' (1999: 56). For our purposes, in addition to the role and character of the state as a 'regulator' and part of a 'steering' action for international trade transactions, we draw from Bourdieu's understanding of the state as a 'bank of symbolic capital' (1999: 66) and access to *capital étatique* (state capital) as a '(meta)authority to validate or invalidate other forms of authority, that is, to have the last word in a territory, to have the last judgment' (Hansen and Stepputat 2001: 6).

Bourdieu's focus on the reproduction of state power through rituals and symbols provides a dynamic framework to make sense of the blurring of lines between public and private institutional actors that make up modern modes of regulation. This approach allows us to consider how domestic and global communication and media policy is increasingly negotiated across the range of policy-making arenas by a variety of institutional actors – most notably state bureaucrats and representatives from transnational firms but also recognized delegates of civil society – who compete over access to resources as well as the very rules of governance. Communications reform is clearly an economic issue, and raising questions of allocation and distribution are crucial to understanding the technical processes of expansion, distribution and efficiency. A meaningful understanding of political transformation of the policy process, however, requires that we confront the symbolic dimension of economic processes. Bourdieu offers an insightful alternative to circumvent tired questions concerning an assumed 'conflict' of material versus ideological interests shaping state actions.

The bureaucratic bodies of national or even multilateral state institutions may process new rules shaping what local and transnational publics watch or how and what they pay for access to information. Nevertheless, the 'business of rule' is necessarily connected to 'the business of creating emotional attachment to the state or "noncontingent" identities' (Berisen 1999: 360). Taking up Anderson's claims, feminists, subaltern studies scholars and other critics from a variety of disciplines have examined the making and unmaking of national culture, citizenship and political identity both historically and ethnographically through various media, from print and broadcasting to the proliferation of new technologies (Abu-Lugodh 2004; Kraidy 2005; Rajagopal 2001).

In turn, the study of the symbolic domain investigated within the broader field of cultural policy studies has drawn from Michel Foucault's writings on governmentality (or the intensified regulation of modern societies whereby human practices became the objects of knowledge, Regulation and discipline), allowing state policies to appear natural in a given cultural context (Burchell et al. 1991). For instance, Tom Streeter (1996) has argued that the US state's regulation of private ownership of the broadcast spectrum with broadcast licences created a system of 'soft property' premised on the specificities of corporate liberalism. From a Marxist tradition based on the work of Antonio Gramsci and Raymond Williams, Jim McGuigan (1996) has examined how historically rooted policy discourses set the parameters for cultural politics and the policing of culture. Feminist scholars have pushed the boundaries of investigation to address the reinforcement and reproduction of power structures that maintain sexism and racism through the gendered logic of communication and cultural policy. For these scholars, the role of the state is explored in its contradictory position to facilitate remedies against discrimination, on the one hand, and also to continue and exacerbate symbolic and structural inequalities on the other (Beale 1999; McLaughlin 2004; Meehan and Riordan 2001). Nowhere is this more visible in the field of communication and media policy than in the very technologies that have been heralded as the panacea of all ills and have been identified as the core defining factors of policy development.

The cultural ingredients in the making of myths: technology

> From advertising to trade shows, from demonstration projects to conferences, there is a widespread effort to market the magic, to surround computer communication with power, speed, and the promise of freedom. There is nothing new here. Students of the history of technology will recall similar attempts to make electricity a spectacle by lighting up streets and buildings in the downtowns of many cities and towns, turning them into miniature versions of New York's Great White Way. (Mosco 2004: 45–6)

Technological advances have repeatedly been seen as catalysts for social change – communications technology in particular. Techno-capitalist and organizational prophets from academia, government bodies, think-tanks and private industry have sanctified the existence and importance of what we today call the 'information society'. Each group has produced its own (predominantly White, and occasionally Asian, male) guru to bring the message of technocracy to their respective audiences. The cooperation of university research with the state and the private sector reshapes public policy discourse to focus almost exclusively on priorities defined by concerns about market expansion. The IT and telecommunications industries, often amalgamated in one mega industrial complex, expand their reign over more traditional cultural economies and are integral gatekeepers in the organization of the Information Society. Gates, Gore and Negroponte were the early (white, male) gurus of an information age that is based on a virtual reorganization of the 'atom' economy. All three of them helped to define the terms of reference of techno- or informational capitalism through their positions in their respective constituencies, in the world of business, politics, research and publication. Bill Gates's *Business @ the Speed of Thought* (2004), Al Gore's *National Information Infrastructure* (1993) and Nicholas Negroponte's *Being Digital* (1995) and *WiReD* constitute the Qur'an in the mythical Mecca of Silicon Valley. Negroponte's visions of the transformation of atoms into digital beings through the 'technologies of freedom' have provided much material to create the myths of this allegedly unprecedented revolutionary era.

Mosco (2004) argues that the building of the Information Society is based on a series of myths that provides the narrative necessary for the implementation of policies, and the acceptance of the organization of the economy and social relations. Mosco explores these myths to show how, historically, every new invention was claimed as 'ahistorical', that is, the first and unprecedented expression of technological breakthrough. All of these 'ahistorical' unprecedented moments of technological revolution were presented as the promise for freedom, peace and wealth. Tracing such myths throughout the development of telegraph, electricity, telephone, radio and television, Mosco shows how each innovation has been accompanied by nested discourses about prosperity and peace embodied by these new technologies, popularized by ideologies of 'magic and awe' and of course of the superiority of Western science and progress.[3] In the cases of electrification, for example, the 'light' brought by electricity became the metaphor that separated progress from underdevelopment, the white colonists from their subjects: 'As the telegraph and electricity demonstrate, the new world of cyberspace is not the first to be christened with magical powers to transcend the present and institute a new order' (Mosco 2004: 125).

For the information society, nowhere more graphically and magically than in *WiReD* magazine, has this mythical information society been celebrated , a publication that Negroponte has helped found. Negroponte, himself a member of the board of directors of one of the most powerful telecommunications industries (Motorola), occupies a position at the nexus of military, regulatory and industrial research and practice. The wonders of the Information Society, but also the fear – of being left behind if one does not embrace this new world order; of becoming obsolete; and even of not being useful anymore in the new economics – are adequately transmitted to the readers of *WiReD*. Melanie Stewart Millar (1998) offered one of the most astute early analyses of the bard of digital technology. The production of further myths to sustain the myth of a computer mediated society is part of the magazine's *raison d'être*. These myths, like the myths that came before them, sustain the 'awe' of the new era and the drive to consume, reinforcing gender, class and racial hierarchies associated with American capitalism. Stewart Millar (1998) analysed the myths that *WiReD* developed to produce the 'hypermacho man'. They are the myths of a deterministic culture of digital technology that is both religious and libertarian in its promise. *WiReD* helped pave the way for the representation of the universal virtuality of cyberspace as a separate and unadulterated place; like the creation of a new market-led Eden where floating cyberidentities are free from the shackles of the physical world and can therefore be formed and transformed. Miller's study of *WiReD* magazine from 1993 to 1998, these most crucial and defining years of the contemporary era of 'information society' and convergence, shows how the representation of technology perpetuates demagogic dilemmas about the relevance and validity of information technologies, rendering its critics as Luddite and retrograde. This is a common strategy against proponents of oppositional politics, especially when critique is addressed to the dominant configuration of the assumed technophile, what Stewart Miller calls the 'hypermacho man'. Picking up a copy of *WiReD* in January 2005, we can see that the political outlook remains constant despite booms and busts within the information industry. The cover page depicts Richard Branson in a space suit, preparing to take us to the final frontier. The article presents Branson, 'The Rocket Man', as an all-conquering (white, male, Anglo) entrepreneur not only embracing but also leading the new information age with his next crusade to conquer the cosmos for his space travel customers. True to the spirit of techno-capitalism, all other major stories in the issue generate odes to masculinist cultures paying homage to technological invention, as a process of controlling or reconfiguring nature (article: O. Morton, 'Life Reinvented' *WiReD*, January 2005).

The celebratory discourse of *WiReD* magazine has influenced the field of global communication and media policy in ways that are both obvious and harder to identify. If we consider telecommunications policy – the backbone of modern communications and media industries (Internet, new media, broadcasting) – as the necessary infrastructure for the information economy, we see how these associated myths translate into legitimate policy practice. For instance, scholarly expertise in policy was increasingly cultivated, most often in US Business and Law Schools, where the consensus about the nature and direction of the liberalization of the telecommunications infrastructure crystallized into practice. The dominant approach in terms of the scholarship on telecommunications communication policy is prescriptive and, particularly from the 1980s onwards, technologically deterministic with the assumption that the market and technology are inherently neutral forces (Pool 1997). This dominant model espouses an evolutionary understanding of technological innovation based on the 'natural' dynamic of a competitive market place. From this perspective, technological innovation is understood as a source or cause of social change, what influential 'futurologists' beginning in the 1970s referred to as the mark of a 'postindustrial society' (Bell 1973).

Much as the technologies before the computer, mobile phone or wireless were, this utopian or idealist vision of technological change is based on two central arguments. First, that technological innovation is increasingly important in shaping changes in society and second that these new technological innovations are autonomous from political and economic processes. Thus technological 'revolutions' in telecommunications networks and computer technologies are seen to have an inherent and singular trajectory of development that will lead to superior social outcomes improving everyday life for all, if left to competitive market forces. The integrated intelligent network is seen as the new basis for the reorganization of education, work, entertainment and all other forms of social interaction, a basis that is both decentralized and connected. The operators of telecommunications networks and services are assumed to be fully accountable to the customer, whereby inefficient or overpriced services are checked through competition in the marketplace. In this context, the need for policy intervention and regulation is minimal, except for the technical arbitration over rates and standards. Similar assumptions are presented as facts in the broadcasting world: here speedy adaptation of technology and consumer sovereignty have dominated the discourses surrounding the liberalization (from the state) of the airwaves and their privatization.

In contrast to the naturalized assumptions about the logic of the market in the dominant approach to tele/communications policy, neo-Marxist critics contend that political and economic interests shape the application and development of tele/communications networks, content and services (Hills 1998; Schiller 2000). Specifically, these critical scholars, who are sometimes viewed as 'dystopian' (Graham and Marvin 2001), argue that technological development is an outcome of social power and cannot therefore be a neutral force in shaping social change. While the technologically centred analysis considers innovation and competition as sufficient in eroding monopolistic control delivering the consumer freedom to choose from a range of services, this approach focuses on the importance of communications and in particular telcoms to the very process of global economic restructuring, on the uneven development and expansion of new communications networks and services and the ramifications of transforming a regulatory model that is organized around consumers as opposed to citizens (Harvey 1989; Mosco 2004).

Moreover, the merger of traditional telecommunications companies with producers of content further reinforces concentration as opposed to competition in overall services, raising new concerns about proprietary standards and intellectual property. Neo-Marxist analysts have argued that the centrality of TNCs in shaping the terms of expansion to fit their needs has led to 'uneven biases' in the development of telecommunications around the world. Finally, the economic centrality of telecommunications services for TNCs puts pressures on national governments to separate the needs of corporate users of high-speed networks and services from the public networks, creating new levels of information disparity and a 'new geography of inequality' (Sassen 1999).

Social constructionists also reject the dominant view on telecommunications policy on the grounds of technological determinism. While this school agrees that social relations shape policy, they are less convinced that political economic structures determine technological outcome. They focus less on broader macro-power imbalances (at the level of capital, nation or class), and more on meso- or micro-power relations at the level of institutional struggle. These critics begin by recognizing that the older model of national telecommunications policy failed to meet anywhere near universal service objectives in most societies in the world, and they seek instead institutional solutions that can identify the causal 'relationships between social, institutional and political factors and the development and applications of technologies' (Graham and Marvin 2000: 151). Although much of this work critiques the simplistic notion that competition is a catch-all alternative to public ownership or regulation, the focus of this research is on the operation of autonomous regulatory agencies that can hold both state and private actors accountable in local contexts. As such, researchers in this tradition propose public-policy solutions institutionalizing competition and innovation while taking into account questions of equitable distribution and access (Mansell 2001). At issue in these analyses of reform is the changing meaning of public interest as an objective of communications policy (van Cuilenburg and McQuail 2003). Not only are new questions being raised about who exactly represents public interest in an era of 'liberalization', but, as the state's role changes from owner to regulator, new concerns are being voiced about the accountability of both state and corporate actors at the local, national and global level.

Historicizing shifts in communications policy and public interest in the West

When describing the historical development of communications policy in the Western world, van Cuilenburg and McQuail (2003) identify three periods of communications policy paradigms that express the definition and understanding of 'public interest'. These periods are identified from the mid-nineteenth century to the beginnings of the Second World War characterized by 'piece meal accumulation of measures, with varying aims, means and scope' (2003: 186); the second period between the Second World War and the 1980s/1990s characterized by the public-service media paradigm and shaped according to political and normative – rather than technological – considerations; and the third is the current period of 'communications policy' where the issue of technological and economic convergence is expressed through decision-making that reflects the connection of telecommunications and media. The authors' basis is that these distinct periods have produced media and communications policy that correspond to particular perceptions of the state about the role of the media. During the first period then, they argue, only the press was seen to have a political, normative function and it was only regulated with rights to report freely on current social and political affairs (freedom of expression). The second period perceived the electronic media as of political and social significance (given their use throughout the Second World War) and extended the pursuit of national cohesion and stability (2003: 191). According to the authors, media policy was dominated by sociopolitical rather than economic concerns (2003: 191). The current third period is one where 'pragmatism and populism increasingly drive policy' (2003: 197) especially following the '"decline in ideology" and the fall of Communism, the increased scope and respectability of the free market and the shift to the right in European politics' (2003: 197). As van Cuilenburg and McQuail rightly point out, in the European terrain, the communications policy philosophy is based on the idea of the market, which is not dissimilar to the priorities of US communications policy and indeed policies imposed by the World Bank and the IMF on the 'developing' world. The authors 'predict' three core values in an emerging communications paradigm: freedom of communication, access and accountability (2003: 203).

From the other side of the Atlantic, Marc Raboy (1995), writing about the public-broadcasting media, echoes some of these predictions. For Raboy, if the public-service broadcasting system is to have any future, it would need to pursue and achieve a status of accountability in the era of fierce competition from private broadcasters. As he notes 'the promotion of the public interest can only come through regulation guaranteeing system access for all with something to communicate, as well as for receivers'(1995:14). Both sets of authors seem to argue for state intervention in the media market but not state control over them. Indeed, state intervention has been identified in terms of policy – whether as a positive or negative strategy – as a determining factor in shaping the course of policy philosophy and ideology, objectives and output.

Communications policy scholars, such as Abramson and Raboy (1999); Collins (1994, 2003); Harcourt (2005); Harrison and Woods (2001);

Humphreys (1996); and Moore (1997), despite their differences, tend to agree on the categorization of communications policy according to the degree of state intervention. The term *dirigisme* for example has been used to describe a philosophy of active state involvement in policy matters, especially in the European Union terrain, as opposed to laissez-faire policies (Collins 1994; Harcourt 2005; Moore 1997; etc.). It is certainly the case, however, that regulating for a neoliberalist framework of media policies involves at least as much state intervention as in the cases of *dirigisme*. Or, as several scholars have pointed out, deregulation of communications has required a new set of regulations (for example, Humphreys 1996), so that we are actually referring to *reregulation*.

The politics of neoliberalism has succeeded in defining the ways in which we debate the role of the state in communications policy to a rather significant degree. *Dirigisme* is considered an ill, to be avoided at any cost in international relations and global policy as some of the most influential neoliberal think tanks advise (e.g. Bandow 1994). The state here is presented as 'corrupt' in the case of the 'developing' world, not to be trusted with funds or other support by the 'international community' or, in the case of the 'developed' countries, as a rather asphyxiating paternalistic nanny that hinders progress and individual freedom. In this book, we try and map the shifting role of the nation-state in relation to the market and society, paying attention to structural similarities as well as historical specificities of this process.

Scholars have attempted to address this changing role, often indirectly by mapping out the institutional changes that take place at the national level, as direct responses to the profound pressures of the processes of globalization. Within the field of communications and media studies, there has been a growing interest in studying cultural and media policy-making, where scholars have focused their attention on the shifting and historically specific relationships between states, markets and social actors who make policy (Lewis and Miller 2002). Also, scholars have concerned themselves not only with the macro-level questions of globalization, neoliberalism and the role of the media (McChesney 2004) but also with 'meso-level' issues of institutional arrangements and policy-making. So for example, Mansell (2001, 2002) points to the institutional processes, strategies and rhetoric to define policy problems related to the 'new media'; Abramson and Raboy (1999) explore the institutional responses of the Canadian state to adapt to the definitions and visions of a global information society; Hamelink (1995) analyses the institutional interactions of international organizations in the process of determining policy paradigms. International and supranational policy developments continue to attract the attention of scholars and activists. More recently, a variety of first reflections upon another significant institutional reform is emerging, addressing the official inclusion of civil society actors in the deliberations of the World Summit on the Information Society.[4] Recent approaches to communications and media policy attempt to sketch the structural and institutional transformations of international and national policy-making from a critical political economic perspective that introduces a synthesis of factors into the equation of communication policy analysis. These are institutional change, legislative reform and process, analysis of legislative, policy and political discourse, the impact of the international policy regime and the relationship with the symbolic cultural domain of identity and expression (for example, Mosco 2004).

In this book, we are exploring the multiplicity of these factors and draw upon theoretical perspectives that address the structural as well as cultural and agency bound domain to analyse policy. We argue that there is a need to move beyond the developmentalist framework of the study of global communication policy based on our previous work on communication, modernization and the postcolonial state (Chakravartty 2001, 2004). We address institutional change building upon previous work on representational politics and parliamentary advocacy within the context of liberal democracy and in response to processes of globalization (Sarikakis 2004c). This book is also informed by postcolonial and feminist scholarship influencing the ways in which we look into other than the obvious spaces, to identify the range of policy formation. And it is in this way that we seek to help extend the rich debate on global communications and media policy.

The logic and organization of the book

Our approach to the study of policy derives from the understanding that communications and media are not just technologies or tradeable goods but also expressions of social relations and power. In this work, we focus on the actors and institutions that have played a significant role historically in defining, challenging, disrupting or reinforcing symbolic power in the policy field – both in terms of influencing outcome and discourse. Our approach to policy is to identify those issues that are of common concern across cultures and geopolitical formations, whether states, regions or other localities, and analyse them against the background of the intensification of market integration at a global scale. The study uses empirical and historical sets of data that relate to policy development in the fields of telecommunications policy, broadcasting and audiovisual policy, as well as information and communication technologies (ICTs) policy. These fields are intrinsically dependent in the way that telecommunications serve as the 'backbone' to the modern broadcasting media and ICTs (on which print media are also increasingly dependent), and has since colonial times served as the vital infrastructure of international trade. Furthermore, they are the physical links to a pronounced 'virtual' reality as a major aspect of the Information Society. Broadcasting similarly has been counted upon to define and construct national and other identities and contribute to cultural and social cohesion historically.

Our aim is to address questions of global communications and media policy that cut across cultures and geographies. One 'unusual' characteristic with our book is that it does not address 'case' studies but moves between 'developing' and 'developed' economies, 'dissimilar' geopolitical power and a wide range of political cultures. Through this logic we address the broader spectrum of capitalist organization while acknowledging the differences in cultural and socio-political locations, traditions and methods of administration. Therefore we move from the study of the dramatic impact of the dominance of the liberalization paradigm in the field of telecommunications in 'developing' countries to the analysis of the effects of privatization and the loss of the normative basis for public ownership of broadcast media in the Western world. We address the complex ideological, cultural and political dimensions of the vision for a 'new world' of information and communication through the study of the powers that shape the policy agenda globally and we show why and how the vision is neither perfect nor panoramic.

In the first two chapters, our aim is to provide the methodological, theoretical and historical context of our approach to the study of communication and media policy, which derives from the understanding that the nation-state remains an important actor in the field of global policy, despite claims announcing its 'death'. It also derives from the position that globalization is not always a helpful concept, although it has gained such widespread popularity that often encompasses a number of complex concepts and assumptions and provides us with a vehicle to communicate the scope of analysis with our readers. In these two chapters we address the role of the realm of ideas, values and language for institutions and any actors with claims to authority and jurisdiction in their pursuit of some form of minimum legitimation, even when this is limited to the purpose of persuading the various publics to accept the shifts in policy through processes of normalization. In the present chapter we have outlined our understanding of the symbiotic relationship between the state and the market, focusing on how advances in communications and media technologies have shaped both public and policy discourse.

In Chapter 2, we argue that the experiences of postcolonial states in the context of the Cold War reveal pertinent lessons for current debates on the globalization of communications and media policy. We trace the broader historical context and normative claims within the changing field of global communication and media policy to show the continuities and ruptures between the Fordist and post-Fordist regulatory eras.

In the second part of the book we explore two major areas where communication and media policy had a transformative effect on media across the world. In Chapter 3 we examine telecommunications as the backbone and infrastructure of the content industry on the one hand and the nervous system of the digital 'revolution,' the carrier of information society on the other. Although we map the changing discourse of public interest in this field from a global perspective, we focus on the experiences of telecommunications reform in the Third World where the pace and scale of transformation has been the most dramatic. We trace why the new discourse of the market managed to overwhelm the nationally defined redistributive role of the state in shaping telecommunications policy in the 1980s and 1990s. While powerful institutional actors like TNCs and Northern states play an important role in this transformation, we contend that claims by citizens for access to the new information economy only become clear if we pay closer attention to local histories and practices, which are themselves embedded in the uneven processes of globalization.

In Chapter 4 we focus on broadcasting policies as they are central to informing the ways in which publics understand their relationship to their media and public space and also their histories and cultures. As such, the story telling capacities of broadcasting industries have grown enormously to become the main media consumed, talked about and used as a cultural practice, sources of information and labour tools across the planet. Issues of content, access, diversity in representation and truthfulness echo values acclaimed almost by all states in the world, as the ratification of UN declarations on human rights and other equity centred policy initiatives allows at least a formal statement to be made. Our analysis places particular emphasis on the role of the EU as an international and supranational actor in communications policies. In particular, because of its institutional organization, which offers more spaces open to citizens' input than other international organizations, it serves as an example of possibilities with more democratic policy orientation than the dominant neoliberal stream of policy direction. Attention is paid to the fundamental commonalities among nations, such as the quest for public-broadcasting communication spaces predominantly expressed through public-service broadcasting and the issues related to the continuous threat of the idea/l and model of PSB. A set of neoliberalist arguments and perceptions, including technological advancement, the era of convergence and consumer sovereignty, are explored through the lenses of public interest and the participation of publics in active self-expression.

Chapters 5 and 6 (Part Three) address the new 'paradigm' of communications policy, one that involves an increasing 'convergence' of policy areas under the rubric of the 'Information Society' and its technologically focused framing, and the increasing attention to non-traditional policy actors in the policy-making process, such as corporations and civil society.

The question of technology is taken up in Chapter 5, which seeks to grasp the concept and object of policy known as the 'Information Society'. On the technology determined front of the knowledge economy hi-tech, futuristic and often dry, incomprehensible language may be closer to the language and everyday experiences of some but its optimistic overtones remain distant to the majority of the citizens on the planet. Increasingly it has come to include everything, from new broadcasting techniques and the digitalization of the content of services to the Internet, from cyberidentities to optic and glass-fibre architectures, determined by the demands of the material not virtual infrastructure. Similarly, the 'Knowledge Economy' symbolizes a transition from the manual/machine-assisted production line of material things to an abstract, placeless interaction between human and electronic brains for the production of services. 'Knowledge', a questionable term, refers to the collection and trafficking of data, in particular personal data, and their analysis for predominantly marketing purposes. These discourses represent some aspects of the condition of the Western industrialized economies but often overgeneralizations made in relation to their usefulness and character overshadow realities and visions that suggest a different almost radical reading.

In Chapter 6 we pick up on the politics of civil society as an institutional actor engaged in global communication and media governance. We trace historically the continuities and disjunctures of this seemingly 'new' social actor, to argue that the presence of civil society organizations, whether locally or nationally delivering services or playing a central role in framing policy at the WTO or WSIS, does not in itself challenge the reproduction of symbolic dominance by traditional actors, nation-states and transnational firms. Assessing the specific case of the WSIS, an institutional site where civil society actors are in theory given unprecedented access, we focus on the gap between policy and politics that exists in current formulations of the normative basis for civil society intervention to argue that addressing issues of recognition are as crucial as redistribution.

Notes

1. These include the 'Asian Tigers' (Hong Kong, South Korea, Singapore and Taiwan) but also China, India, Mexico, Brazil and other emerging economies that have relatively stronger bargaining power vis-à-vis G8 nations and foreign capital. But these sites also include the Philippines, Indonesia and the Dominican Republic whereby TNCs enjoy a 'modern form of colonial trading privileges' (Gordon 1994).
2. Across Europe and North America, civil rights are under attack, including abortion rights, state benefit and unemployment support, freedom of expression when exercised for dissent, such as in the case of Indymedia shut down in London in 2004, restriction of the free movement of citizens within and across countries and the exploitation of private data collected on borders, such as at US entry points. Demonstrations and protests are heavily policed, and policies of 'shoot to kill' and unlawful imprisonment and detention of individuals without trial or access to legal aid are some of the policies taken under the ideological construct of 'war on terror' or 'anti-terrorist' strategies by the state.
3. These discourses of scientific superiority, often used as a justification for colonial rule or neocolonial expansion, had their own valences and reinterpretations in colonial and postcolonial societies which are significant but beyond the scope of this chapter to address. For more see Gyan Prakash 1999.
4. We refer to this work in greater detail in Chapter 6.

2 Revisiting the history of global communication and media policy

This chapter provides a broad overview of the shifts in the field of global communication policy as the nation-state's regulatory power itself is reconfigured from the post-World War Two era to the current era of global integration. In historicizing the shift in global governance we highlight the various factors which led to the rise and ultimate decline of the Fordist mode of regulation. In the first section, we consider the continuities as well as the ruptures of the shift by focusing on the specific experience of the postcolonial state. We contend that these states, unlike their welfare state and state-socialist counterparts in the First and Second Worlds,[1] were already integrated into an uneven international system of governance, well before the pressures of globalization. The post-World War Two project of 'national development' and modernization of Third World economies and cultures were very much at the heart of the most significant struggles in the field of global communication policy and provide a particularly interesting vantage point to consider the ideals and failures of the state's role in representing public interest. In the second section, we account for the turn toward the neoliberal[2] information economy focusing on the transformation of the state in shaping national policy. We trace the evolution of North–South relations in this 'flexible' post-Fordist regulatory era by laying out the material and symbolic dimensions behind the 'reregulation' of global communication policy. Specifically, we consider how the field of communication policy is transformed as the nation-state loses relative autonomy just as the object of regulation and accountability shifts from nation-states to markets and civil society. We conclude the chapter by arguing that we need to rethink the normative claims about public interest and social justice in a transnational, if not post-national era of policy practice.

Developmentalism, Fordism and the shadow of the Cold War

> The eras of the *Pax Britannica*, the *Pax Americana*, or the *Pax Soveitica* – the era of states inclined to prophetic visions of their own grandeur and the unshakeable affirmation of their superiority – gave rise to the tendency to look at the world from the point from which power radiated outwards. The East–West confrontation has left its imprint in the form of a bipolar division of the planet that fuelled the imaginary with a metaphysical contest between the forces off good and evil – at least until the day when the bloc conception crumbled along with regimes thought eternal and omnipotent. And yet the Manichean vision of the planet has not vanished from mentalities. The Cold War had scarcely been buried when a regional war broke out, and this religious conception of grand international oppositions made a spectacular resurgence. The havoc it has wrought is visible even among the most enlightened intellectuals. (Mattelart 2002: 242)

In an exhaustive historiography, Armand Mattelart writes of the enduring legacy of military and economic power in shaping the role of modern media and information systems. These arguments remain resonant today as new foreign and civil wars are rationalized as an 'exceptional' response to terrorism, whether in Iraq, Afghanistan, or at 'home' in the West (Agamben 2004). Mattelart cautions against the 'fading memory' of past internationalization, the way in which conservatives and liberals alike assume that today's multipolar and networked world marks a distinct rupture from previous modes of governance and technological order (Friedman 2005; Ohmae 1999). In this tradition, we trace how the bipolar ideological division of the world as defined through the Cold War remains central to the current definition of 'free' media and information flow. We also consider how the brutal encounter and legacy of colonialism continues to shape the problems and solutions in the field of global media and communication policy.

We start with the end of the Second World War, when multilateral governance was codified with the founding of the United Nations (UN). The UN charter provided for the establishment of specialized bodies like the United Nations Education, Scientific and Cultural Organization (UNESCO) which has dealt explicitly in regulating international communications and media industries, as well as the World Bank and International Monetary Fund (IMF) and the General Agreement on Trade and Tariffs (GATT), which would eventually play a prominent role in these areas. Although multilateral governance of communication industries has a longer history – for instance, the International Telecommunications

Union (ITU) has its origins in 1865 but came under UN supervision in this period – 1945 marked a new era of global governance. The UN was established with the specific mandate of mitigating the recurrence of another major war just as the US and the Soviet Union emerged as the two military superpowers in 1945. These UN bodies set the normative grounds for international cooperation from regulating the terms of trade and transfer of technology to establishing a universal commitment to 'the right to freedom of opinion and expression'.[3] Shortly thereafter, the first steps were taken to establish the European Union (EU), which would prove to be an influential actor in the field of global communication policy.

In this period, debates over the merits of two competing systems of media governance – state-owned media reflecting the Soviet model versus the privately owned commercial media system reflecting the US model, recur within the UN bodies, tension between the multilaterally mandated right to freedom of information against the principle of national sovereignty. In practice, Eastern and Western blocks were not obliged to follow each others' rules, so the fora of international governance had less direct effect in shaping actual domestic policy in either the First or Second Worlds. In contrast, the formerly colonized world now configured as the Third World, became the physical site of 'hot wars' and the political battles over competing systems governance. It is in this context that 'development' as a project emerged to be carried out through multilateral institutions of governance where 'Communication and its technologies were called on to occupy a key position in the battle for development'.[4] For this reason, the most significant struggles over international communication policy actually took place between the newly configured Third World nations whose weight in numbers challenged the economic and military clout of First World nations (Western nations along with Japan) resulting from decolonization in Africa, Asia and the Middle East between the 1940s and 1970s.

Many of these newly sovereign nations along with their postcolonial counterparts in Central and Latin America embarked on projects for national integration as a way to counter the negative effects of the colonial division of labour. Colonial nations were invariably locked into communications and transportations systems that were 'designed mainly to evacuate exports' as opposed to promote internal economic exchange (Hopkins 1973, cited in Graham and Marvin 2001: 84). For most postcolonial political leaders, nationalizing communications infrastructure and using mass media to integrate fractured colonial nation-states was high on the agenda. These national policy objectives were mediated through multilateral institutions and bilateral agreements that set the normative framework for the terms of domestic 'development'. By the 1960s, the Cold War was explicitly forcing national political elites in the Third World to choose sides, and multilateral bodies such as UNESCO, the World Bank and the IMF began to focus on communication, promoting modernization and Westernization based on the already 'developed' experiences of Western Europe and the US (Lerner 1958; Schramm 1964; Tunstall 1977).

In the First World, the rise of the Fordist welfare state meant greater state intervention in markets and welfare provisions, and a discourse of discrete national economies as the object of national government regulation. Fordism was characterized by a correlation between the geography of economic regulation and the nation-state that legitimated the 'central state's claim to be the penultimate source of power' (Steinmetz 1999: 34). In terms of communication policy, the Fordist mode of regulation reinforced a sense of national cohesion, as Graham and Marvin (2001) write:

> Strategies such as the New Deal initiative in the United States, which did much to support the extension towards national phone, electricity and highway grids, sought to use integrated public works programmes to 'bind' cities, regions and the nation whilst bringing social 'harmony', utilizing new technologies and also creating much needed employment... Taking control over the supply of networked infrastructure supplies to production, the territorial roll-out of networks over space, and the application of new services to modern consumption, were therefore essential components of the growth of the modern nation-state itself. (74)

Mattelart (2002) has shown how the US took the lead in developing 'strategies for organizing mass consumption', not as a result of technological advancement, 'but rather because the media had, throughout this whole period, become the very cornerstone of a project of national integration' (71). State ownership of broadcasting and telecommunications industries as practised in Western Europe, Canada and Australia and state regulation of private monopolies in broadcasting and telecommunications industries as practised in the US, created the terms of a 'Fordist class compromise' of guaranteed employment for a highly unionized but stable workforce. A gendered division of labour in terms of both production and consumption complemented this era of mass production. For instance, through the growing reach of network television, advertising targeted white middle-class 'housewives' who were schooled in the practice of mass consumption.[5] Scholars have compared national experiences in communication and policy-making in the Fordist era, often assessing the differences in the parameters and distributive consequences of public welfare and public interest between Western European, Canadian and Australian corporatist modes of governance in contrast to the US model of corporate liberalism (Calabrese 1999: 275; Garnham 1990; Horwitz 1989; Mansell 1994; Streeter 1996; Winseck 2002).

The Fordist era of national integration and economic expansion produced a very specific understanding of the state within the international state system. Fundamental to the formation of the rules of international governance was the assumption that 'all states in principle are, or will become, similar, or at least mutually intelligible, in their structures and in the rationalities governing their actions' (Hansen and Stepputat 2001: 10). Political elites from across the postcolonial world were eager to embrace this understanding of the state as the central institutional actor capable of delivering national development, whether these states chose central planning, a mixed model of national private industry and state participation, or early forms of export-led expansion. Third World political elites embarked on the project of development, attempting to move forward and shed the 'flawed' characteristics of pre-modern institutions (Huntington 1968). The state itself was understood as the 'modern sector' to be supported by multilateral agencies, foreign governments and donors with little reflection upon the fact that these were inherited colonial institutions designed to control as opposed to serve the 'native' populations. Mahmood Mamdani (1996) has shown how newly independent African nation-states, diagnosed by development experts as 'weak states', were barely dismantled versions of colonial administrations, which had been purposely centralized, without independent judiciaries and meant to be oppressive towards the colonial subject population. Instead of addressing the roots of these institutional imbalances, or questioning how colonialism led to 'underdevelopment' (Golding 1974; Schiller 1992), social scientists based in the US took the lead through UN agencies to resolve the problem of development through new technologies of progress, including communication and the mass media.

In 1958, Daniel Lerner's *The Passing of Traditional Society* consolidated and made explicit the prescriptive link between exposure to commercial mass media and the requisite social and psychic preconditions – the revolution in rising expectations – that would propel a linear mode of development. Sociologists like Lerner, and eventually scholars of the emerging discipline of international communication, identified a series of non-economic 'agents of development' – urbanization, literacy, exposure to the media – that would serve the dual purpose of erasing the negative effects of 'traditional values' while creating the conditions for modern market subjects who would be equally at ease as citizen and consumer.[6]

The mass media would consequently be seen as an agent for individual mobilization as well as social cohesion – appealing to postcolonial political leaders who had to contend with the difficult project of national integration. The modernization mandate was based not only on an idealized and ahistorical understanding of the state but also on a deeply gendered logic of 'institutionalized individualism' (Kabeer 2003; 16). The 'modern man' would be driven to achieve as an individual as opposed to follow ascribed norms or customs, thereby spurring development, whereas the modern woman was presumed to have even more to gain from development, 'emancipated from the seclusion of the household' and 'exercising her mind and her talents in the same way as men' (Kabeer 2003: 19).

With national liberation struggles spilling over to civil wars spurred on by the rival superpowers, national development organizations such as the United States Agency for International Development (USAID) and UNESCO began to make communication policy in the developing world a priority, beginning in the early 1960s.[7] Throughout this period, the Third World became a social laboratory for development scholars and policy-makers in general, including communication scholars experimenting on 'diffusion of innovation' to see if peasants could imagine being entrepreneurs, if slumdwellers would use condoms and if 'nation building' could take place without the threat of land redistribution and political revolution. Private firms based in the US and Western Europe saw opportunities for expansion in areas such as telecommunications equipment and transfer of technologies, advertising and trade in film and television within the larger objectives of promoting development.[8] By the end of the 1960s, USAID along with the National Aeronautics and Space Administration (NASA) introduced satellite television in large developing countries like India and Brazil. By the early 1970s when these projects were implemented, increasingly authoritarian national leaders in both countries were anxious to stem political unrest in the form of emerging social and political movements, allowing these agencies to test the hypotheses of development communication on the largest of scales with the promise of national integration. In both countries the state deployed the 'panacea of televized education' (Mattelart 2002: 160) while simultaneously opening the doors to the lucrative spoils of commercial television for domestic private industry.[9]

Many scholars have documented the violence and failures of the development decades with worldwide poverty far from disappearing and the Orientalist discourse of development condemning the Third World forever to the 'waiting room of history' (Chakrabarty 2000: 22; Escobar 1994; Kabeer 2002). We argue that postcolonial political leaders adapted the deeply Eurocentric normative assumptions of development communications assuming a linear road to modernization and progress. The integration of national culture often meant state censorship of minority perspectives or the smoothing over of historically sensitive social divisions. The diffusion of radios to farmers and expansion of satellite television failed, of course, to take into consideration the experiences or participation of the very people they were supposed to modernize. This would be the basis of the critique by reformers arguing for new participatory approaches to development communication (Melkote and Steeves 2001), often by former modernization scholars such as Everett Rogers (1995). We are arguing that nations in the Third World in the Fordist era were already integrated into an international system of development and modernization defined by the West. National regulation of infrastructure investment and expansion in the areas of telecommunications, electronics and broadcasting followed the objectives of development, with minimum participation from and often at the direct expense of the vast majority of any given nation's population. Moreover, national elites throughout much of the Third World tightened their grip on the regulation of mass media for the ostensible objective of national development, often with the implicit backing of the US and other Western powers, who set aside their commitment to 'freedom of information' and instead supported authoritarian regimes faithful to a modernization agenda without social upheaval.[10]

It is in this historical context that we turn to the most significant struggle over international communication policy in the Fordist era: the call for a New World Information and Communication Order (NWICO) in UNESCO. NWICO had its roots in the non-aligned movement (NAM), formed by a group of prominent African and Asian national leaders who met in 1955 in Bandung, Indonesia, to promote an independent vision of development outside the constraints of the bipolar framework of the Cold War. The key players of the NAM movement like Sukarno (Indonesia), Nehru (India), Nkrumah (Ghana), Nasser (Egypt), Nyrere (Tanzania), Ho Chi Minh (Vietnam), Chou En-lai (China), outlined a philosophy of non-interference in matters of international relations. This movement was not promoting neutrality in international relations; rather, it laid out an explicit critique of 'colonialism, neocolonialism, imperialism and racism' (Gupta 2001; 183). In 1961, a summit in Belgrade – with the leadership of Yugoslavia's Tito – launched the new movement against the intervention of both Soviet aggression in the Eastern block and the growing military involvement of the US from Cuba to Sub-Saharan Africa to Southeast Asia. By the mid-1960s, a new group of 77 (G77) nations within the UN emerged that by 1974 would call for a New International Economic Order (NIEO) with the explicit objective of overturning the structural dependency of Third World nations on First World powers. Drawing from dependency theory – a critical school of thought based on the Latin American experience of underdevelopment – intellectuals and policy-makers within the non-aligned nations challenged the assumptions about the universality of the development paradigm and set out to reverse the neocolonial rules governing aid and the terms of trade.[11]

International communication policy became an area of interest for national leaders, who saw 'decolonizing information' and reversing 'cultural imperialism' as vital to the New Economic Order, in the light of growing US corporate domination of news and cultural flows at the expense of mass media produced in the Third World (Nordenstreng 1984). Throughout the 1970s, debates within UNESCO criticized the US vision of a 'free flow of information' as opposed to the 'quantitative imbalance' in news and information flow across media, the gaping lack of information exchange between Third World nations and the social and cultural costs of 'alienating cultural influences' of commercially based media (Gross and Costanza-Chock 2004: 24–6). The idea of a New International Information Order (later becoming the NWICO) was laid out in 1976 in Colombo, Sri Lanka. Initially, the call for NWICO criticized the five major news agencies that dominated international news flows. An immediate outcome of this critique was the creation of the News Agency Pool, which aimed to create an alternate news distribution system within the Third World. Criticisms initially raised by radical Latin American scholars against US commercial media imperialism were echoed and reinterpreted by national leaders across both the North–South as well as East–West axes of tension: 'The East ably succeeded in fusing its position on the possibility and thus the intervention of the state in defense of national sovereignty with that of countries of the Third World fighting for their cultural self-determination' (Mattelart 2002: 181). In the end, the MacBride Commission Report, published in 1980, after several years of heated international deliberation, raised important questions about global information inequality, media concentration and national cultural determination, marking a significant departure for UNESCO. However, the final outcome was a source of frustration for most of its supporters, many of whom felt that the MacBride Report presented a contradictory and inherently impractical set of prescriptions for policy reform.[12]

The muddled prescriptions of the MacBride Report and the failures of the NWICO debates to radically alter the course of international communication and media policy has been rightly blamed on the overwhelming political economic power of the US media industry to launch an aggressive attack against the 'politicization' of UNESCO (Preston et al. 1989). This is further evidenced by the fact that both the Reagan and Thatcher administrations withdrew from UNESCO in the mid-1980s, taking with them their financial dues and thereby crippling the organization and the NWICO agenda. However, to fully make sense of the NWICO debate, we must also take into account the disparate demand by political leaders for the democratization of multilateral institutions without any reference to internal democratization. The credibility of national leaders, who were passionate about Third World solidarity on the world stage while brutally promoting development at home by silencing expressions of local culture and discussions about economic and human rights, was limited to say the least (Mattelart 2002: 182–4; Servaes 1999).

Akhil Gupta (2001) has argued that efforts at Third World solidarity through the Nonaligned Movement and the call for a new economic and communication order 'represented an effort on the part of economically and militarily weaker nations to use the interstate system to consolidate the nation-state' (191). The point here is neither to deny the substantial achievements of the NWICO era nor to underplay the extraordinary influence of media industries and the US in opposing any moves to challenge the development paradigm. Rather, recognizing the legacy of the postcolonial state and historicizing this specific mode of transnational imagining of a coordinated nationalist response to Western cultural dominance, exposes the gaps in the international communication and media policy debate. When during the NWICO debates political leaders from large sections of Africa and Asia argued that 'democracy was a luxury that could wait for the serious business of development' (Alhassan 2004: 65), the legitimacy of the nation-state to represent public interest was certainly open to question.

As the NWICO debates began and ended with little resolution, the Fordist era – based on the legitimacy of national regulatory autonomy – was already in decline. Financial liberalization and the relocation of manufacturing industries 'shedding' production from the First World to the fast-growing 'East Asian Tigers' meant that the collective unity of the Third World was itself in jeopardy by the mid-1970s. By the time the MacBride Commission Report was published the nation-state faced a crisis of legitimacy whether in debt ridden Africa and Latin America, the crumbling Soviet Block, and even within the fiscally strapped borders of the welfare state where Reagan and Thatcher began their strategic assault against the perils of 'big government'.

Neoliberalism, post-Fordism and the deterritorialized information economy

> During the second half of the twentieth century, economics established its claim to be the true political science. The idea of 'the economy' provided a mode of seeing and a way of organizing the world that could diagnose a country's fundamental condition, frame the terms of its public debate, picture its collective growth or decline, and propose remedies for its improvement, all in terms of what seemed a legible series of measurements, goals, and comparisons. In the closing decade of the century, after the collapse of state socialism in the Soviet Union and Eastern Europe, the authority of economic science seemed stronger than ever. Employing the language and authority of neoclassical economics, the programs of economic reform and structural adjustment advocated in Washington by the International Monetary Fund, the World Bank, and the United States government could judge the condition of a nation and its collective well-being by simply measuring its monetary and fiscal balances. (Mitchell 2002: 272)

Many of the national leaders arguing for Third World solidarity and cultural sovereignty on the UNESCO stage were simultaneously opening their arms to accept unprecedented levels of foreign private bank loans thanks to the newly deregulated financial markets in the early 1970s. The beneficiaries of these loans included ruthless autocrats like Zaire's Sésé Seko Mobutu, the Philippines' Ferdinand Marcos, Indonesia's General Suharto, Chile's Augusto Pinochet and Iraq's Saddam Hussein.[13] The Bretton Woods institutions of the World Bank and IMF encouraged large-scale borrowing in this period, ostensibly to spur national development, including infrastructural development in telecommunications and broadcasting. It was also between 1973 and 1975 that the Group of Seven (G7) states formed an official alliance of 'developed' nations, whereby the finance ministers of the US, the UK, France, West Germany, Japan, Italy and Canada met regularly to coordinate economic development strategies and 'crisis management' in response to the increased financial liberalization unleashed on the world market (McMichael 2003: 121–2).[14] By the early 1980s, a deep recession in Western economies and a monetarist turn in economic policy meant that credit was suddenly in short supply. By 1986, Third World public debt was at $1 trillion, and with interest rates suddenly soaring these nations were held in a kind of debt bondage having to pay back these loans at whatever cost (George 1992).

It is at this point that the World Bank and IMF become central institutional actors involved in not merely guiding, but actually designing and enforcing development policy, including communication and media policy in both the Second and Third Worlds. In practice this has meant the push to liberalize, deregulate and privatize domestic communication and media industries. McMichael (2003) argues that the debt crisis consolidated two trends that were already in place in the 1970s: First, the crisis caused 'the undoing of the Third World as a collective entity' based on the distinct trajectories of the rapidly expanding economies of the Asian Tigers or Newly Industrialized Countries (NICs)[15] in contrast to the debt-ridden nations in need of 'restructuring'; Second, these events legitimated global governance by the World Bank and IMF who took charge of evaluating the well-being of national economies based on whether or not they followed the principles of structural adjustment which included undoing expensive social programmes for health and education, removing barriers to investment and trade, devaluing national currencies and promoting export-led development.[16]

With the end of the Cold War in clear sight, the US and its allies quickly shifted the locus of international policy debates from the wider 'politicized' fora like UNESCO to narrow technical venues where First World nations held more clout and Transnational Corporations had access to manoeuvring favourable policy outcomes. In terms of the specifics of the NWICO debate, the US and its allies shifted the discourse of information inequality and cultural sovereignty to creating requisite regulatory conditions for an 'information society' in the ITU and the World Intellectual Property Organization (Kleinwächter 2004a). A much more significant shift in venue would take place in the Uruguay Rounds of the GATT. The GATT was established in 1947 through pressure from the US, and had grown from an organization of 23 members in 1947 to 128 members in 1984 (Siochrú et al. 2002: 54). The purpose of the GATT was to remove tariffs and promote trade – mostly focusing on manufactured goods until the 1980s. The Uruguay Rounds, which began in 1986, significantly broadened the scope of the GATT to include trade in 'services' where 'developed' nations had an obvious initial comparative advantage in selling the hardware and software necessary for entry into the information economy including telecommunications equipment and services, television and film products, advertising and marketing services, and networking and database services.

In addition to broadening its scope to include agriculture and passing the controversial General Agreement on Trade in Services (GATS), the eight years of negotiation that made up the Uruguay Rounds also created a new set of binding rules for member states based on liberalizing investment (Trade-Related Aspect of Investment Measures, TRIMS) and protecting property rights (Trade-Related Aspects of Intellectual Property Rights, TRIPs). These agreements would be the basis for replacing the GATT with the permanent institutional structure of the WTO in 1995. The WTO is essentially a multilateral regulatory agency based on member nation representation (currently at 148 members)[17] that coordinates trade policy, negotiates trade disputes and has the legal power to sanction member nations through an empowered Dispute Settlement Body. In contrast to the GATT, which was exclusively a treaty that dealt with trade, the WTO has jurisdiction like the UN to enforce its rulings in the much broader realm of 'trade-related' issues. In effect, the WTO 'harmonizes' trade policy between member nations such that individual states can be sanctioned for any kind of regulatory intervention that is seen as discriminating against the 'free' movement of goods or services. In practice, this has meant unprecedented challenges to national labour, health, environmental and other public interest legislation that is now deemed a violation of the rules of 'free' trade. While any member nation has the right to lodge complaints through the WTO against another nation-state that is 'distorting trade obligations,' the highly technical and opaque structure of the WTO explicitly favors the most economically powerful member states and the transnational firms that are the biggest beneficiaries of the 'harmonization' process (Jawara and Kwa 2004). Since the last failed WTO ministerial meeting in Cancun in 2003, a Group of Twenty Southern (G20) nations including Brazil, China, Egypt, India and South Africa, among others, have 'joined forces to defend the interests of developing countries in multilateral trade negotiations'.[18]

The authority of the World Bank and IMF in transforming the role of the state in the 'developing' and former Socialist world, along with the rise of the G8 nations and the WTO gave credence to the argument that national elites and policy-makers across the world had now come to agreement over the 'Washington Consensus' of neoliberal reform for both strategic reasons and out of economic necessity. This transformation was also, however, a result of the failures of most postcolonial states to deliver the promise of modernization and progress to its citizens as discussed in the previous section. In this case, it is not so much the institutional failures – which became the myopic focus of policy reform initiatives by the World Bank and others who would now manage 'good governance' – but rather the symbolic violence enacted by state institutions on behalf of the public that lent a degree of legitimacy to whatever external pressures there existed for reform. These gaps in the symbolic authority of the nation-state to represent public interest allowed a variety of civil-society organizations, ranging from religious nationalists to new social movements, to offer competing political solutions to the problems of modernization and development. Within the 'developing world' there has been consistent opposition by social movements and political parties from the Left (and occasionally the Right) against neoliberal policy reforms beginning in the 1980s, but many of these critics tend to argue that the state's relationship to its citizens has to be reimagined in contrast to the development decades of state intervention.

In both former state-socialist and Western welfare state economies, the culture of the state and the legitimacy of national integration and economic growth faced significant challenges.[19] In the West, the welfare-state capacities of national governments to regulate media and communication changed in response to the changing needs of private industry which was focusing on global production and sales. This changed the 'object of economic management' to focus on balance of payments as opposed to national full employment. However, equally important to these structural macro-economic changes are the constitutive role of race and gender in transforming the legitimacy of the state in any national policy arena. For instance, the increasing reliance of European welfare-state economies on foreign immigrant labour from former colonies or Southern or Eastern Europe posed a threat to the 'Fordist class compromise'. In the US, the welfare state faced more profound crises based on the migration of African Americans from the rural south to the industrial North and the arrival of Mexican and other Third World migrants who were often excluded from the benefits of the welfare state, regardless of citizenship. In the same way, the growing feminization of the labour force across welfare states in the 1970s challenged how citizenship rights were constructed around the patriarchal nuclear family, stressing the limits of the social contract.

It is crucial to recognize that the crisis of legitimacy of the nation-state as the arbiter of public interest happens just as pressures from private capital and multilateral institutions of governance are eroding its power. This combination of political economic and cultural change helps explain the transition from Fordism to 'post-Fordism' and the rise of a new discourse of enterprise culture and privatization (Jessop 1992). In the post-Fordist era, the demands for redistribution of communications resources and cultural sovereignty raised during the NWICO debates were swept aside in international policy-making circles. We contend, following Jessop, that the profound changes that take place in the field of communication and media policy should be seen as a kind of 'reregulation' of neoliberal governance. This reregulation has meant that the nation-state loses autonomy in relation to supranational regimes and regional and local governance bodies. It has also meant the reorganization of the functions of the state to include 'partnerships' with parastatal, non-governmental bodies as well as private capital. Finally, reregulation also includes the 'internationalization of policy regimes' in effect blurring the distinction between domestic and foreign policy.

The expansion of the GATT, the creation of the WTO and the reinforced role of the World Bank, the IMF and the G8 are clear examples of supranational regimes, along with the growing institutional power of regional trade agreements in areas such as trade in cultural products and harmonization of technology standards and intellectual property rights. The three most significant groupings are referred to as the triad regions of the North American Free Trade Agreement (NAFTA), centred around the US economy and established in 1994, the Asian Pacific Economic Community (APEC), centred around Japanese and Chinese economies and established in 1989, and the EU. In subsequent chapters, which provide an extended discussion of the EU, we argue that the loss of national autonomy is very much a source of political contest in the present moment where the 'business of rule' has not corresponded easily with national identity.

The loss of the nation-state's autonomy happens in relation to the expansion of regional and local governance structures, as national governments decentralize governance of local networks that serve as links to a larger global economy. Sassen (1999) and Castells (1996) have written about the new geography of centrality and marginality that make up network societies, whereby local and state governments invest in developing strategic spaces within a global city or region to serve as crucial nodes of production or management for a variety of transnational firms, while bypassing other spaces that are considered less lucrative. The expansion of private information and communication technology (ICT) networks following the logic of 'premium networked spaces' has created new regulatory parallels between business districts, 'techno-poles' and 'high-tech innovation clusters' across the North–South divide (Graham and Marvin 2002). The relative loss of national autonomy should therefore be understood as a dynamic process, where the new translocal linkages between firms might be challenged by regional or translocal state and non-governmental actors that have the potential to disrupt the very terms of global expansion and integration.

The reorganization of the functions of the state is evident in the shift from a centralized notion of government to a decentralized mode of governance:

> This trend concerns not so much the territorial dispersion of the national state's activities as a reorganization of functions in the broader political system on whatever territorial scale the state operates. It

> involves movements from the taken-for-granted necessity of varied forms and levels of partnership between official, parastatal, and non-governmental organizations in managing economic and social relations. (Jessop 1999: 389–90)

Current discourses of global communication and media policy speak of *governance* in this precise way, where the object and actors that define state intervention have changed from centralized state bodies focusing on domestic performance of the national economy to 'partnerships' between private actors, non-governmental organizations (NGOs) and state bodies to coordinate the delivery of social goods and services at the local level. Although the nation-state plays a crucial role through public spending, enforcing national laws or contributing other kinds of resources, private investment, knowledge and expertise become important in shaping social policy. Within the institutions of global governance, this process is evident with the growing formal presence and participation of transnational corporate actors who have deep pockets to conduct research, send delegates to international meetings and press for changes at policy-making forums. Civil Society Organizations (CSOs) have also gained more access, albeit often with less financial and technical resources than their corporate counterparts, who also represent themselves as part of civil society depending on the forum or body. NGOs have historically been recognized as part of the UN since its formation, but their roles only became formally recognized through the UN Economic and Social Council (ECOSOC) in 1968. NGO participation within the UN began in earnest in the 1970s, and then 'exploded in the 1990s with the 1992 Earth Summit in Rio de Janeiro', reflecting the growing presence of both local and international NGOs (INGOs). In 1996, ECOSOC formalized the already-existing guidelines spelling out the basis for a 'consultative relationship' between 'accredited NGOs' and UN bodies (Siochrú 2003: 38).

In the following chapters we will interrogate these supranational sites of global governance – the World Bank and the IMF, the WTO, the ITU as the host of the World Summit on the Information Society (WSIS) – keeping in mind the growing tensions between the multilateral UN agencies that have historically focused on political consensus versus the market-oriented multilateral bodies. US-led pressure to shift power in line with the 'Washington Consensus' away from UN bodies towards the trade-oriented organizations have transformed the rules of global communication governance. Private firms advocate 'self-regulation' in these fora, providing technical and market expertise while NGOs might take the lead in delivering services – a function that was previously limited to state bodies. This devolution of national state power is less hierarchical and centralized , reinforcing the legitimacy of 'flexibility,' a central feature of post-Fordist discourse in the policy field.

The relative loss of national autonomy and the reorganization of the state's functions have taken place as policy regimes themselves have become increasingly intertwined with the objectives of international competitiveness (Jessop 1999). In terms of communication and media policy this means that previous national policy objectives – cultural sovereignty, universal service, national integration, national employment schemes – are 'subordinated to labour market flexibility and/or to the constraints of international competition' (392). The degree that individual nation-states are subject to the internationalization of policy regimes varies with political, economic and also military power – such that powerful nation-states like the US can choose to opt out in ways that are unimaginable for most nations in the South. But this obvious imbalance in the rules of the game has led to debates about the accountability of the different social actors involved in governance as well as the 'governance of governance' and the failure in most cases to create legitimacy for internationalized policy regimes themselves.[20]

The legitimacy of governance: rethinking normative claims for social justice

The new actors and institutions of global governance face a legitimacy crisis because of the dislocating effects of rapid global integration, reinforcing and also creating new divisions based on race, gender and sexuality, as well as ethnicity, religion and nationality. Foremost among these effects is the growing inequality both within and across national economies measured in terms of the increasing disparity between society's marginalized and affluent populations. Contributing to the rising inequality and instability in people's everyday lives is the rapid financial instability in nations jolted by financial crises, growing rates of casualization and feminization of labour, and the diminished capacity of states to fund health and education to the growing cross-border movement of displaced peoples in the form of migrant labour and refugees. In the midst of these transformations, and despite the shifts in its institutional capacity, the nation-state remains the major site of ongoing competition over social conflict and cohesion and redistribution, precisely because supranational and local and regional bodies do not possess the requisite 'popular democratic legitimacy' (Jessop 1999: 395). It is in response to this disjuncture between the nation-state as the enduring site of political legitimacy despite the expansive internationalization of policy practice that Habermas and Held argue for cosmopolitan democracy in a 'postnational' political world where transnational networks of communication, NGOs and popular political movements form the basis for global sovereignty and citizenship (Habermas 2001; Held 2004).

A wide range of oppositional movements has responded to the dislocating effects of globalization that has not simply challenged, but actually transformed the course of global integration, raising fundamental questions about the legitimacy of the mechanisms of global governance. In 1998, Joseph Stiglitz, then Senior Vice President and Chief Economist for the World Bank, acknowledging the power of this response, spoke of a 'Post-Washington Consensus' signalling the end of an era of blind faith in markets and US dominance in promoting neoliberal trade . While far from radical in his prescriptions for reform, it is instructive to consider the following principles of the new consensus that Stiglitz outlined:

> One principle of these emerging ideas is that whatever the new consensus is, it cannot be based on Washington. In order for policies to be sustainable, they must receive ownership by developing countries. It is relatively easier to monitor and set conditions for inflation rates and current account balances. Doing the same for financial sector regulation or competition policy is neither feasible nor desirable. The second principle of the emerging consensus is a greater degree of humility, the frank acknowledgment that we do not have all of the answers. (Stiglitz 1998)

Stiglitz's comments preceded the mass mobilization against the WTO in Seattle in 1999, and the subsequent protests at global summits and trade talks that along with the creation of the World Social Forum in Porto Alegre, Brazil, in 2001, became recognized as part of an organized global justice movement directly challenging the legitimacy of the neoliberal trade paradigm. These comments were instead responding to both the rapid expansion of new economic powers like China, Brazil, India and Russia as well as to the financial crises, social and economic dislocation and mass mobilization against the violence of structural adjustment and trade 'harmonization' across Africa, Asia and Latin America since the 1980s.

The faltering legitimacy of neoliberalism has many manifestations relevant for scholars critical of global communication and media policy. On the one hand, the rise of religious fundamentalisms and xenophobic nationalisms in both the North and South mobilizes support around arguments for cultural integrity or purity in response to foreign or 'alien' cultural influences. It becomes vital in this context to consider how the political culture of nationalism as a response to globalization shapes policy debates, even if the institutional world of rule making may falsely appear immune from these forces. On the other hand, a variety of progressive new social movements have themselves become transnational – from environmentalism to feminism, new labour movements, movements for human rights, to name a few – and are seen to embody modes of 'globalization from below'.

These movements explicitly address the inequities of the neoliberal information society, by confronting the market logic of intellectual property rights or negotiating the tensions between universal human rights on the one hand and cultural rights to determine gender and sexuality, norms or societal standards for 'decency', on the other. They are but a few examples of political contests over global communication and media policy within the larger struggles over the governance of globalization that highlight, once again the need for a cultural theory of the state – even as the role of the state is drastically transformed. We have argued that the experiences of the postcolonial nation-state revealed the constitutive role of colonialism in shaping the limits of the state to represent the public, or more precisely multiple publics. We must also pay attention to the ways in which the intensification of 'social suffering' and the 'humiliation' associated with globalization remain 'unrecognized' and outside of a public political debate (Bourdieu and Accordo 1999; Chatterjee 2004).

The need to acknowledge difference as we rethink the relationship between state institutions and public representation and deliberation has been at the centre of debates within feminist theory for the last decade (McLaughlin 2004). Feminist political theorists like Nancy Fraser have argued that post-Fordist claims for justice are multifaceted along at least two recognizable, interrelated dimensions of redistribution (claims around economic equality) and recognition (claims around cultural difference). Fraser has argued that while redistributive claims dominated claims for justice in the Fordist era without adequate attention to gender, race or nationality, claims for recognition have overshadowed egalitarian claims in the post-Fordist (post-Socialist) era (Fraser and Honneth 2003). There has been disagreement and criticism about the rigid separation of these categories among feminist theorists,[21] but for our purposes it is useful to note that most feminists agree that the presumed antithesis between the material (distribution) and the cultural (recognition) dimensions of politics needs to be rethought (Benhabib 2004; Young 2000; Butler 2004; Mohanty 2003). Feminist theorists have long argued for the need to theorize justice outside questions of distribution alone. Fraser points to the 'materiality of genocide, violence against women, hate crimes against sexual and ethnic minorities', and argues that claims on behalf of 'exploited classes' and 'despised sexualities' are at once about recognition and redistribution (Fraser and Honneth 2003).

In this context, actors seeking to make these claims for justice or seeking to engage in progressive politics face three dilemmas, according to Fraser. First, there is a problem of 'reification', or giving the impression that an abstract category represents something concrete. While some struggles for recognition seek to adapt to condition of increased complexity by emphasizing 'respectful differences in multicultural contexts' others embrace forms of communitarianism, drastically simplifying or reifying group identities and encouraging 'separatism, group enclaves, chauvinism and intolerance, patriarchalism and authoritarianism' (Fraser Honneth 2003: 91–2). In the field of media policy, reified notions of community in response to globalization complicate earlier claims of 'cultural imperialism' and 'cultural diversity' as expressed in the NWICO era. Today, Christian fundamentalists and xenophobes, pan-Islamic nationalists, conservative Zionists and Hindu Chauvinists have *all* deployed arguments against the globalization of culture by focusing on the threats to 'local' and 'national' culture. These reinterpretations of the older cultural imperialism argument legitimate deeply unequal social orders by strategically reifying local cultures as monolithic.

Second, Fraser argues that there is a problem of 'displacement' where conflicts over recognition dominate just as 'neoliberal capitalism exacerbates economic inequality' (Fraser and Honneth 2003: 91). In their study of transnational social movements in the 1980s and 1990s, Keck and Sikkink argued that the most successful global campaigns mobilized around negative freedoms that associated 'bodily harm to vulnerable individuals, and legal equality of opportunity' – in each case human rights claims for recognition. They pointed out that despite agreement between activists across borders over rights based norms like these – ***structural inequality*** of outcome remains a source of tension ***between*** activists from the South and the North. In other words, their study found that campaigns around negative freedoms such as the rights of women to live without threats of violence, the rights of minority communities to live without discrimination by the state (in Fraser's terms, claims for recognition), have greater 'transcultural resonance'. They found, however, that activists from the South were equally concerned with positive freedoms (in Fraser's terms redistributive claims) associated with 'poverty and inequality in an internationalist framework,' where the political and institutional power of the North to set ***and*** challenge the rules of globalization is paramount.[22] We will argue in subsequent chapters that these tensions are a persistent feature of current struggles in the field of global communication policy.

Finally, Fraser identifies the problem of 'misframing' where social movements impose a 'national frame on a global problem'. For social movements claiming recognition, this might lead to demands for 'secure ethnic enclaves' – restrictive immigration policy or violence against 'outsiders' – just as migrations of populations increase both within and across national borders. Similarly, Fraser argues that 'defenders of redistribution are turning protectionist at precisely the moment when economic globalization is making Keynesianism in one country an impossibility' (Fraser and Honneth 2003: 92). The problem of misframing is evident in the struggles over the regulation of work in the global information economy. Now that white-collar workers – the flexible knowledge workers of the post-industrial economy – have been negatively affected by the insecurities of the global economy through the off-shoring of work, temporary migration and competition from emerging markets, there are renewed calls for 'national' regulatory solutions against 'Third World labor standards'. The 'double standard' that allows social actors from dominant powers to make protectionist claims after two decades of evangelical preaching to Third World nations about the benefits of deregulated labour markets, hardly seems like an effective political strategy in the long-run.

Instead, there is a compelling need for a global frame for what are increasingly 'post-national' problems. For Fraser, the dilemma of misframing corresponds to the issue of representation as the third political dimension of social justice alongside of recognition and redistribution (Fraser and Naples 2004: 117). The legitimacy of social actors to represent the interest of citizens and their relationship to state institutions democratically becomes a pressing concern as democratic politics framed within the context of the nation-state expands (Chandhoke 2005). In the post-Fordist era, the terrain of political claims has expanded beyond class as has the scale of contest beyond that of the sovereign nation-state. The uncertain correspondence between the state and public interest or the complex relationship between state and nation are not peculiar pre-modern features of 'underdeveloped' societies, but rather point to the need for a cultural theory of the state whether examining the rise and fall of public broadcasting within the British or Canadian welfare state or the seeming disappearance of the state in the post-Soviet era.[23]

In chapters 3 and 4, we will examine historically specific empirical areas of policy reform in the fields of telecommunications and broadcasting policy. We focus on how various actors compete for symbolic power within the institutional bodies of local, regional, national and multilateral governance to make sense of the outcome of global communication policy struggles. In chapters 5 and 6 we will consider the postnational ideal of the governance of the global information society, as multiple stakeholders formulate the rules of Internet governance through specialized bodies such as ICANN (Internet Corporation for Assigned Names and Numbers) or even reimagine the 'governance of governance' at the WSIS. We argue that while we must explore why there is limited public awareness of these issues, much less public participation in these institutions and processes, we should not too quickly assume that the fault lies with uninformed global citizens who are disengaged or hopelessly misinformed about communication and information resources or media access, content and accountability. And in fact we argue quite the contrary position later in the book. Throughout *this* chapter we have argued that political, economic and technological transformations have altered how national governments regulate communication industries and content in ways that defy older forms of national regulation. In the next chapter, we address the reregulation of public interest in the field of telecommunications policy, seen by many commentators as the central nervous system of the global information economy.

Notes

1. In the postwar era, social scientists and development experts divided up the world according to stages of development. The First World was the industrialized, capitalist nations in the North (with the addition of Japan), the Second World was the Socialist Bloc of nations in Eastern Europe and the Third World was the former colonized world in Africa, Asia, Latin America and the Middle East. The First World also correlated with the term 'developed' world while Third World stood for 'undeveloped' or the 'underdeveloped' world. We will discuss the making and unmaking of the 'Third World' as a collective political voice in the international arena in subsequent sections of this chapter.
2. Neoliberalism refers to the shift in thinking as well as in macroecomic policy from Keynesian welfare or state-led models of economic growth which were dominant in the postwar era, towards the adoption of monetarism, privileging the role of markets over state intervention. We discuss this transition in much greater detail in the second half of this chapter.
3. Most significantly, in 1948 the UN passed the Declaration of Human Rights. Article 19 of this document states: 'Everyone has the right to freedom of opinion and expression. This right includes freedom to hold opinions without interference and to seek, receive and

impart information through any media regardless of frontiers.' See: http://www.un.org.overview.rights.html

4. Mattelart writes: 'It was in 1949 that the notion of "development" appeared in the language of international relations, designating by its antonym "underdevelopment" the state of the part of the planet that did not yet have access to the benefits of progress . . . The expression was born in the White House and passed into history via the 1949 State of the Union speech given by President Truman, in a section entitled "Point Four". This program aimed to mobilize energies and public opinion to combat the great social disequilibria that threatened to open the door to world communism. The ideology of progress metamorphosed into the ideology of development.' (Mattelart 2002: 148).
5. The gendered construction of mass consumption was a necessarily complex process that involved evoking desire, comfort and convenience as well as negotiation on the part of female consumers as discussed by Spigel (1992) and others (Meehan and Riordan 2001). Although beyond the scope of this chapter to explore the gendered dimensions of Fordist public policy in greater depth, it is important to point out that the paternalistic and patriarchal images of 'housewives' as grateful consumers also reinforced gendered 'distinctions between the (female) domestic private space and (male) public space' as a broader objective of public policy (Graham and Marvin 2001: 70).
6. Following in the tradition of dependency theorists in communications and other fields, Mattelart provides much-needed geopolitical context for the timing of the interest in communication for development. For instance, Lerner's research was based on a study of six Middle Eastern countries in the 1950s, after the US became concerned about democratically elected political leaders such as Iran's Mossadegh, who nationalized the oil industry in 1951, which was reversed thanks to the CIA-backed coup d'état in Iran in 1953. For more see: Mattelart 2002: 148–50.
7. UNESCO was associated with development communication as early as 1948. However, it began focusing on helping 'develop media of information in underdeveloped countries' in 1958, with a series of 'expert meetings' in the early 1960s. The organization prepared a report that it presented to the General Assembly in 1961, entitled *Mass Media in Developing Countries*, where it was estimated that 70 per cent of the world population lacked the 'minimum levels of communication capacity'. This marked the beginning of indexing communication needs as a development problem to be solved through aid and First World Assistance. For more on the institutional history

of international development communication see: Hamelink 1994: Chapter 7.

8. The power of transnational corporations to shape communication policy was especially strong in the Caribbean and Latin America, partially because of the US' overwhelming influence in the region economically and militarily (Martin-Berbero 1993). The experiences of these nations in the 1960s would lead to the dependency movement which itself spurred many of the first critiques of international 'development' within the field of communications (Mattelart 2002).
9. In Brazil, domestic private capital in the form of the Globo multimedia group played a more direct role in shaping policy with the backing of both the authoritarian Brazilian state in the 1970s and 1980s, and the US' tacit support. In contrast in India, despite the growing popularity of commercial television in the 1980s, the state remained the dominant player in shaping broadcasting policy until the 1990s with the unexpected entry of satellite television. For a rich account of the institutional and cultural history of television in India, see Rajagopal 2001.
10. Mattelart (2002) notes that between 1967 and 1972, the number of countries governed by military chiefs of staff more than doubled. In the US, technocratic development 'experts' like political scientist Lucian Pye initiated a series of studies on the role of mass media in ensuring national development through military administrations. In this period, the US government actively promoted 'nation-building' whereby modernization and authoritarian rule went hand in hand in Egypt, Indonesia, Brazil, Chile and Peru. See: 153–6.
11. Objectives of the NIEO included democratizing multilateral agencies like the World Bank and the IMF, institutions that functioned primarily in Third World nations with very minimal Third World participation or management. Other objectives included opening northern markets to southern exports, improving terms of trade for agricultural and mining exports, establishing codes for technological transfers, and codes of conduct for multinational corporations (See Mattelart 2002: 180; and McMichael 2003: 120–1). While the NIEO was radical in its calls for redistribution at the international level, it was silent on internal inequalities, including gender inequalities (Kabeer 2003: 71).
12. The NWICO debates as well as the politics of conducting research for and publishing the MacBride Commission Report have been analyzed by several researchers involved in the UNESCO process. For more see: Hamelink 1994; Braman 1991, 1999; Servaes 1999; and Nordenstrang 1984.
13. It was only once the debt crisis was officially diagnosed by the World Bank and the IMF – institutions that had been centrally

involved in 'brokering' private bank lending in the 'developing' world (McMichael 2003: 125) – that corruption as a disease endemic of Third World states began to be diagnosed. It was only then that corrupt military strongmen were seen as easy targets embodying failed states as opposed to failed international development policy.

14. This group did not go 'public' until 1986, and became the Group of Eight (G8) in 1997 when Russia officially joined the organization. The G8 meetings reflect the growing influence of private transnational firms on shaping policy, and the G8 serves to 'guide' the policy expansion within the WTO. For more from the organization's own website see: http://usinfo.state.gov/ei/economic_issues/group_of_8.html
15. The NICS, also referred to as the 'Asian Tigers' or 'Asian Dragons' are Hong Kong, Singapore, South Korea and Taiwan.
16. The Bretton Woods institutions played a significant role in making the Asian NICS a model for state reform across the rest of the Third World in the 1980s and 1990s. The premise that the Asian NICS had grown rapidly because of their commitment to free trade glossed over the strategic role of these states during the Cold War which guaranteed access to American and Japanese markets, as well as the combination of authoritarian rule and redistributive function of the 'developmentalist' state. For more on misperceptions about the NICs developmentalist strategies see: Amsden 1989; Wade and Veneroso 1998.
17. For more on member nations of the WTO and its organizational structure see: http://www.wto.org/english/thewto_e/whatis_e/tif_e/org6_e.htm
18. There are a number of issues of contention that currently divide Northern and Southern delegations within the WTO including intellectual property protocols, trade in agriculture and the basic structure of the WTO rule-making process. Marin Khor, the director of the NGO Third World Network argues that 'it was the WTO's untransparent and non-participatory decision-making process that caused the "unmanageable situation" that led to the collapse of the Cancun Ministerial'. For more see: http://www.choike.org/nuevo_eng/informes/1236.html
19. The argument here is based on Bob Jessop's analysis of the 'contradiction in the field of social reproduction' in his discussion of the reasons for the erosion of the Keynesian Welfare state (Jessop 1999: 385–6).
20. A variety of groups within civil society have raised questions about the accountability of state and multilateral institutions as well as transnational corporations in relation to the needs of citizens. However, critics have also raised questions about the accountability

of civil society organizations, in contrast with state bodies that are in theory representative (Held and McDrew 2002). Moreover, the issue of accountability has been central to critiques of the internationalization of policy regimes, with those who advocate for the diminished capacity of multilateral/supranational institutions versus those who advocate greater accountability within the WTO, NAFTA, EU and other bodies of supranational governance (Keohane 2002).

21. Nancy Fraser's writing on 'recognition' versus 'redistribution' led to an extensive debate within feminist political theory about the relationship between democracy and difference. Feminist scholars like Judith Butler and Iris Young who argued convincingly that Fraser devalued the politics of 'recognition' met Fraser's initial conceptualization with intense criticism. Fraser's more recent work highlights the inter-related aspects of the two dimensions and the hybridity of the categories such as gender and race that are equally about redistributive and recognition claims. Feminists from the postcolonial and ethnic studies traditions have also forwarded similar arguments, in what is recognized as transational feminism in the works of Chandra Mohanty (2003); Kaplan, Alarcon and Moallem (eds)(1999). For an overview of this debate see interview with Nancy Fraser by Nancy Naples (*Signs* 2004; and Lisa McLaughlin 2004).
22. The discussion of the limits of 'transcultural resonance' in Keck and Sikkink's work is insightful but brief. The authors make it clear that 'sterile debates' about power inequalities between the North and South are less interesting than meaningful coordination of campaigns. The major part of their book examines the means by which effective networks of cross-national advocacy groups function. Only in one of the subsections of the conclusion do they consider what seems like a crucial concern for such cross-border activist coalitions. See Keck and Sikkink 1998: 203–6.
23. When social scientists have traditionally considered culture as integral to theories of the state, they have focused primarily on the unique features of non-Western societies, in the Orientalist Weberian tradition (Steinmetz 1999: 15–17). In line with contemporary critical theorists of the state, here we are proposing embedding analysis of the political economy of communication and media policy-making in a cultural framework (Chakravartty and Zhao [eds] 2007).

Part Two

The policy domains

3 Governing the central nervous system of the global economy: telecommunications policy

Telecommunications infrastructure has been described as the 'central nervous system' of the very process of globalization (Castells 1996; Mansell 1994). Access to telecommunications services is increasingly assumed as a minimum condition of participation in the 'new economy' with the telecommunications industry as the foundation for Information Technology (IT), new media and financial services. Global advertisements plastered on television screens and billboards are replete with images of seamless high-tech networks that instantly link stock markets, urban centres and ethnically diverse consumers together, erasing national economic as well as cultural boundaries. Beneath the glamour and the breathless pace of these new technological transformations are the equally stunning, if less celebrated, changes in the ways in which telecommunications as an industry is governed. Beginning in the 1980s and throughout the 1990s, the deregulation and liberalization of national telecommunications markets was seen as imperative by policy-makers across the globe. Today, we see a shift in policy discourse in at least the recognition that there are social obstacles associated with rapid global integration. The 'United Nations Millennium Development Goals' (see Table 5.2) acknowledges the centrality of access to communications technologies as vital to the eradication of global poverty and hunger. As such, access to communications is seen as a basic human need linked to participation in modern economic as well as political activity (ITU 2003: 73).

We have seen dramatic changes in the field of telecommunications governance in the past two decades, influenced most significantly by the change in the balance of power against national governments and in favour of the 37, 000 transnational corporations that emerge as a

Table 3.1A Infrastructure: top 5 by fixed telephone subscribers per 100 inhabitants

1	Sweden	65.25
2	United States	65.02
3	Cyprus	62.44
4	Canada	61.30
5	Taiwan, China	57.45

Source: ITU World Telecommunication Indicator Database. Reproduced with the kind permission of ITU.

dominant force by the early 1990s (Graham and Marvin 2001: 95). Telecommunications firms have been aggressive and effective at influencing policy outcomes at both the national and transnational levels, with growing official presence in multilateral bodies from the ITU to the WTO. As discussed in Chapter 2, the domain of national regulation has become increasingly interlinked to transnational institutions of governance such as the WTO. Meanwhile the object of telecommunication regulation has expanded from basic telephone services to information and communications technologies which facilitate the transnational production and distribution of goods and services, including the proliferation of financial markets and new media technologies. The impact of these changes is visible in national indices measuring technological modernization, and recent figures show the prominence of select Asian markets as compared with their European and North American counterparts (See Tables 3.1A–3.1D).

As discussed also in Chapter 2, state bodies increasingly rely on 'partnerships' with private-sector and civil-society organizations to deliver services and ensure equity in terms of access to new technologies, especially in the multilateral policy-making arena. For example, in the G8 2000 summit when global attention first turned to the issue of the 'digital divide', political leaders from the North spelled out that private industry

Table 3.1B Infrastructure: top 5 by mobile cellular telephone subscribers per 100 inhabitants

1	Taiwan, China	106.5
2	Luxembourg	105.4
3	Israel	95.5
4	Italy	92.5
5	Hong Kong, China	91.6

Source: ITU World Telecommunication Indicator Database. Reproduced with the kind permission of ITU.

Table 3.1C Infrastructure: top 5 by broadband Internet subscribers per 100 inhabitants

1	Korea (Rep.)	21.9
2	Hong Kong, China	14.6
3	Canada	11.1
4	Taiwan, China	9.4
5	Belgium	8.4

Source: ITU World Telecommunication Indicator Database. Reproduced with the kind permission of ITU.

and civil society would take a leading role in addressing the global problems of access to communication resources:

> Bridging the digital divide in and among countries has assumed a critical importance on our respective national agendas. Everyone should be able to enjoy access to information and communications networks. We reaffirm our commitment to the efforts underway to formulate and implement a coherent strategy to address this issue. We also welcome the increasing recognition on the part of industry and civil society of the need to bridge the divide. Mobilising their expertise and resources is an indispensable element of our response to this challenge. We will continue to pursue an effective partnership between government and civil societies responsive to the rapid pace of technological and market developments.
>
> Okinawa Charter on the Global Information Society, 22 July 2000; http://www.g8.utoronto.ca/summit/2000okinawa/gis.htm

The charter established the Digital Opportunity Task (DOT) Force, which commissioned a report on 'ICTs for Development' (ICT4D) that was authored by 'Accenture, the world's top private consulting firm, [the] Markle Foundation (a non-profit in the US oriented toward US civil society concerns) and the UNDP'. In tracing the road from Okinawa to the World Summit on Information Societies (WSIS), Anita Gurumurthy, the

Table 3.1D Infrastructure: top 5 Internet users per 100 inhabitants

1	Iceland	64.9
2	Sweden	57.3
3	Korea (Rep.)	55.2
4	United States	55.1
5	Japan	54.5

Source: ITU World Telecommunication Indicator Database. Reproduced with the kind permission of ITU.

director of a NGO based in India, writes about the impact of this report as follows: 'With neat private sector efficiency, the DOT report gave some key concepts to what came to be known as ICT4D, and notably, these form the basic framework of ICT4D thinking even today' (2005a: 2). The emphasis on 'business models', the involvement of private industry with the corrective presence of civil society organizations and the assumed neutrality of communications technologies are some of the key features of this new global policy framework. The Okinawa Charter is an important document because it asserts newfound attention to the growing global 'digital divide' and acknowledges that the emerging Information Society requires some mode of social policy to be determined and implemented by multistakeholders. The charter also explicitly reproduces the symbolic dominance of Northern nation-states and transnational capital in setting the parameters for the new rules of global governance by coordinating the limits of national or local regulatory intervention.

Following our overview in Chapter 2, we argue that it is crucial to consider how notions of public interest and accountability emerge and transform within a given national context, even as the functions of governance might shift from the national to the transnational spheres. In this chapter, we assess the changes in the field of global telecommunications governance but we return to the experiences of nations in the South to consider more closely the specific political economic and cultural context of telecommunications reform – the liberalization of the telecommunications sector – in regions where the pace and extent of change has been the most dramatic in the last twenty years. We argue that this focus allows us to pay attention to both the external global factors which explain the push for reform as well as the historically rooted local factors that account both for the legitimacy and contestation of the changes in the rules of governance. In the next section we outline the shift in logic of the national public-interest model of telecommunications regulation.

Global telecommunications policy today: reregulating public interest

Between 1990 and 2000, the number of 'independent' national telecommunications regulatory agencies multiplied from 12 to 101, in effect regulating the new terms of economic liberalization – the opening up of national markets to foreign investment and introducing competition – into practice (Samarajiva 2001). In 1997, the WTO passed the Agreement on Basic Telecommunications (ABT) culminating fifteen years of debate over the terms of the new rules of trade with the liberalization of telecommunications services. Meanwhile, between 1984 and 1999, somewhere between $250 billion and $1 trillion of state owned telecommunications networks were sold to private investors and some half of the 189 member nations of the ITU had partially privatized their domestic telecommunications sectors (McChesney and Schiller 2003: 18).[1] In order to make sense of these dramatic changes, we outline the basic economic assumptions that have historically guided telecommunications regulation on the basis of national public interest.

In contrast to top-down, one-way mass media, the regulation of telecommunications is based on the assumption of shared resources. In the case of telephone services, calls made by individual subscribers are routed through a local exchange, where, using a common connection, the calls are connected to a bigger regional exchange that uses high-capacity connections that link major exchanges in order to distribute calls. The assumption in this model is that the value of this network grows as each additional user joins the network, precisely because it spreads the fixed costs around a larger number of users and because it expands the numbers of people each existing subscriber can contact. Economists argue that because the network can enhance social benefits beyond the members of the network, telecommunications should be seen as a 'public good' because of 'positive externalities. In other words, the greater the number of people connected to a network actually increases the worth of that network' (Garnham 2000). Putting this into practice, public-policy experts have historically argued that the telecommunications network should be seen as a 'club' based on members with mutual interests, as opposed to a market composed of members with competing interests. Until relatively recently, these 'members' or, in more current language, 'stakeholders' have included different institutional actors within and between national government bodies and, to a lesser extent, domestic and transnational firms, labour unions and consumer organizations and public interest groups (Mansell 1994; Singh 1999). Regulation here should be understood as a dynamic political process, part of a larger regularization practice that in this case normalizes among others the changing roles of private telecommunications industries. As we have seen, corporate stakeholders began to exert growing influence in both national and transnational telecommunications policy arenas that had historically been dominated by state actors, whereas today, many analysts contend that civil-society actors are emerging as empowered stakeholders in policy arenas.

The impact of all of these changes has meant a dizzying rate of expansion and transformation that has been recognized by a variety of critics as deeply uneven (Castells 1996; Sassen 1999, 2001; Schiller 1999). Corporate actors have taken the lead in pushing for *glocal* telecommunications services – global to local networks that bypass national networks – linking research and development and ultimately privatizing the delivery of premium capacity networks for large users. In this way national governments delegate authority to private infrastructure and service providers, often through tax exemptions provided by the national and/or regional government to attract foreign investment within specific segmented markets. Graham and Marvin (2001) describe the logic of the glocalization of the segmented telecommunications sector:

> Multiple providers offer private fibre optic networks that are configured to bypass local networks and interconnect sites on global corporate networks seamlessly and reliably. These networks are highly selective; they tend to be limited to the top fifty business and finance cities and are configured to meet the needs of the largest corporate users. In specialist 'back office zones' in the Caribbean and Ireland, meanwhile, specialist telecommunications operators offer multiple networks to allow the insurance, retail and financial service sectors to export routine administrative functions from low-wage enclaves. In addition, a wide range of private Internet 'pipes' are being deployed to bypass the constraints of old Internet trunks so that content delivery networks can be operated which enable the high-speed delivery of media and e-commerce services to selected affluent markets by the major media conglomerates. (2001: 172)

This form of segmentation results from the 'erosion' of the universal service model resulting from the changes in the field of telecommunications policy governance at the national level. In tracing the history of telecommunications reform in Canada, Winseck (1995) has argued that beginning in the mid-1980s, the 'means/end relation between competition and social policy changed. Competition became an end in itself, marking the transformation of regulation from social policy to industrial policy.' Graham and Marvin (2001) argue that these transformations are part of an overall shift away from national 'public works monopolies' within infrastructure industries – including water, energy and transportation – towards glocal premium networks creating a new form of 'splintering urbanism'. Critical urban studies scholars like Michael Peter Smith (1999) argue that these new inequalities that arise within major urban areas and across cities globally should be studied with an awareness of translocal networks that connect and marginalize communities across national boundaries.

Throughout the 1990s, telecommunications and media conglomerates took unprecedented financial risks to build these translocal telecommunications networks.[2] Intense competition to buy licences to operate basic telephony in emerging markets, as well as massive investments in broadband, cellular and satellite networks catering to transnational corporate users, translated into hundreds of billions of dollar of debt for these same firms since 2000. The massive investment corresponded with increasingly rapid and complex patterns of conglomeration, mergers and transnational alliances between local and long-distance service providers, broadband and digital cable companies and firms specializing in satellite and wireless services.[3] Beginning in 2000, a global glut in telecommunications capacity, combined with a series of highly public corruption scandals involving telecommunications giants like WorldCom, raised new concerns about corporate accountability in the sector.

Today the industry is once again undergoing a series of transnational mergers where national regulators are encouraging a new round of consolidation after two decades of promoting deregulation on the normative grounds that competition improved services for consumers. Perhaps the most telling example is the current status of AT&T, the US private telecommunications monopoly that triggered the global deregulation process in 1984 when national regulators allowed the company to be broken up into multiple regional 'baby bell' service providers (Horwitz 1989). In 2005, AT&T's monopoly has been replaced by an oligopoly made up of four regional telecommunications providers including SBC, the 'baby bell' that is 'swallowing its former parent' AT&T which will 'live on as the business division' providing services for corporate clients (Belson 2005). Similarly, Verizon is in the process of buying up MCI, therefore reversing the twenty years of competition between local and long-distance providers that served as the model for reform for most other nations.

The processes of consolidation that we see today are taking place in a multipolar universe of telecommunications giants based in Europe and North America, but also the Asia Pacific and Latin America (see Table 3.2). In order to make sense of the normative basis for this global shift, we turn to the historical context of the evolution and disintegration of the national public-interest model of telecommunications regulation.

Historicizing telecommunications policy and national public interest (1950–1980)

The colonial legacy of international telecommunications policy dates back to the 1865 when the (then) International Telegraph Union (ITU) emerged as the first international organization established by twenty European countries to coordinate common technological standards and protocols between member nations, including their colonies. The US and other sovereign nations continued joining the organization as telephony

Table 3.2 Top 20 telecommunications operators – ranked by revenue (1999)

	Rank	**Telecommunication**	**Revenue**	**Total**	**Net**	**Income**
	Operator (Country)	Total (US $Million)	Change 98–99**	Total (US $Million)	Change (98–99)**	Total (000s)
1	NTT (Japan)	97,953	**6.7**	**2,821**	**–46.0**	**223.9**
2	AT&T (US)	62,391	17.2	3,428	–34.5	147.8
3	SBC (US)	48,489	7.1	8,159	6.1	204.5
4	MCI Worldcom (US)	37,120	104.3	3,941	#	77.0
5	Deutsche Telekom (Germany)	35,750	1.1	1,309	–40.9	195.8
6	BT (UK)	34,955	20.2	3,264	–31.9	136.8
7	Bell Atlantic (US)	33,174	5.1	4,202	41.7	145.0
8	China Telecommunication (China)	27,539	14.5	. . .	. . .	444.5
9	France Telecommunication (France)	27,344	10.5	2,786	20.5	174.3
10	Telecommunication Italia (Italy)	27,229	8.2	1,745	–12.2	122.7
11	GTE (US)	25,336	–0.5	4,033	87.5	99.0
12	BellSouth (US)	25,224	9.1	3,448	–2.2	96.2
13	Telefonica (Spain)	23,051	31.4	1,812	38.0	118.8
14	Sprint (US)	19,928	18.0	–935	#	77.6
15	DDI (Japan)	14,396	22.4	–99	#	2.6
16	Vodafone AirTouch (UK)	14,183	26.6	166	#	29.5
17	US West (US)	13,182	6.3	1,324	–11.0	58.3
18	Telstra (Australia)b	12,046	5.3	2,305	16.0	52.8
19	Telmex (Mexico)	10,132	23.1	2,643	53.2	63.9*
20	KPN (Netherlands)	9,169	14.9	832	20.5	34.8
	Top 20	**599,591**	**12.9**	**47,202**	**14.1**	**2,506**

Note: US dollar values obtained by using operator supplied exchange rates or ending period exchange rate. Net income is after tax. # indicates that Net Income was negative in 1997 and/or 1998. A Year beginning 1 April. B Year ending 30 June. * = 1997 data. ** = percentages.

Source: ITU PTO Database 2001. Reproduced with the kind permission of ITU.

was first incorporated in 1903, and, by 1947, the ITU became a specialized agency within the United Nations (Lee 1996). Following the Second World War, newly independent nations in Africa, Asia and the Middle East, as well as many nations in Latin America, replaced the private monopolies with ties to colonial powers with state-owned monopolies. Until the 1980s, international telecommunication policy was regulated by a stable set of norms that allowed for the setting of standards, tariffs, allocation of radio frequencies and satellite orbital positions.

While this was a period of relative stability in the international regulatory arena, that is not to discount political tensions within the ITU, fuelled by both the Cold War and the growing divergence of opinion between the minority 'developed' and majority 'developing' nations. Both factors were important in terms of the transnational coordination over the allocation of satellite orbital positions and radio frequencies (see, for example, Hamelink 1994: 74–94).Throughout this period, although the ITU was the most important multilateral regulatory body in the arena of telecommunications policy, it was designed as a 'weak' institution by member nations reluctant to 'cede sovereignty over potentially strategic areas of communication' and thus focused primarily on technical matters (Siochrú et al. 2002: 41). International coordination of policy reflected the 'modern ideals' of national integration and standardization evident in welfare-state objectives in the West promoting a public, or in the exceptional cases of the US and Canada, a private, national monopoly over networks and services. In the Soviet Union, across Eastern Europe but also other countries 'belonging' to the Western Block, telecommunications networks were centralized and regulated directly by the state. In the developing world, the postcolonial state linked the growth of infrastructures with national development.

In the Fordist regulatory era, the dominant policy discourse assumed that telecommunications networks functioned most efficiently as natural monopolies because of the enormous fixed costs required to build and upgrade any national network. The rationale for monopoly in telephone manufacturing and services was based on the understanding that centralization of operations would be more reliable because monopolies could best tap economies of scale and scope to better achieve growth and equity. Much of the world therefore relied on state ownership and operation of their Post and Telecommunications Operator (PTO), investing revenues to provide national standardized services.[4] Networks were regulated at the national level through a system of cross-subsidy, whereby urban areas subsidized rural areas, long-distance rates subsidized local rates, large (corporate) users subsidized residential users, and telecommunications revenues subsidized the postal system. Given this economic logic, regulators and policy-makers were concerned, at least in principle, with how best to achieve national public interest through the equitable distribution of service at the most reasonable prices: 'The arrangement served the important goal of interconnecting society and operated as a means of redistribution' (Noam 1992: 3).

Slow rates of technological change coupled with national monopoly control over the network and monopsony (single buyer) control over equipment ensured a period of relative stasis in the arena of national telecommunications policy. In the US, the Federal Communications Commission (FCC) was established in the 1920s as an independent body 'with a high degree of autonomy from executive government power' (O'Siorchu et al. 2002: 13). The FCC was composed of government-appointed experts who were to serve as 'neutral' commissioners 'insulated form the winds of politics by formal institutional boundaries and rules' (Streeter 1996: 122). AT&T as a state-sanctioned private monopoly, was required by the FCC to fulfill specific 'public-interest' obligations with the most important goal being universal service, explicitly making telecommunications services economically viable for all citizens.

In much of the rest of the world, with the state directly involved in the operation and provision of telecommunications services, there was no need for a separate regulatory agency monitoring the private sector. In Western Europe, for example, the corollary for 'universal service' as monitored by the FCC was the broader notion of 'public service' provided through the state-operated telecommunications services. As Nicholas Garnham has argued, public interest is assumed to be synonymous with the interests of the state:

> Within this tradition the State, by definition represents, through the political process, the best interests of all citizens. Thus the delivery of a public service by the State, whether directly or by delegated authority, does not require a more specific universal service remit nor is there a requirement for the State to be held accountable for its actions, legally, or otherwise, to individual citizens. (Garnham and Mansell 1991: 29)

In most cases, the state also fulfilled what was assumed as a public-interest mandate in its role as employer and/or mediator in a sector that has historically been highly unionized around the world. Although national telecommunications unions have varied histories of militancy and cooperation (Dubb 1999), it is fair to generalize that this was a largely stable era of industrial relations with job security for those who had access to what were mostly permanent unionized positions. Writing about the Canadian telecommunications sector, but with relevance for the experience of telecommunications unions the world over, Bernard and Schnaid argue that 'the symbiotic relationship that existed between phone companies and their workers was reflected in the fact that telecommunications unions often sided with employers at regulatory hearings. They felt that their members' wages and job security depended on the companies' prosperity' (Bernard and Schnaid 1997: 166). In the case of the US, the main trade union confederation, the American Federation of Labor and Congress of Industrial Organizations (AFL-CIO) was directly involved in CIA and State Department funded foreign policy campaigns against Third World unions labelled as communists during the height of the Cold War (Moody 1988; Ross 2004).

In developing countries where rates of urban unemployment and underemployment were high, national governments looked at telecommunications as an area for job creation. Although an extreme case, the example of apartheid South Africa is illustrative of the racialization of labour within the highly unionized telecommunications sector. Horwitz (2001) writes that the South African state's 'job reservation system' promoted the 'expansion of the white public sector workforce':

> As the apartheid policy of white uplift succeeded, Afrikaners moved into technical and managerial ranks, and nonwhites began to occupy the lower job grades of the parastatals [state-owned monopoly enterprises]. A gradual shortage of white labor meant corresponding increases in the employment of blacks . . . But this increase was not a matter of course. At the SAPT [South African Posts and Telecommunication] it required agreement by the white staff associations (the name for the postal trade unions) over the number of non-whites who could be taken into service for training each year. (81)

Racist hiring and promotion practices were codified in apartheid state policy, but similar formal and informal practices existed within telecommunications unions in many parts of the developed and developing world, highlighting that there were real limitations of the national monopoly model (Bernard 1982; Chakravartty 2001; Green 2001). While workers benefited from union membership in terms of wage increases and job security, feminist research reminds us that sexism and racism featured prominently in the history of labour movements in both the North and South.[5]

As a service, telecommunications density increased above the 60 per cent mark in all First World nations by the late-1970s. For much of the rest of the world, however, state control of the telecommunications infrastructure did not necessarily translate to the state's prioritization of the sector. This was especially the case for nations where other more vital areas such as energy and water as well as health and education were more pressing priorities for governments with limited resources. By the late-1970s, the logic and scope of the national monopoly model of telecommunications began to be seriously challenged by the post-Fordist regulatory shift. Technological advances stemming from research in the defence-related electronics sector introduced new satellite, cellular radio, fibre-optic and digital exchange technology, which became increasingly vital components of all sectors of economic activity. This was true not just in the First World where most transnational firms were based but also in Asian and Latin American economies where firms began to relocate production. These new technologies led to the potential for the provision of segmented and differentiated services, thereby undermining the assumptions about the need for a 'natural' monopoly in the sector.

For most Western nations, these technological changes coincided with the fiscal crises of the 1970s, creating a crisis of legitimacy for the welfare state. The failures of the postcolonial state to deliver equitable modern telecommunications infrastructure became acute, compounded by the debt crisis of the 1980s and new pressures for privatization of national monopolies. The eventual collapse of Eastern European communism further reinforced the need for reformulating the state's role in regulating industry, especially infrastructure areas like telecommunications that were by the 1980s recognized by powerful governments in the West as well as multilateral organizations as crucial to new developmental imperatives.

Leading the charge for reform in deregulating and ultimately liberalizing telecommunications policy were politically powerful states led by new conservative political forces, embodied in the Reagan and Thatcher period. Despite the successful expansion of telecommunications services in the US and the UK, influential policy experts gained authority to espouse 'the moral superiority of individual choice compared to the "tyranny" of collective decision-making'(Graham and Marvin 2001: 91). For the organization and supply of telecommunications services, reformers from the US, the UK and in the World Bank and ITU argued that cost-based tariffs should replace the regulatory logic of cross-subsidy; in other words, business and other larger users of services should not have to subsidize smaller, less remunerative users or 'customers'. In this same period, transnational telecommunications firms found a receptive climate for their demands to enter 'untapped' national markets and for advanced networks that were seamless in order to facilitate coordination of production as well as transactions across national borders. The dominant global policy consensus posited that state regulation and ownership stunted innovation and led to inefficiencies in resource allocation and distribution. The sudden focus on the negative effects of the corrupt behaviour of regulators and bureaucrats transformed the rules in the field of telecommunications governance, thus questioning the role of state actors as legitimate guardians of public interest.

While the influence of corporate lobbying in the Reagan–Thatcher era of supply-side economics surely contributed enormously to the shift in telecommunications public-policy discourse in this period, other factors played a role in challenging the state's failure to protect the public interest. In the US, consumer rights and other public interest advocates were integral to the eventual deregulation of AT&T's national monopoly (Horwitz 1989) and, in Europe, Japan and elsewhere in the First World, inadequacies and unaccountability of state-provided services fuelled a legitimacy crisis of state-owned infrastructure (Graham and Marvin 2001). The tangible outcome of these policy shifts was the FCC's decision to break up AT&T into twenty-two local companies, with AT&T focusing on long-distance and 'value-added' services. In 1985, 51 per cent of the British Telecommunications was sold to the private sector, and in 1985 Japan broke up its telecommunications monopoly through Nippon Telephone & Telegraph (NT&T), and liberalized its overall telecommunications market (Hamelink 1994: 68–9).

The paradigm shift in regulatory norms favouring market-based competition had a profound impact beyond the national boundaries of the Northern nations. With the end of the Cold War and the post-Fordist discourse of 'free' markets, policy-makers around most of the world fell in line with the strategic consensus about the failure of state-operated monopolies, promoting instead a new faith in free trade. In terms of telecommunications policy, traditional concerns for establishing what is considered 'fair' prices and maximum access to services was replaced by a new emphasis on the performance of home-based corporations in global trade, procuring favourable balance of payments and ensuring consumer sovereignty in a competitive market.

This shift in the rules of governance was carried out most dramatically in the developing world where the debt crisis and the changing geopolitical order led to a swift transformation in national development goals. We are exploring the experiences of postcolonial nation-states in negotiating the terms of reform, keeping in mind that external pressures only partially explain the political outcomes associated with these changes, in the rest of the chapter. We argue that the aggressive tactics used to pressure national governments in the South to adopt telecommunications privatization schemes have to be assessed within local political contexts. Although we see new forms of 'splintering urbanism' and inequality emerge following these regulatory shifts, we argue that the view from the 'margins', and in a global scale the South, reveals opposition and contestation of the legitimacy of the new rules of governance.

Privatization as salvation: the view from the South (1980–95)

This shift in policy framework was particularly significant for nations in the South, where liberalization of state-operated telecommunications networks and services often went hand in hand with the overhaul of their national economies in the 1980s and 1990s. Within the course of a decade, a majority of nations in the South had already implemented or were in the process of implementing liberalization policies which opened strategic sections of their telecommunications markets to foreign investors, in most cases, well beyond what most Western nations were willing to do in the same time period. The shift to privatization in the North was based on the rationale that the inefficiency of monopolistic state enterprise coupled with advances in technology undermined the argument for natural monopoly in telecommunication. Unlike their developed counterparts, states in the South began to privatize national telecommunications primarily as a means to reduce debt burdens and invite in foreign capital and expertise. Experts based in multilateral organizations promised that the rapid adoption of new technologies offered a means of 'leapfrogging' development, literally allowing developing nations the possibility of 'skipping' the industrial revolution for the benefits of the 'new' post-industrial economy (Singh 1999).

The fact that telecommunications services were not recognized as an economic priority in most of the South until the 1980s was reflected in very low rates of telephone density (between 1 and 10 per cent) and very slow absorption of new technologies. In most nations, the state owned and operated the PTO, and the network was regulated on the basis of cross-subsidy principles. Domestically, nearly all governments advocated the ideals of universal or public service, although other, more pressing, economic priorities relegated state-operated telecommunications networks to low levels of penetration, especially in rural and low-income areas. In the multilateral arena, the growing numbers of 'developing country' members in institutions like the ITU, led to new tensions over the allocation of satellite orbital positions and radio frequencies (Hamelink 1994). As we have seen in Chapter 2, the negotiations within the ITU and other UN bodies represented a specific moment of collective solidarity for Southern nations in the 1970s that culminated in the call for NWICO. In this same period, transnational telecommunications firms – recognizing that markets in the North were increasingly saturated – began to exert greater influence within the ITU to pressure member states in the South to open their markets to foreign firms (Lee 1996: 176). The growing influence of corporate actors in multilateral policy-making bodies like the ITU corresponded with a renewed focus and concern about telecommunications disparity in the South, an issue that became paramount in development circles in the mid-1980s.

Although the ITU had officially recognized the 'special character' of telecommunications as a 'medium of economic and social development' as early as the 1950s (O'Siorchu et al. 2002: 40), it was only in the 1980s that the ITU along with the World Bank and the IMF began to promote the 'Missing Link' between economic development and 'telecommunications penetration'. The 1984 publication of the ITU-sponsored influential *Maitland Commission Report* condemned the extreme inequalities of telephone access between rich and poor nations. Although the report drew global attention to the relatively novel issue of information disparity, its recommendations pressed for the need to reform inefficient national public monopolies and promote the transfer of technologies from advanced to developing nations. The ITU report argued that investment in telecommunications should no longer be seen as a luxury service for corporate and national elites, but rather as an essential service that directly leads to economic growth. Reflecting the new technologically driven consensus in policy circles, the report overemphasized the causality between 'telephone penetration' and economic growth (Samarajiva and Shields 1990). Policy experts in the ITU and the World Bank claimed that investment in the newest telecommunications technologies would allow developing countries to actually 'leapfrog' over stages of development (Wellenius and Stern 1994).

The first phase of reforms in the South consisted of the liberalization of the equipment market but, by 1986, discussions within the Uruguay Round of the GATT introduced the economically more significant area of trade in telecommunications services. US-based transnational firms ranging from credit card companies to telecommunication, media and computer service providers had been lobbying the US government for over a decade to include services along with manufactured goods in the purview of the GATT. This would mean that member states would agree to reduce and eventually eliminate tariffs and trade barriers in the area of services – including telecommunications services. An initial overwhelming comparative advantage held by Northern industries in the area of services prompted eight years of opposition and negotiation between 'developing' economies such as India and Brazil against the US and its Western European and East Asian allies. Ultimately, opposition gave way to agreement, as developed countries conceded to open their markets to agriculture and textiles while developing countries found it harder to argue against the basic tenets of neoliberal trade, reinforced by mounting pressures from the World Bank and IMF.[6]

Critics of this process point out that the ITU, along with the more powerful World Bank and the IMF, began promoting the expanded role of the private sector in telecommunications development just as transnational telecommunications firms began to play a greater role in influencing policy with the objective of entering new, lucrative markets especially in Asia, Eastern Europe and Latin America. Jill Hills (1998) argues that transnational equipment manufacturers like Alcatel, NEC, Erickson, British Telecommunication, US West and others, worked with the World Bank and the IMF to direct foreign investment at concessional financing to governments that opened their markets. According to McChesney and Schiller, the intense corporate lobbying and the 'promise of access' to the US corporate telecommunications market explained why much of the rest of the world eventually agreed to what accounted for a total overhall in the way that the telecommunications infrastructure was organized and regulated (2003: 18). However, for advocates of reform, the shift among policy-makers in both the North and the South was a response to the failures of the state to promote growth, expansion and consumer choice. The same reformers have argued that it was the very 'success of neoliberal economic reform in Asia and South America [that] put even the most politically untouchable forms of monopoly up for consideration by the mid-1990s'. Moreover, they contend that, 'the soaring US economy, symbolized by its resurgent information industry' served as 'added stimulus for other nations following the US lead' in liberalization (Cowhey and Klimenko 1999: 3).

Corporate pressure, backed by the US and other G7 nations lobbying intensely at the GATT and the ITU, was reinforced by the conditions imposed by the World Bank and the IMF, whose lending was contingent on liberalization. For smaller economies with less political influence, the outcome was one of being forced to privatize in order to maintain investor confidence. Based on his study of the experience of the Caribbean economies, Hopeton Dunn (1995) has shown that smaller debt-ridden states had little power in negotiating the terms of telecommunications reform against the influence of the US and the UK, which lobbied intensely on behalf of their home-based telecommunications transnationals. Gerald Sussman (2001) has argued that Mexico implemented a 'radical reform process' when NAFTA rules went into effect in 1995, leading to the statutory lifting of foreign ownership restrictions and the introduction of laws that required telecommunications companies to lower long-distance rates while raising local rates. At the same time, all segments of the telecommunications market were opened to competition from American and Canadian firms, including radio, satellite orbital slots and local and long-distance telephony. Although foreign ownership was restricted at 49 per cent for basic services, cellular telephony was not bound by this restriction. Mexico's reforms took place a few years earlier and were more radical than many other nations in the South because of NAFTA, but this mode of reform was reinforced by the World Bank where telecommunications privatization became a central conditionality within the Structural Adjustment Policy (SAP) programmes, as evident by the privatization schemes initiated in Brazil, Chile, India, Ghana and Kenya, among others.

These external pressures for national reform have to be weighed according to the bargaining power of Southern nation-states, and it would be faulty logic to assume that the expansive range of reforms can be explained by the power of multilateral institutions and the G7 nations alone. In explaining the internal factors for reform, we argue that the symbolic failures of the previous state-led model of telecommunications provision in much of the South coupled with the allure and speed of modernization promised through the global integration must be taken into account (Chakravartty 2004). In considering these internal factors, we hope to show the grounds for both the legitimacy and contestation of these new rules of governance.

During the period of nationalized telecommunications operations in the South, World Bank and ITU experts repeatedly highlighted both low rates of telephone density – numbers of phones per population – and long waiting lists for new services and records of consistent patterns of poor service (Wellenius and Stern 1994). For example, World Bank studies drew frequent attention to the number of years people who had to wait for phone installations in 1986 and 1991, when reforms were launched in these countries: Argentina (4.1), Chile (5.7), Jamaica (9), Malaysia (1.6), Mexico (4.9), the Philippines (14.7) and Venezuela (2.5)(Galal and Nauriayal 1995; Noll 1999: 12). Low rates of telephony along with soaring rates of unmet demand and poor service allowed domestic neoliberal reformers to make a convincing case that the state had failed to serve the public interest. While it is very clear that large corporate users were the main constituents lobbying for reforms, increasingly vocal urban middle-class users of telecommunications and other state-provided infrastructure services supported the new regulatory logic of market-based expansion and efficiency.

By the late 1980s and certainly into the 1990s, a new globalized middle class of 'highly educated salaried professionals, technical specialists, managers and administrators' in the private and public sectors rejected previous models of state intervention, embracing the post-Fordist discourse of markets, flexibility, consumption and choice (Pinches 1997: 24–6).[7] Many in these new middle classes saw telecommunications reforms as crucial to the infrastructure overhaul necessary for participation in the new global economy. In contrast to the constituency for jobs in the public-sector telecommunications unions, the promise of jobs in a new information economy appealed to younger workers, including young women, who were targeted by transnational firms in the new gendered division of labour associated with the post-Fordist economy (Mitter and Rowbotham 1997). Ultimately the jobs that would open up in the 'new' economy would also be segmented by class, gender and other sociocultural divisions (Baldoz, Koelbler and Kraft 2001). But the initial appeal of the reforms lay in the prospect of overcoming the failures of the previous development model which had offered rapid economic opportunities, for a more technologically savvy generation (Freeman 2000). By the 1990s, access to commercial media – especially television – was expanding rapidly in the developing world as was the influence of diasporic communities who were returning 'home' with more frequency to influence local tastes and practices (Appadurai 1996; Ong 2001).

The fact that the new middle classes who backed these reforms have made up a minority, and in many cases a small minority, of the overall population of most nations in the South did not undermine the resonance of the new discourse about failed state capacity, especially as reformers turned to issues of state inefficiency and corruption. Experts in the World Bank and the ITU routinely compared the inefficient performance of state-based operators in the South with their successful counterparts in the developed North and the rapidly 'emerging' economies represented by the Four Tigers of Hong Kong, Singapore, South Korea and Taiwan. The overwhelmingly poor performance of state-operated telecommunications services in the South coupled with inefficiency – measured by such indicators as the relatively high numbers of employees per telephone line – demonstrated the problem with government 'interference' (Wellenius and Stern 1994; Wellenius 1997). The implicit anti-union sentiment dovetailed perfectly with the promise that state-of-the art liberalized telecommunications infrastructure would provide modern flexible jobs beneficial to both employees and employers.

For consumers, the state's monopoly in this increasingly important economic sector was seen by reformers as fertile grounds to raise the issue of corruption – a concern that would drive policy-making from the mid-1990s until the present.[8] Inefficiency and corruption were real concerns for citizens of many postcolonial nations where, as we discussed in Chapter 2, governments in power for decades deployed empty populist rhetoric of development in the economic realm to justify corrupt practices, in many instances reproducing colonial technologies of governance. In the area of telecommunications this meant everything from influential politicians or bureaucrats taking bribes from foreign equipment manufacturers to politicians reserving telephone lines for friends and family, and much in between. For the news and emerging business media in urban centres across the developing world, it was issues like these that catalyzed important sections of public opinion against the state and towards market solutions to expand and modernize services (Chakravartty 2001b).

Domestic policy-makers, often 'experts' trained in US business and law schools with stints at the World Bank and the ITU, consequently explained that the urgency of reforms was a direct result of the failing performance of state enterprises. The solution spelled out by numerous World Bank and ITU policy reports was to implement a comprehensive reform process that would enable competition and technological modernization, promising to balance the concerns of equity with those of efficiency. In theory this included the deregulation of the state-operated network with the ultimate goal of privatization, liberalization of the supply of services, and the separation of the government's policy and regulatory arm from its responsibilities as a network operator. In effect, most governments in this first period of liberalization implemented some form of privatization whereby state-operated telecommunications monopolies were either sold to private investors or re-organized as private corporations (corporatization). Early reformers such as Chile (1988) and Argentina and Mexico (1990) led the way in allowing a certain amount of foreign ownership in basic networks, followed up in a few years by allowing foreign competitors to enter long-distance and other value-added markets, with other countries quickly adopting similar strategies (Singh 1999; Tigre 1999).

In this way, privatization almost always came *before* regulatory reform, which might have allowed the possibility of balancing efficiency and equity and demonstrates that the impetus for reform was driven by the need to 'generate revenue' for national governments 'strapped for funds'. Economist Roger Noll writes plainly:

> Thus part of the impetus for neoliberal reform in telecommunications and other infrastructure sectors had nothing to do with performance, but instead the possibility to use their reform as a means to ease the pain of the larger neoliberal reform agenda. (Noll 2002: 13)

Although influential urban middle classes supported neoliberal reforms on the grounds of state inefficiency, opposition to privatization schemes was a common feature of broader public sentiment against globalization. In Argentina, Brazil, Mexico, Puerto Rico, India and South Africa, to name a few examples, trade unions mobilized public protests, work stoppages and strikes against the state's privatization plans. Proponents of neoliberal reforms have discounted unionized opposition arguing that these represent 'narrow' vested interests (Noll 2002; Petrazzini 1996a). Union opposition, nevertheless, often paved the way to larger public negotiations over the terms of neoliberal reform – including raising concerns about foreign ownership and regional inequality, and drawing attention to the issue of corporate accountability. Intense opposition by unions in these cases led to a recognition by state reformers, however reluctantly, that organized labour was indeed an important 'stakeholder' in future policy debates (Chakravartty 2004; Dubb 1999; Horwitz 2001). A common theme raised by organized labour across the South was concerns about neocolonial patterns of ownership that would emerge as state enterprises were replaced by foreign transnationals. In most cases, national governments, while liberalizing access to value-added services, maintained strict restrictions on foreign and private ownership in basic telecommunications services in this first stage of reforms, allaying fears of foreign and private takeover of a strategic national sector.

As these reforms were carried out, rapid growth in the sector was not a result of the moral superiority of competition alone, since in practice telecommunications services remained a monopoly or at best a duopoly in most instances. Although a plethora of new corporate players entered the expanded telecommunications markets offering a range of new services, there was little competition between providers of basic telecommunications services within a defined geographic area. Consequently, it was not competition that drove sudden expansion of the sector in much of the world, but rather massive new investment in the number of main telephone lines and the digitalization of switching and networks. In almost all cases, a combination of privatization schemes and higher rates of public investment led to double-digit growth in teledensity figures throughout the 1990s and continuing today (see Table 3. 3).

Private telecommunications operators were drawn to emerging markets like Brazil, China and India, among others, because technological innovation coupled with policy reforms promised access to lucrative high-density business and urban middle-class consumers. In each of these three cases, national institutional actors continued to raise concerns about domestic political and economic priorities in negotiating the reregulation of the sector according to rules inscribed in the arenas of global governance. The few comparative studies of telecommunications reform in the South show that the political environment – whether the state is responsive to democratic public interest – and its relative power vis-à-vis foreign capital and G8 nations have shaped the terms of reform.[9]

Table 3.3 Telecommunications indicators in selected emerging economies (2001–3)

Country	GDP per capita 2001 (US$)	GDP per capita 2002 (US$)	Total telephone subscribers (k) 2001	Total telephone subscribers (k) 2003	Telephone per 100 inhabitants 2001	Telephone per 100 inhabitants 2001
Brazil	3,544	2,603	66,176.5	85,595.3	38.51	48.65
China	833	963	325,188.0	532,700.0	24.77	42.38
Egypt	1,544	1,260	9,488.7	14,533.2	14.70	21.17
India	459	488	44,964.7	75,071.4	4.38	7.10
Mexico	5,871	6,328	35,531.7	46,408.8	35.83	45.44
Nigeria	423	409	1,000.3	4,002.5	0.86	3.25
Russia	1,709	2,370	41,028.7	73,493.0	27.96	50.20
South Africa	2,982	2,293	15,711.5	18,546.0*	35.26	40.80
South Korea	11,127	11,481	54,837.2	59,392.1	115.83	123.93
Turkey	3,062	2,630	38,477.4	46,804.3	56.15	66.19

*2002 figures

Source: compiled by authors from ITU statistics. http://www.itu.int/ITU-D/ict/statistics/

In this last section we consider how the new institutional reality of the WTO in 1995 posed new challenges for national governments in the South. In order to follow these changes more carefully, the next section provides a brief overview of three relatively powerful emerging economies, and the shifting role of the nation-state as it liberalizes telecommunications policy, while facing pressures from both translational capital and multilateral policy convergence.

Corporate discipline and unruly publics (1996–2005)

Pressure from TNCs to play a bigger role in multilateral telecommunications reform was acute throughout the 1980s, but became formalized within the ITU in 1994. At this time, a 'second tier of membership was created to facilitate greater participation of the private sector and NGOs' (Siochru et al. 2002: 49). In reality, telecommunications companies have driven the policy agenda with minimal participation by NGOs, who have less power, fewer experts and access to the privately funded meetings that increasingly define policy goals. A recent study found that 'more aid money now goes into creating governance regimes than to developing the communications networks and services that people will actually use'. This same study points out that within the ITU, the private sector has come to 'out-number governments 450 to 187' (Winsek 2002: 24–5).

The pressure for reregulating telecommunications to reflect neoliberal trade norms is most apparent when we turn to the new multilateral institution of telecommunications governance: the WTO. The Uruguay Rounds of the GATT ended in 1994 with sixty nations committing to liberalization of value-added services – cellular phones, paging, private-leased networks etc. – but only eight willing to liberalize basic telecommunications and public-data networks (Siochrú et al. 2002: 57). It would take another three years of negotiations within the newly created WTO to establish the ABT, which would require all sixty-nine signatories to liberalize gradually their telecommunications service markets fully, as well as establish independent regulatory agencies similar in form to the US FCC. With US policy-makers and corporate lobbyists leading the push for liberalization in the WTO, it is not coincidental that the 1996 Telecommunications Act commits to opening up competition in all markets in telecommunications services, thereby fundamentally altering the domestic legal framework that had guided universal telecommunications provision (Aufderheide 1999). The explicit commitment to liberalization in basic services, and the transformation of regulation as a 'technical' function to ensure efficient operation of markets, is a drastic departure for most states in the South. The WTO agreement elevated the mode of liberalization to the transnational level, 'And there is no going back without risking possibly severe sanctions, the result being constant pressure to extend commitments' (Siochrú et al. 2002: 58).[10]

Brazil, China and India are all currently signatories of the ABT, and a brief overview of reforms in each country provides tangible examples of the implementation of the new norms of public interest in the telecommunications field. We have argued throughout that the relative power of nation-states to negotiate the terms of global governance varies significantly with political economic and military clout. As we saw in Chapter 2, Third World solidarity in multilateral institutions has ebbed and flowed since the mid-1980s when the debt crisis reinforced divisions between emerging economies and what some refer to as the 'Fourth World', most often associated with the most impoverished nations left outside the circuits of global capitalism, including much of Sub-Saharan Africa (McMichael 2003: 139). Competition between Southern nations for foreign investment marked the early stages of global integration. In the last five years, at the date of writing, there have been a number of new efforts at South–South collaboration and solidarity led by emerging economies such as Brazil, China, India, Mexico and South Africa. We are not suggesting that the experiences of these relatively powerful nations are illustrative of the whole developing world. Instead, our focus here is to highlight the experiences of three of the emerging powers in the global economy from the South to illustrate the magnitude of the implied changes, and the political and social costs that this transformation entails.

In contrast to the early and more radical reformers of Latin America such as Argentina, Chile and Mexico, Brazil had a longer and more substantial history of public investment in telecommunications infrastructure as well as research and development linked to its electronics sector (Evans 1995). The multilateral push for reforms coincided with the end of Brazil's twenty years of authoritarian rule in 1985, which had produced powerful domestic corporate interests along with a range of social movements critical of both state power and foreign capital (Evans 1979). Although the Brazilian economy was a victim of the debt crisis and hyperinflation in the 1980s, the newly democratic state took a more cautious approach toward reform compared to its regional neighbours. The new constitution set up in 1988 'adopted exclusively public-controlled models' for basic telecommunications operations, reinforcing a commitment to a public monopoly model as other nations were moving towards privatization (Evans 1995).

Attempts by President Collor to introduce telecommunications privatization by decree in 1992 was partially responsible for his impeachment and led to further public distrust of rapid privatization schemes imposed by the state (Hughes 2002). With a much broader base of political support, President Cardoso introduced a constitutional amendment allowing private investment in the telecommunications sector without ending Telebrás's public monopoly in 1995. In the same year, the government reversed the cross-subsidy system of telecommunications regulation and introduced incentives for competition between different subsidiaries of Telebrás. One commentator noted that 'at one blow, the Brazilian government increased the residential subscription by a factor of five, and the cost of local calls by 80 per cent' (Pinheiro 2003: 3). Brazil was a signatory of the WTO's ABT and in 1997 the government passed the General Telecommunications Act, which opened the door for the restructuring of Telebrás into twelve regional companies, as well as into local, cellular and long-distance companies. Privatization was introduced in 1998, and was met with opposition from political parties, unions and other social movements whose case was reinforced by a major corruption scandal that erupted over procedures having to do with the sale of regional licences.

The Cardoso government was able to argue that it was committed to 'universalization' as it laid out a range of obligations that private firms had to meet in order to gain access to the Brazilian market. In the same year, the government created the National Agency of Telecommunications (Anatel), insisting that Brazil was taking a more cautious and moderate road to privatization, balancing concerns of universal access and competition with privatization strategies (Hughes 2002). Private investment has targeted niche consumers and high-end business users in Brazil's notoriously unequal economy, and costs for basic and local services have increased substantially. The unprecedented electoral victory of the Workers Party (Partido dos Trabalhadores [PT]) in 2002 generated panic amongst private foreign investors about the future of Brazil's commitment to neoliberal reforms. The outcome in terms of policy issues related to access to telecommunications and ICTs is complex. In the international arena, the Lula administration has played a pivotal role in mounting a challenge against the symbolic dominance of Northern institutional players through the endorsement of the World Social Forum (WSF), as well as through its leadership in South–South alliances in global trade talks, especially in the area of intellectual property rights. Domestically, a series of corruption scandals coupled with a visible retreat from its initial economic agenda in order to appease fears about investor confidence has seriously weakened the party's credibility to meet the needs of its own political base of unionized workers, landless farmers, the urban lower-middle classes and the urban poor (Baiocchi 2005). Despite these very real limitations, we will discuss in later chapters how the Brazilian state has taken an unprecedented lead among Southern nations in including civil society participation in information policy design as well as in advocating for greater 'digital inclusion' through the promotion of open-source software. The point here is that redistributive claims for access continue to play an important role in shaping the parameters of policy outcome.

Similar to the Brazilian experience in some ways, the Indian state has also negotiated a slower pace of reform when compared to the rapid liberalization undertaken by neighbours in the subcontinent as well as throughout much of Southeast Asia. The democratic legacy of the Indian state has meant that it has had to mediate political interests, ranging from domestic capital to trade unions and new social movements that have emerged since the 1980s (Chakravartty 2004). Although efforts to reform the sector internally began in the mid-1980s, it was an unprecedented balance of payments crisis in 1991 that forced the Congress government to consider more drastic steps towards telecommunications liberalization. This included the liberalization of the equipment market, and opening up value-added services in the same way that cellular phones and paging were to private investors in 1992. After several years of internal negotiations between competing bureaucratic interests within the state, the government passed the controversial 1994 National Telecommunications Policy (NTP) in 1994, which opened basic services to limited foreign competition. Policy-makers and business leaders alike bemoan interference from 'vested interests', characterizing the Indian case as 'privatization without deregulation', with the state continuing to play a substantial role as policy-maker, dominant operator and adjudicator.

Although initial corporate interest in the Indian telecommunications market was euphoric, with unexpectedly high bids for cellular licences and basic service licenses in lucrative regions, the entry of private and especially foreign private investors was regulated on the basis of principles of national and public interest. The implementation of reforms in India was a drawn-out negotiated process between different institutional actors within the state, competing interests between domestic and transnational capital and growing public scrutiny of the liberalization process from organized labour, consumer advocates and the media. While reformers and corporate actors argued that public interest would be best served by foreign investment and technology entering India's vast untapped market, critics held that the nation's disparate information economy required safeguards for the majority of low-income subscribers. The private firms that entered the telecommunications market in India concentrated their investment in urban areas, in many cases paying penalties to the state rather than rolling out expensive infrastructure in areas deemed 'unremunerative'. The aftermath of the initial liberalization scheme included a national strike, two 'Telecommunications Scandals', dozens of public-interest petitions, a stalemate in both houses of parliament, and (however indirectly) the electoral defeat in 1996 of the Congress Party that had introduced the reforms.

In 1999, the right-wing BJP coalition government introduced a new NTP (1999) in order to meet the WTO commitments by corporatizing the largest state-owned operators (2001), reinforcing its commitment to an independent regulatory agency (the Telecommunications Regulatory Authority of India (TRAI)), liberalizing long-distance services (2003) and introducing new mechanisms to force private operators to provide minimum rural connectivity. As in Brazil, telecommunications density expanded exponentially between the mid-1980s and the late 1990s. Building on several decades of state-funded research in electronics and software, the government began to link telecommunications expansion to high-tech growth aimed at the export of software services in cities like Bangalore, Hyderabad and New Delhi. Unsurprisingly, the most rapid transformations have happened in urban areas with large corporate users and a growing number of middle-class consumers linked by high-speed networks and new communications services to counterparts in the North and South. The highly skewed expansion favouring urban markets is clearly unsustainable in a nation where over 740 million people (some 12 per cent of the world's population) live in rural areas. In 2002, the government 'removed rural obligations' for private operators, once again raising the ire of a range of opponents protesting against the state's skewed development agenda (Jhunjhunwala et al. 2004). The electoral defeat of the Bharatiya Janata Party (BJP)-led government in 2004 has been closely associated with its failure to promote the benefits of 'high-tech India' beyond the interests of the globalized urban middle classes. Once again, public pressure from civil-society organizations including hundreds of prominent non-governmental organizations (NGOs), a variety of social movements, including labour unions, have kept questions of redistribution on the negotiating table.[11]

In both the Brazilian and Indian cases, we see that the negotiation of telecommunications liberalization has taken place in the context of public debates about the promises and costs of rapid global integration. In both cases, a longer legacy of state investment in domestic research and development (R&D) in the telecommunications and electronics sectors (Evans 1995) has meant that the issue of appropriate technology and the cost effectiveness of reliance of patented imports are recurring concerns in public debates about the costs of global integration. In the case of the Chinese authoritarian state, it has not been explicit political opposition or public protest that has shaped the terms of domestic telecommunications reform, but rather the nation's enormous market power which in itself acts as a means to discipline TNCs. Yuezhi Zhao has argued that the Chinese state has played a unique role in both muting public protest against the neoliberal reforms while at the same time implementing its version of competition without privatization. In contrast to analysts who see an inherent tension between China's 'capitalist practice and socialist ideology' (Singh 1999), Zhao argues that socialist ideology and capitalist practice reinforce each other through the Chinese nation-state.

Reform in China began in the 1980s when the state 'prioritised the development of telecommunications networks in coastal areas to facilitate transnational capital's access to cheap labour in China' (Zhao 2005: 66). The state's strategic prioritization and investment in telecommunications saw rapid unprecedented expansion, with telecommunications transnationals entering in joint venture operations with different state-operated bodies to produce equipment and deliver services. China today has become the second largest national telecommunications market with its 'highly digitised fixed line and mobile phone networks' that saw an increase in access to telephony from a mere 2 million in 1979 to 200 million by 2000 (Zhao and Schiller 2001: 141). At the same time, China is also experiencing some of the most drastic disparities in terms of access, for example, with teledensity rates between rural and urban centres growing at an alarming pace.[12] The Chinese state's role in regulating the terms of reform is undergoing a period of transition as it has become one of the most recent and noted members of the WTO. China agreed to allow foreign investment in joint ventures (up to 25 per cent in 2002, 35 per cent in 2003, 49 per cent in 2005) and to eliminate all geographic restrictions by the end of 2005 (Siochrú et al. 2002: 58). Zhao and Schiller (2001) have argued that the different institutional actors within the Chinese state are wary of the liberalization process, therefore proceeding with these pressures from above in a cautious manner. Meanwhile, the legitimacy of the Chinese state to implement policies that are associated with increasing social and economic inequalities is likely to face its own internal tensions. Reflecting similar trends in India and Brazil that are less known outside of China, Zhao writes that:

> The reform process has met with vibrant forms of social contestation at the grassroots level. Localised protests by laid-off workers, impoverished pensioners, overtaxed farmers and urban residents displaced by real estate developments have become a permanent feature of the Chinese scene, and the scope and frequency of these protests are intensifying. (Zhao 2005: 78)

The discussion of these three cases provides a small glimpse of the wider and much more varied experiences that make up the specific process of telecommunications reform in the developing world. The objective here is to suggest that the legitimacy of reregulation of telecommunications governance is not assured in the local contexts where they are applied. We should also point out that opposition to new modes of governance takes place in the context of disillusionment and discontent with what existed before, in these cases, the failings of some form of state-led models of development and modernization in the telecommunications sector.

Beyond telecommunications policy and towards the fractured Information Society

We began the chapter by discussing the Okinawa Charter and the G8 nations' new-found concern with the growing 'global digital divide', remedied through private-sector participation and civil-society engagement. We argued that the symbolic power of the neoliberal rules of governance embodied in documents like the Okinawa Charter have to be located in a historical context. We have traced the dominance of and ultimate challenge to the Fordist regulatory discourse in the field of telecommunications governance in order to show the coherence as well as the gaps in the logic of national public-interest models. We also outlined how Northern political actors, transnational corporations and policy-makers from G8 nations and in multilateral organizations played a pivotal role in designing and implementing the reregulation of the industry across the world at rapid speed since the 1980s.

The second part of the chapter focused on the experiences of the South as national governments implemented telecommunications reforms in order to highlight the political, economic and cultural conditions that explain the internal legitimacy of these reforms in practice. We must qualify that, in speaking of the experiences of the South, we are less interested in generalizations, but try instead to map and explore common features of the ways in which postcolonial states negotiate the terms of telecommunications policy. The cases of Brazil, China and India are of importance not only because of their relative economic power as emerging economies but also because they offer us different kinds of examples of support as well as visible resistance to the norms of global governance.

Today throughout much of the world, state telecommunications monopolies have been replaced by a small handful of transnational firms who primarily target the most lucrative markets – business users and the internally stratified category of the globalized and 'new middle classes' who live in the 'splintering' global cities described above. We have argued that the massive expansion in telecommunications infrastructure was not a result of the moral superiority of competition but rather the prioritization by nation-states of the sector as a development priority in the context of global integration. In many cases, governments generated revenues by selling licenses for telecom services, with private firms bidding extravagantly for the most highly valued emerging markets, such as Brazil's privatization of Telebrás that raised an estimated $18.85 billion in 1998 (Singh 1999).

The targeting of the relatively wealthy sections of the population within national economies does not discount the explosive growth in overall access to telecommunications worldwide since the 1990s, with the most spectacular increases in the spread of mobile telephony. Impressive rates of expansion in access to mobile telephony and community-based Internet kiosks in urban as well as some rural areas have been seen by organizations like the ITU as well as many NGOs involved in development as central to combating poverty and inequality and encouraging accountability from both public and private institutions. Beyond the measurable objectives of development, access to these new technologies has transformed everyday life for the majority of the world's urban population, in ways that we are only now recognizing in new studies of global urban culture and politics.[13]

Our focus on the experiences of postcolonial states showed us that the lack of legitimacy of the previous model helped mobilize public support for a liberalization paradigm pushed by Northern institutional actors. Nevertheless, scepticism by multiple publics about the cost of rapid global integration and the growing gap between the promise and reality of the fractured information economy helped slow down the pace of reform where national governments had manoeuvring power. In 2005, we saw that the legitimacy of the market as a solution to the failure of the state seems to be increasingly questioned in both the South and the North. The era of telecommunications privatization actually witnessed the proliferation of corruption, and, with the telecommunications bubble bursting officially in 2000, public attention turned to both state and corporate accountability (See Table 3.4). Even in the US, the 1990s euphoria associated with the deregulation and privatization of infrastructure industries like energy and telecommunications has vanished with a series of highly public corruption scandals that began in 2000. Today, images of former C.E.Os, like WorldCom's Bernard J. Ebbers, walking to court in handcuffs serve to restrain the market triumphalism, justifying reforms in these sectors throughout the 1990s.

Table 3.4 Corruption index: privatization and telecommunications corruption

Date	Country	Scandal
May 1996	India	India Federal police discover US$1.3 million in cash and a stash of jewellery during raids on two homes owned by Sukh Ram, former telecommunication minister under Rao. Diaries obtained during the raids indicate that Ram had undeclared assets of US$8.5 million. Ram, who until the recent elections supervised US$25 billion worth of tender offers for the privatization of the Indian telephone system, stands accused of accepting bribes from a company, and remains a fugitive until his arrest in September. The charges are later dropped.
November 1998	Brazil	*Veja* and several other newsmagazines release taped conversations of high-level government officials discussing how to influence bidding in the privatization of Telebrás, the national phone company. The tapes include Luiz Carlos Mendonça de Barros, the minister of communications, and André Lara Resende, president of the National Development Bank (BNDES – Banco Nacional de Desenvolvimento Econômico e Social), discussing how to convince the Telemar investment group to underbid, and thus likely lose the auction, for Tele Norte Leste, one of the sixteen companies formed during the privatization of Telebrás. Although not charged with any illegality, both men resign by the end of the month, as do BNDES Vice President, José Pio Borges, and Foreign Trade Secretary, José Roberto Mendonca de Barros.
July 2000	Kenya	KACA charges the minister for water development, Kipng'eno arap Ng'eny, with fraud and abuse of authority for actions when he was head of the now-defunct Kenya Posts and Telecommunication Corporation in 1993. KACA accuses Ng'eny of defrauding the telecommunication organization of 186 million shillings (US$2.4 million).

Table 3.4 (*Continued*)

Date	Country	Scandal
February 2002	Ghana	The government stops the sale of Ghana Telecommunication to Telecommunication Malaysia on the grounds that members of the former government had allegedly received free shares.
June 2002	USA	WorldCom Inc. admits that it inflated its earnings by US$3.8 billion. The figure is later amended to US$11 billion. The Securities and Exchange Commission immediately files fraud charges against the company and top officials. The following month WorldCom Inc. files for bankruptcy, a surprise move that eventually costs investors more than US$175 billion.

Source: compiled by the authors from data available at: http://www.publicintegrity.org/

After two decades of telecommunications policy reform, the ITU in its most recent development communication initiative called *Connect the World* acknowledged the following about the very real limits of the dominant policy discourse:

> At present, the 942 million people living in the world's developed economies enjoy five times better access to fixed and mobile phone services, nine times better access to Internet services, and own 13 times more PCs than the 85% of the world's population living in low and lower-middle income countries. But while figures do show a clear improvement over the last ten years in bridging the gap between information 'haves' and 'have-nots', they nonetheless fail to paint a true picture for many rural dwellers, whose communities are still often unserved by any form of ICT. (ITU *Connect the World*, 16 June 2005 http://www.itu.int/newsroom/press_releases/2005/07.html)

The liberalization of telecommunications infrastructure and services has been integral in creating the 'splintering urbanism' that very visibly divides the world between the 'wired' and those left behind, criss-crossing nations and continents, linking high-tech neighbourhoods within cities and industrial regions together, bypassing socially and economically marginalized communities, especially rural communities, across the North and South. In other words, the earlier promise of reformers that societies would 'leapfrog' development, bypassing the industrial stage of development altogether, has clearly had contradictory outcomes. We can see how similar arguments are made today about wireless, satellite and broadband technologies, with the promise of technological and market-driven solutions to the global digital divide.

Financing affordable telecommunications access and ICT competence for low-income communities has become a pressing area of concern for policy-makers in the field of global communication governance more broadly. In the next two chapters, we consider the policies that shaped traditional media on the one hand, with an emphasis on the audiovisual sectors, and the most current, futuristic expressions of communications, the 'Information Society', on the other. The relationship between the media and telecommunications sectors is quite visible in the light of technological convergence, which becomes the object of new regulatory reforms at an international level. As we will see, the development of technology has been systematically utilized to further the aims of neoliberalism with considerable success. The conflicting ideas about public interest, communication and cultural rights and that of emphasis on market-led normative framework for the shaping of communications are discussed as they are found in the development of broadcasting and the Information Society (IS).

Notes

1. For current information about privatization of basic telecommunications see ITU figures: http://www.itu.int/ITU-D/treg/profiles/MainFixedOps.asp
2. For current information about conglomeration, mergers and cross-ownership in the communication and media industries see the 'Who Owns What' URL of the Columbia Journalism Review website: http://www.cjr.org/tools/owners/
3. For current information about changes in ownership the US telecommunications industry, which has historically influenced changes in other parts of the world, see: http://www.openairwaves.org/telecommunication/industry.aspx? act=phone
4. A 'first wave of privatization' took place in the 1930s, especially in Latin America and the Caribbean, but most countries nationalized their telecommunications sectors in the 1950s and 1960s. See Hills 1998.
5. Feminist historical and ethnographic research has produced mounting evidence about the gendered history of labour movements throughout much of the world. The role of racial discrimination, as well as discrimination and exclusion based on caste and ethnicity,

has also been explored by recent critical researchers. For more, see: Chaterjee 2004; Freeman 2000; Kabeer 2002; Voss and Linden 2002.

6. The North–South split that occurred during the Uruguay Rounds of the GATT far from disappeared in 1994 (See: McDowell 1997). As discussed in Chapter 2, the WTO is the main institution where these debates about trade take place, and, as evident in the 2004 meetings in Cancun or the 2005 G8 meetings in Scotland, access by Southern nations to developed markets in long-subsidized areas like agriculture continues to be grounds for disagreement and negotiation.
7. The 'new middle classes' constitute a minority of the population in most of the emerging economies in Asia and Latin America, but their purchasing power in sheer numbers has been the source of great interest for telecommunications transnationals since the early 1990s. Studies of the growing and new inequalities between these middle classes (or 'new rich') and everyone else reveal complex divisions based on class, but also ethnicity (that is, the backlash against the diasporic Chinese population in Southeast Asia following the Asian financial crisis) religion (that is, the rise of Hindu fundamentalism among the globalized elites of India) and gender (that is, nationalist middle class assertion of Asian 'family values') which requires careful empirical study. For more, see: Sen and Stivens 1998; and Pinches 1997.
8. Corruption and its solution, 'good governance', are terms that began to dominate the World Bank and other development agencies from the mid- to late 1990s (Marquette 2001). However, the argument that state 'interference' in economic development causes corruption was the explicit assumption that guided the telecommunications reform from the mid-1980s.
9. Researchers have pointed out the paucity of comparative empirical studies of telecommunications policy reform, especially given the scale of reform all, within the course of one decade (Noll 2002). However, Singh (1999) and Evans (1995) both provide comparative frameworks to study institutional differences between emerging economies engaged in telecommunications reform and IT development focusing primarily on the 1980s and the first half of the 1990s.
10. For current WTO commitments see: http://www.wto.org/english/tratop_e/serv_e/telecommunication_e/telecommunication_commit_exempt_list_e.htm
11. In India, the issue of rural access has been paramount in discussions about national public interest given the fact that the overwhelming majority of the nation's citizens live in areas that have literally been untouched by the 'high-tech' revolution that has very much

suggestions for current policy solutions favouring private and civil society participation in 'bridging' the urban-rural telecommunications divide in India, see Jhunjhunwala et al. 2004.

12. For example, teledensity rates in Chinese cities were 19 per cent as compared to 4.3 per cent in the rest of the country in 1996. This was a wider gap than Brazil, which is recognized as one of the most unequal societies in the world – with teledensity at 16.5 per cent in cities compared to 8.7 in the rest of the country (Winseck 2002: 29).
13. For more on the ITU's accounting of development 'success' stories in the telecommunications and ICT see: http://www.itu.int/ITU-D/e_card/index.asp

    Scholars have recently taken an interest in examining the role of telecommunications and ICT in shaping everyday cultural and political practice in Asia, Africa and Latin America. See: Rafael 2003; as well as postings on http://www.sarai.net/

4 Governing the backbone of cultures: broadcasting policy

A whole generation of urban young people now in their 20s grew up with only a vague memory of a media system that consists of two or, at a maximum, three television channels. In Europe, children born in the 1980s have reached young adulthood with MTV and to a significant extent have learned about human relationships – and fashion – through *Friends*, *Frasier*, *Big Brother* and *Sex and the City*. The idea alone that their media lives could be limited to wildlife and historical documentaries seems absurd. The very thought that they – or more possibly their parents, since they still live at home – have to pay monthly fees to receive channels they do not watch is illogical. The suggestion that, not so long ago, there used to be a state monopoly over television seems archaic at best. Often, in the classroom it is difficult to generate support for Public Service Broadcasting (PSB) among students, who although they may know to appreciate that private television is largely about Hollywood and imitations thereof, do not necessarily have PSB on their agenda of glamorous entertainment. In the United States, where the project of public service television seems to be financially suspended in a vegetative state, because of the firm hand of commercial broadcasting, the whole concept of non-commercial broadcasting has been pushed to the margins of public discussion. This is not to say that Americans or young Europeans are oblivious to the politics of commercialization of the media. However, in the eyes of Hollywood-raised audiences, non-commercial media have not managed to escape the dry language of their past, the same way that criticism of the big bully – Capitalism – has not escaped its association with colourless and monotonous left-wing politics that have ceased to inspire and excite young blood. Whether the above described images correspond to reality or stereotypes is possibly relevant to the ways in which the questions about public service broadcasting and publicly owned media in general have been framed. Is Gramsci's analysis of hegemony in maintaining the domination of capital pointing to a haunting prediction of absolute domination, where resistance becomes coopted as a 'trendy' part of finding pleasure in the consumption of lifestyle programmes? Has Fukuyama been right all along? Have we passed the end of the history of ideas – other than the idea of consumption? Is this the last breath of grand ideals for the noble causes that publicly owned media, at least in theory, claim to stand for? And how can this be explained at the times where the fragmentation of audiences, conflicts of interests and the gap of inequality are increasing? But, most importantly for the purpose of this book, how have these changes shaped the field of media policy?

If the struggle over the telecommunications regulatory reform is largely defined by the realignment of resources and direct material access to these resources, the infrastructure of telephony and computer networks, and the resistance to oligopolies based upon claims for redistributive justice, then broadcasting policies are characterized by an overwhelming attachment to issues of symbolic significance. As we shall see, the development of broadcasting policies reflects a struggle for a 'place under the sun' for cultures and languages whose cultural products in the global markets do not share the same privileges of access and distribution as for example those of the Western world or the 'North'. A relevant concept for the debates surrounding the regulatory reform of broadcasting and the concept of cultural or media imperialism has held a prominent presence, both in academic and policy circles, since Nordenstreng and Varis's report commissioned by UNESCO in 1974 (Chadha and Kavoori 2000), which eventually led to the MacBride Report and NWICO. Arguments about cultural imperialism have experienced a 'life-after-death attraction' (Kraidy 2005: 27) deployed today by conservative nationalists and progressives alike, spanning the North–South divide. In Europe and in Canada, claims about cultural imperialism demonstrate renewed anxiety over the popularity of US content on television and cinema screens today, as will be discussed at greater length below. The effect of US cultural exports, especially in the form of television programming, varies tremendously, based on the size of national audience and regional and transnational trends in trade in television programming (Iwabuchi 2002). Without abandoning a critique of the structural dominance of both Northern states and TNCs to shape audiovisual policy, recent critical research emphasizes the importance of local context and televisual practices. These works on broadcasting practice in the post-Fordist era draw our attention to 'hybrid' and 'transcultural' forms that defy strict segregation of local 'folk' culture from commercial Western cultural flows (Abu-Lughodh 2003; Rajagopal 2001).

Across broadcasting policy debates, the pull towards a liberalized audiovisual industry without the strings of social accountability is challenged by claims for representation and recognition in the production of cultural goods. 'Culture' as a terrain where these claims are expressed and experienced becomes a core, albeit contested, component in global policy. In the case of broadcasting policy, debates about culture and identity function around claims for the recognition of difference in contrast to the universalizing tendencies of the market. At the same time, the claims for the recognition of cultural presence and existence against the standardizing effects of much of the internationalization of capital are ab/used for fascist and other totalitarian and reactionary agendas across the world.[1] In these cases, 'culture' and 'identity' are used to express new forms of racism, sexism and xenophobia, advocating the 'purity' of cultural practices as opposed to the polluting character of globalization. Therefore, although the underlying demands for 'recognition' (of the validity of non-dominant cultural positions) become more prominent than those of redistribution in the realm of broadcasting content and meanings (of the democratization of the mode of production and ownership of cultural and media industries), they echo some of the problems cautioned by Fraser (2001), such as the treatment of culture and identity as fixed and clearly defined and the failure to address domination within national 'traditions'.

In the following pages we explore the changes in the policy field of the European Union where two forms of organization of audiovisual media with particular effects for content, the system of public service broadcasting and the development of non public media, appear to be in conflict. We turn our attention to the contexts and conditions within which driving assumptions about policy have been adopted and contested against the background of the global liberalization of telecommunications (Chapter 3). In the case of broadcasting policy, we focus on the European Union because it serves as the most politically integrated institutional site of global governance, allowing for some measure of democratic deliberation in contrast to the WTO or even NAFTA. Furthermore, broadcasting is the field where the struggle for cultural hegemony becomes most visible and acute, not only for competing corporate interests within national economies but also among policy-makers at an international level. These issues are attracting increasing attention in studies of communication policy from a regional perspective (for example, Harrison and Sinclair 2000; Iwabuchi 2002). For our discussion, the role of the European Union is of particular interest to civil society and policy actors in favour of a protective climate of cultural survival through the defence of cultural goods, not only within the EU or the wider European space but also within the international terrain of trade agreements and the emerging global governance of content.

The battlefield where public service broadcasters were (nearly) slaughtered

It is true that PSB is greeted as a European institution, which, free from the pressures of market competition, bases its foundational principles on the noble ideals of education, information and high-quality entertainment. Or at least this is part of the myth of PSBs. An integral part of the European model of welfare society, the PSB emerged at different times in Europe (with the first one being the BBC in the 1920s) under the organized efforts of European governments to use radio and television for the education of their citizens. Programming was meant to bring the arts to those with the least knowledge about – and possibly lowest interest in – high culture, informational programmes for farmers, morning household-focused magazines for housewives, children's programmes and a variety of other genres of information and entertainment. Public and state-owned media also served to reinforce a sense of homogenous national culture – a tangible imagined community – by bringing home the government's voice as news, transmitting Sunday Mass and broadcasting speeches of royalty, colonizers and political strongmen. It is of no surprise then that commercial broadcasting became partly associated with the negative freedoms associated with the free print press in the late 1980s and 1990s. From the prime minister's hour in London to the oath to the Führer in Nazi Berlin, and from the Armed Forces-run television channel in Athens to the Franco-ruled television in Barcelona, state-controlled PSBs provided plenty of examples of unfree media and a range of propaganda strategies. Overt propaganda as well as covert persuasion has been used as one of the main functions of public service media, despite differences in the political principles behind totalitarian regimes and liberal democracies. State actors have repeatedly demonstrated hostility to community, pirate and citizens' media throughout the twentieth century by criminalizing radio transmission on unlicensed frequencies. This situation continues today whereby government policies push pirate radio stations out of available frequencies, in order either to make room for commercial enterprises or otherwise to control the distribution of airwaves.[2] Even in the era of digital, infinite spectrum for broadcasting, spaces for non commercial media are neither guaranteed nor protected.

Despite their various degrees of autonomy, PSBs were rather closer to the government than to 'impartiality'.[3] Having been financially supported largely by state funds and taxpayers' contributions, European PSBs were allowed to function in a nearly monopoly geared communications system. Unlike in the US, where public service broadcasters have relied largely on voluntary contributions, European PSBs have had relatively greater freedom from market imperatives but with the price of dependence upon and control by national governments. In the 1980s, with the wave of liberalization of the broadcasting spectrum and the privatization of the airwaves, private broadcasting corporations had two powerful arguments on their side. The first was the lightness and glamour – comparable to the Hollywood stories that postwar Europe grew up with – and the associated symbolic power of non-state media as the 'free' media. This has proved to be an undeniably powerful argument, particularly in the former Soviet Block nations. The discourse of 'liberty' and 'free media' has been used quite extensively in policy, to provide the normative justification of the liberalization of airwaves, licences and other means of communications transmissions, especially by neoliberal, right-wing governments who played a significant role in this process.

Since the late 1980s, the governments of the US and the UK have pushed hardest for the liberalization of broadcasting policy within the EU. Media conglomerates of both nations are some of the leading and most powerful corporate actors in the global economy. The US is the largest global player in terms of the export of cultural products, and its film industry remains culturally and economically dominant in most of the world (Miller et al. 2001). The US is also the headquarters of some of the most powerful telecommunications and cross-media industries in the world.[4] Indeed, the majority of the British media is owned by US-based media, which spread their enterprises to the newly liberalized markets of former Eastern Europe in the 1990s. In Britain, although ownership is shifting to American hands for the majority of the conventional media, the market itself is booming. The strength of the British context lies in the fact that London has the busiest and most central 'hub' of correspondents and foreign media outlets in Europe. It is followed in significance by Germany whose market functions as the indicator of audiences' preferences to US-originated material for the rest of Europe. Furthermore, the BBC has a powerful presence across the world, with particular success through its educational programmes.

Certainly, the imperial domination of an Anglo-Saxon model of media culture is directly related to the political economic dominance of the British communication systems in the last two centuries. The US media have followed a comparable trajectory, where the notion of a commercially based 'free' media associated with the New World stood in contrast to a shattered postwar Europe.

A second and related argument employed against the financial assistance for PSBs is based on the notion of market sovereignty. The 'free' market depends on the discourse of 'fair' competition among market forces. Through this competition of interests, neoliberalism holds that the best (or most popular, strongest, adequate etc.) solution will prevail. 'Fairness' derives from the assumption that participants know and can defend their own interests, while competition offers stability through a self-organizing, spontaneous order of the system. The claims of 'fairness' of competition in media landscapes echo the post-Fordist context of contestation of welfare state and all things related to that. At the same time, the need for legitimization maintains its power through concepts that are held high in Western democracies and administrations, such as freedom and 'merit' (or fairness) and individual 'choice'. Previous modes of PSB funding are seen as breaching the social contract as it renders the competition between private and public media unfair. This argument makes sense only if understood within the logic of 'free market' and only if the PSB system is understood as a foremost market actor. The circularity of these arguments fails to address the serious objections as to the role of public service media and as to the achievement of a free market, and the total withdrawal of the state as a regulating actor, assuming that this is a consensual goal of societies.

Questioning PSB legitimacy at the supranational level

Despite their obvious weaknesses, arguments against the support for PSBs became an increasingly dominant position by policy-makers and critics within the international field of communication policy through a series of interventions promoting the liberalization of communications industries and 'services' through the GATI. Although it is not surprising that industrial lobbies turned their attention to Brussels, it is nevertheless indicative of the lengths to which the private sector was prepared to go to secure as much profit and control as possible in the newly constructed markets (Hartcourt 2005; Sarikakis 2004c). The more technocratic and market inclined directorate of the European Commission,[5] the Director General for Telecommunications (DG4) responded to this challenge with a proposed set of guidelines that sought to redefine the function of PSBs (Sarikakis 2004b).

The continuous pressure by media conglomerates for the abolition of any support for PSBs in Europe reached its high point with an 'ultimatum' to national PSBs to follow competition rules and rationale in the late 1990s. Before that, a decade of de facto liberalization had taken place, accompanied by the neoliberal governments of the UK and other EU countries. PSBs would have to choose and stick to a single form of funding and programming, according to the guidelines issued by DG4. More concretely, PSBs would have to choose either a single source of funding, such as state support without the possibility of seeking outside revenue, or would choose dual funding and therefore compete for revenues in the market, while at the same time being obliged to fulfil their public service mandate or depend for their funding from private organizations interested in tendering for public services on public tenders. These options offered few choices to states and PSBs for the meaningful development of public service broadcasting systems in Europe in the twenty-first century. The first option would have placed PSBs under the direct control of their respective states, potentially further damaging the effort of journalists and media workers generally of pursuing independent and progressive media work. Even if nation-states avoided interference with broadcasting plans, it is unlikely that the increased running costs of national PSBs would be met by state finances, especially in an era of state withdrawal from the funding of public institutions. The choice of competing in the free market would have also proved to be unrealistic for PSBs, especially when they are expected to fulfill non-commercial obligations. Finally, the choice of funding through public tenders would have brought PSBs into a situation comparable to the tenuous state of public broadcasting in the US, lacking a steady stream of funding and therefore without stability and resources to plan for long-term objectives. In response to these pressures, and through the collaboration of PSBs, states and the European Parliament, EU policy came to define the institution of public service broadcasting as a cornerstone of European societies in the Amsterdam Treaty rationalizing its mode of service vis-à-vis the market-driven private media. This response has become an item of public debate as well, however, that will neither be resolved nor disappear quicly from the agenda of state policy.[6]

According to the Amsterdam Treaty:

> THE HIGH CONTRACTING PARTIES
>
> CONSIDERING that the system of public broadcasting in the Member States is directly related to the democratic, social and cultural needs of each society and to the need to preserve media pluralism
>
> HAVE AGREED upon the following interpretative provisions, which shall be annexed to the Treaty establishing the European Community: The provisions of this Treaty shall be without prejudice to the competence of Member States to provide for the funding of public service broadcasting in so far as such funding is granted to broadcasting organizations for the fulfilment of the public service remit as conferred,

> defined and organized by each Member State, and that such funding does not affect trading conditions and competition in the Community to an extent which would be contrary to the common interest, while the realization of the remit of that public service shall be taken into account. (para j Treaty of the European Community 1997)

Despite the positive declarations of the PSB Protocol, as it became known, support for PSBs is still restricted by their relation to private communication industries by the clause that 'funding does not affect trading conditions and competition' in the EU. This is yet another example of the powers at work at a supranational and fundamental level of the constitutional definition of rights. The 'spirit' of European integration is captured in this paragraph as perhaps nowhere else: this fundamental piece of European identity, the concept of PSB, is renegotiated and reintroduced in the internal politics of nation-states. However, this time, PSBs, a matter clearly of national importance, are subject to market-led conditions of competition and transborder mobility of goods and services, as established by the European project. On the one hand, the official recognition of the special role of publicly owned and run broadcasting systems constitutes an important public statement about the political responsibility to protect public spaces, although for a variety of not always compatible reasons, on behalf of nation-states, parliamentarians, broadcasters and media workers in Europe. On the other hand, neither PSBs nor the normative ideal of publics-centred communication 'services' (that is, content) came out of this battle unbruised. Once on the agenda, the case of state or public support and financing of PSBs will require the constant alertness of advocates in elite formal politics and behind-the-scenes deliberations, especially where private interests are particularly strong.

Across Europe, PSBs had to defend their position and role in European societies anew and situate themselves within the market and a competitive communications system. The two main problems that PSBs have commonly had to deal with have been political interference and political dependency on the one hand and declining, inadequate financing on the other. As Burgelman and Perceval (1996) argue of the Belgian PSB, it is 'absurd to discuss the crisis of public service broadcasting in terms of programme quality or public perception' (101) when the problem of lack of political autonomy remains largely unresolved. For these authors, funding is part of this same question of political dependency that has rendered even adequate amounts of financial support insufficient. Following the general collapse of the state's capacity in the public domain, the declining support for PSBs presents a major obstacle to an independent and public interest focused determination of the role of communication services.

Common concerns across the Atlantic: the Canadian context

Without doubt however, underfunding – and the lack of political commitment to a public broadcasting ethos – is the haunting companion of Public Broadcasting Service in the USA. Political economists and critical policy studies analysts have examined at length the competing social actors that set the parameters of modern US broadcast policy embedded in the ideals of 'corporate liberalism', an attempt to balance a faith in individual rights in market society with the dominance of 'giant, impersonal corporations' (Streeter 1996: 51). Social movements that struggled for community access to the radio spectrum in the 1920s and 1930s lost to private industry with the passing of the Communication Act of 1934, which would have reserved one-fourth of broadcasting frequencies for non-profit organizations (McChesney 1993). In the decades to come, the FCC would reserve one or two channels in most markets for non-commercial broadcasters, in both radio and television, with the issue of the financing of these stations under consistent threat since the 1980s.[7] Although public broadcasting in the US has done much to 'change the character of broadcasting available to the American public', it has been severely constrained by the fact that the FCC has historically argued that non-commercial stations should provide 'programming that is of an entirely different character from that available on most commercial stations' (Streeter 1996: 88). Instead, with some exceptions, public broadcasting in the US is largely relegated to serve as a paternalistic (and unpopular) educator of audiences as 'apolitical consumers' (Streeter 1996: 204).

In North America, the symbolic dominance of commercial broadcasting has defined the limits of possible public broadcasting. The struggle for the maintenance of a form of publicly owned and public interest centred broadcasting system is best exemplified in the case of Canada. Underfunding has been one of the major problems of the public service broadcasters, despite their long history in coexisting alongside commercial broadcasters since the 1950s (Raboy 1996). During the era of increased private media activity, the Canadian government reframed its approach to broadcasting policy through the Department of Communications, in an attempt to identify 'technology' rather than 'free market' as the driving force behind regulatory changes (Raboy 1990; Young 2000).

From very early on, convergence between broadcasting and telecommunications became a policy issue[8] in Canada that promoted the creation of media markets and media enterprises. In the 1990s, following the shift in discourse in European policy circles, enthusiasm about the 'Information Society' and the Information Age became popular discourse in Canada. Policy-makers pushed for a greater role for the private sector in defining everything from the appropriateness of technological standards to the terms of service provision (Canada 1997). The era of digital technology became the defining policy factor that directed policy discourse, object and objectives for both sides of the Atlantic. The 1990s witnessed the reorganization of the jurisdiction of the institutions designing policy for broadcasting and telecommunications. The previous authority for communications, the Department of Communications and Culture, became Industry Canada, responsible among others for policy-making for Telecommunications and the Information Society. Another authority, the Department of Canadian Heritage was put in charge of issues relating to content, broadcasting and culture. This sharp segregation of what used to be a more integrated institutional approach to communications and media comes in contrast to the claims that technological development drives policy. In this case, previous claims about the determining power of technological convergence raise the question whether the jurisdiction over communications would be more efficient had it 'converged' to address the technological realities of the new media. Indeed, this is one of the main recommendations of the report on cultural heritage commissioned by the House of Commons and completed in 2003. According to the 1,000 page report, the recommendations, deriving from a wide consultation with community media and advocacy groups, media organizations and civil society organizations as well as academics and other consultants, stress that decisions about content should be made by a centralized body. Furthermore, it is recommended that the public service broadcaster, the Canadian Broadcasting Corporation (CBC), is guaranteed long-term funding with a clear plan for the transition to digital made available.

The CBC has not been helped by state policies and debates that emphasize as a measuring standard of success the popularity of content and the proportion of audience share in comparison to commercial media. Moreover, the Canadian PSB in general has not been supported in its aims of universality and catering for minorities due to the fragmentation of policy. Again, as a remedial procedure, the report recommends the treatment of the broadcasting system as a single system with further recommendations for the creation of appropriate mechanisms and independent bodies that can promote the development of local programming and regional broadcasting policy (Canada 2003).[9] Canada, as does the EU, has a wide array of institutions and policies supporting cultural and media production, such as the National Film Board and the Council of the Arts, while it also has a dedicated regulator, the Canadian Radio-television and Telecommunications Commission (CRTC). However, despite its positive image in international circles, the Canadian state has allowed further disintegration of its 'social contract' with citizens, through the gradual slippage of support and care for its public cultural institutions. As many scholars and activists argue, the segregation of policy between 'profitable' commercial (telecommunications, digital technologies) and non-profitable (PSB, cultures and arts) sectors compounds to the institutional weakening of the policy-making trajectory for PSBs. The chronic underfunding of the arts in general with which often PSBs are closely linked is a direct symptom of this problem. Industry Canada has deeper pockets and greater negotiating power and is much closer to commercial actors with considerable effectiveness in representing their interests at the policy level. The same cannot be said for the Department of Canadian Heritage, which deals with the softer 'cultural' dimensions of policy. The case of Canada shows the immense difficulties that PSBs and non-commercial communications organizations generally face in a climate of increased liberalization.

Something old, something new? Defending and seeking public service

In this global environment, the EU Protocol to the Treaty of Amsterdam is a lonely but significant statement about the role of public media services and their relationship to citizens. The protocol was the result of a fierce struggle of an alliance among competing actors (state, broadcasters and civil society) that saw in the prescriptive actions of the Commission and the private sector the danger of losing control over public service broadcasting. At the same time, at a symbolic level, the concept of public property and public, free from commercial interests, communicative space is seen to come under attack anew (Sarikakis 2004c). However, although commercial media have a simple and powerful argument for their legitimacy, the logic of profit making and consumer sovereignty, public service actors are juggling with a variety of national and cultural mandates that can be impossible to fulfil. Hoffmann-Riem (1996); Burgelman and Perceval (1996); Jakubowicz (1996); Vipond and Jackson (2002); and Born (2003), among others, point out the difficult, yet crucial, role that PSBs are called to play in the current era of a reregulated competition-driven communications market. PSBs are called to provide programming that helps build cultural cohesion, yet offer a forum for the representation of 'minorities' and special groups, succeed in providing balanced political coverage and educational programmes, fulfil journalistic values of impartiality and objectivity and act as a watchdog of the government. A public service broadcasting system is expected to cater for quality and work for universality. It is also seen as one of the most important 'commons' alongside independent and community media. Its role in safeguarding democracy or at least its role in serving as an indicator of democratic participation belong to the normative debate regarding the future of PSBs as well as constituting part of their assessment. Although the functions of the public service broadcasters are relevant or fulfilled at various degrees in various countries, they remain common characteristics that distinguish this form of broadcasting from the commercial one. Across Europe, but also in countries with similar concerns of financial viability, this domination of US-originated content in domestic markets, political dependence and the shrinking of the social 'safety' net, in the form of the welfare state, have severely destabilized the position of PSBs in domestic politics and society. This is manifested in attempts to change the structural organization of PSBs (exemplified in the case of the BBC) and reevaluate the conditions under which PSBs are supported in their mandate.

Not only Western Europe but also the 'transitional' democracies of Eastern Europe are facing these dilemmas. The liberalization of the communications sector has affected PSBs at multiple fronts. In several Eastern European countries, the transition of their social and economic organization into a system that embraces Western capitalism has proved wrong in its claims that media market liberalization goes hand in hand with democratic media as the dominance of political elites over state media continued undisturbed. This time, the new discourse bases its legitimacy on the ideas that PSBs are pivotal in ensuring diversity, an idea that is used 'as a cover for paternal or authoritarian communication systems' (Williams 1976: 134, cited in Splichal 1995: 63). New political elites (some of which derive from the previous regime) base their rule over the media on the rhetoric of ' "democratic" organs of the new "pluralistic" party state, that is, in the same way it was regarded by the old authorities' (Splichal 1995: 63). The emergence of public service broadcasting systems adhering to the ideals of servicing the public rather than the state is caught between state control and the market and there is little evidence to suggest that a social or public broadcasting system is flourishing in Eastern Europe (Jakubowicz 1996; Vartanova and Zassoursky 1995; Zernetskaya 1996). In most Eastern European countries, broadcasting policies have been successful in introducing media liberalization to their system but have failed to articulate an 'idealistic' form of public service broadcasting, the 'civic' or 'social' broadcasting system that has been the aim of critics of the old regime (Jakubowicz 2004). Instead, a 'transfusion' of Western guidelines and formats was introduced that is not compatible with the participatory model of public broadcasting envisioned by the intelligentsia – and not necessarily the civil society, if we accept that there is a lack of such a society, at least as understood in the West. Nor does it manage to overcome the problems of control by political elites. Differences in the political but also professional, in particular journalistic, cultures in central and eastern

European countries present additional difficulties in the definition and function of PSB systems (Gross 2004). Importantly, although these differences may be problematic to the neat categorization of PSBs among the Western 'family', the variety of visions and professional cultures may offer the potential of enrichment of PSBs in the West.

Despite the shortcomings of partisan media cultures in these countries, it is hardly the case that Western media, whether in the form of PSBs or private companies have maintained an impeccable record of impartiality or objectivity in their coverage and representation of world affairs and minority social groups. Similarly, the *de facto* and *de jure* acceptance of the EU norms and standards for acceding countries leads to the import and enforcement of particular visions and ideas about social relations and of course the role and function of the media and communicative spaces (Sarikakis 2005). In that respect, it seems that the opportunity for a democratic organization of PSBs in East European countries, but also for their Western counterparts as a breath of fresh air entering the EU sphere, has probably been defeated by the dominance of authoritarian politics coupled with the politics of the market.

The pressure for the redefinition of the role and function of PSBs has expressed not only the interests of industrialists but also the intentions of governments to reshape the media landscape in favour of market driven communications industries. This discourse is not as novel an idea as it is often argued to be nor is it a need that arose because of the availability of communication technologies that offer access to media other than those controlled by PSBs. In one form or another, especially in Britain, the redefinition of the role of the public service broadcasting system has resurfaced almost every time a broadcasting committee met to make recommendations. The debate over the role of the BBC, for example, is a continuing pressure item on the policy agenda. In Britain, public opinion is split in half between supporters and non-supporters of the licence fee according to the Lord Burn's report (DMCS 2004). It is understandable that given a choice most people would not choose to pay for services, which could explain the split 'vote'. However, in context, the opinion that there is 75 per cent satisfaction with the BBC offering value for money should indicate that despite criticisms the broadcaster is perceived as a valuable and integral part of British society (*The Guardian* 21 July 2004).

Despite this surprising support for a public broadcaster, the British state has repeatedly attempted to 'reevaluate' the role of the BBC. The latest decision to bring the quality of the BBC under the microscope of a national survey is another action in the series of evaluating exercises, committees and reports with the task to find the best formula for a responsive public institution. Since the establishment of the BBC in the 1920s,

British governments assigned the role of scrutiny and policy proposal making to a number of independent committees. From Sykes (1923) to Beveridge (1951) and from Pilkington (1962) to the Peacock Committee (1986) and to the Communications Act of 2003, British governments have sought to define the 'problem' within specific discursive frameworks that reflect the ideological dispositions of the dominant groups of British society. Therefore the definition of public service broadcasting in Britain as a 'national service' was represented by the Sykes Committee in a period when the politics of the country was geared towards democratic representation and universal suffrage. The beginnings and development of a welfare state in the country were also created under conditions friendlier to broadcasting decentralization (proposed by the Ullswater Committee in 1936) than the totalitarian regimes of Germany and Italy that sought to exercise absolute control over broadcasts.

The fall of British colonial rule gave an impetus to reassessment of the role of the BBC. Compounded by the beginnings of the cold war era and the intensification of a capitalist economy, the conservative government supported the establishment of commercial broadcasting (1954), withdrawing its support for a PSB monopoly and introducing an immature television programming to the competition environment of the market. A series of government interventions since the 1950s has extended the liberalization of the media market in Great Britain and, with every step, the 'issue' of the BBC is addressed anew. This sustained state hostility has not managed to marginalize the corporation, as it evolved and maintained its position as the most successful public service broadcaster in the world and has increased its revenue and strengthened its position in international communication systems. The added risks caused by deregulation of both the market and the use of new technological possibilities and in particular the digitization of communications were pointed out in the early days of television digitization in Britain (Chalaby and Segell 1999). Largely owing to its commercial ventures, the BBC succeeded in reorganizing its structure and priorities and is currently offering a number of digital services alongside private entertainment or highly specialized channels. The other European broadcasters, however, often struggle with decreased audience shares and little development-oriented policy.

Protecting one's own: cultural expression and policy hegemonies

Broadcasting policy has impacted upon European market integration like few other policy areas in the EU. It has created a market for private European media conglomerates and has allowed cross-ownership and increased ownership concentration despite strong objections from the

European Parliament and critics. Broadcasting in general has defined the EU as a single market contributing to the biggest and most impressive experiment in territorial economic integration in the region. The Television Without Frontiers Directive (TVWF) introduced in 1989, amended in 1997 and currently under revision still remains the definitive document of broadcasting policy (EP and Council 1987; Council 1989) because it sets out the general principles that rule transborder media services market today, with a particular emphasis on the unrestricted movement of media content. Broadcasting policy and in particular the audiovisual arm of the industry became the means that tested the functionality of the single market, but also boosted its operation. It has been the ultimate test for the circulation and market validity of products that cannot be understood in physical terms, such as cars, oranges and coffee makers that are easier to circulate. The exceptional thing about 'symbolic' products, or in other words 'cultural' products, is that in most cases they can be reproduced, distributed and broadcast for an almost unlimited number of times. Apart from taste, which changes with time, very little else can affect negatively the profit-making ability of these products. The powerful commercial arm of the film industry repackages products that have lost their novelty and reintroduces them in a variety of ways that help maintain their market value, in forms such as special 'seasons' dedicated to Hollywood stars, according to genre, or releasing different versions of perceived 'cult' films (the 'director's cut' are some of the best examples). The audiovisual sector, currently boosted by the increasing prominence of the electronic sector and e-commerce, is in a unique position to reproduce goods at minimal cost, which is not the case with other products, such as the automotive industry. Digitization and the expansion to the 'virtual' realm, where storage and connection to receivers and therefore customers, are theoretically at least infinite, and provide content providers and media owners with the conditions to move in (almost) unlimited market spaces. For that of course access to nationally controlled markets is necessary.

Sometimes referred to as 'cultural goods' and more often defined as 'services', broadcasting content became the object of liberalization in European societies and markets in the last two decades of the twentieth century. At an EU level, a battalion of neoliberalists working together with the telecommunications companies put forward reports and policy proposals for the full liberalization of telecommunications and broadcasting as the drivers for economic progress. Under this light, the TVWF directive became a major document of mainly competition policy, which treats content as a 'service' partly because juristically the EU's competencies did not expand to non-economic sectors. Additionally, the dominance of market-driven objectives are partly due to the fact that the interests of intensified globalization have proved to be too powerful to disregard. The combination of deregulation (and subsequent reregulation in favour of the private media) and the heavy dependence on competition policy to deal with the consequences of liberalization have led to intensified concentration of ownership not only in the EU space but also within the newly acceded countries. Ownership concentration is reaching alarming levels in Central and Eastern European countries, where major German, US and other transnationals are acquiring local and national media and establishing themselves in the audience market.

Deregulation has benefited the major transnational media corporations through their expansion of ownership and programming into national markets. Obviously US-based corporations from films to Internet providers have seized the opportunity for which they have been waiting. National capital, however, also needs to care for its interests and in this effort very often alliances are formed among cultural and media workers, producers and national capital that in most cases are not comparable to the size and influence of Hollywood. For these countries, broadcasting policy has to be accompanied by measures that offer some protection and establish a 'favourable' position in the market. Possibly the best example of national policy that reached the supranational and international level has been the insistence of France on excluding cultural goods from international trade agreements. Although it has been the will of the vast (but not 'absolute')[10] majority of the European Parliament to include the content quotas in the TVWF directive, a clause which would have forced commercial broadcasters to seek out and promote indigenous (European) content for at least half of the airtime, France's role was central in this battle. The defeat of the EP's noble cause to protect domestic cultural products vis-a-vis the Hollywood industry was neither easy nor smooth, as the tensions between 'protectionists' and liberalists resurfaced as fiercely as ever. Despite the rather vague formulation of the TVWF directive about content quota, which left it up to the individual broadcasters to deem when it is 'practicable' to devote the majority of programming to domestic content, the objections against unregulated liberalization of cultural goods continued. Broadcasting (liberalizing) policy for most countries did not automatically provide their national cultural or media industries with access to borderless markets.

One of the few ways for media companies to survive and indeed expand in the market is by the concentration of ownership, through mergers and acquisitions, that rationalizes (that is, reduces costs) in areas of production and distribution whether vertically, horizontally or both. Cross-ownership has gradually become the accepted norm in policy terms, despite strong opposition by civil society about the detrimental effects it has on genuine diversity of opinions and market entry. Digitization is a costly business, whether it is radio or television, and is most likely to lead to further consolidation of media companies and services (Hendy 2000). Indeed, the Canadian broadcasting industry successfully lobbied for the consolidation of ownership from only one AM and FM station to a multiple license model from 1998 (Parnis 2000: 237). Thus, the Canadian regulator CRTC facilitated and shaped the radio landscape through changes in ownership requirements, as well as the format of broadcasting, which also changed to simulcasting, that is, broadcasting the same programme on more than one station at the same time (Parnis 2000).

The normative framework for this direction of reregulation was offered through the context of 'replacement technology' – this allowed the CRTC to make exceptional allowances of consolidation and simulcasting thereby largely breaking away from accepted restrictions (Parnis 2000). The importance of framing policy problems and objectives is addressed by scholars who point out the significance of 'naming' not only at the early stages of an agenda-setting process but also throughout the course of policy-making and its representation to the public. Through the discourse of 'replacement technology' the CRTC was able to move towards policy that was easier to justify and therefore legitimize in the eyes of critics. This was particularly important as the CRTC had to rule effectively against its own tradition and principles of ensuring a diverse media landscape.

Favouring existing industries and blocking the entry into the market of new broadcasters was the Australian government's broadcasting policy in order to drive the development of High Definition Television (HDTV) (Brown 2002). Evidently, it was not a successful market policy as audiences have shown little interest in investing in HDTV sets (which are more expensive than conventional digital or digital terrestrial sets). Despite the outcome, which represents a typical 'market failure' case (Brown 2002: 284), the intentions of the regulator (heavily influenced by the commercial broadcasters in the late 1990s) to ensure commercial viability for private interests and the maintenance of a broadcasting oligopoly were matched by its rhetoric of taking into account the 'expensive transition to digital television' (Alston 1998, cited in Brown 2002).

The combination of deregulatory policy and the lack of restrictions over ownership concentration has created a regulatory vacuum in Europe that has been used by media conglomerates to assert and secure their position in the market and also to expand to new ones (Central and Eastern Europe). For any future 'successful' policy, the aim to impose some restriction or control over the degree of concentration will be a pointless or at best a decorative exercise in rhetoric, as it will be almost impossible for the European legislator to reverse existing patterns of ownership. It is always more difficult to reverse a phenomenon rather than prevent its spread in the first place. Given the powerful position of most of these media and their powerful positions within their own countries (in the respective German, Finnish or Greek markets) and the role of the media in affecting and generally influencing voting behaviour and elite politics, it is rather hard to imagine how any policy can be pursued that can break away from the now well-secured status quo of ownership. The EP has maintained a public (albeit elite) debate on the need for regulation at an EU level and has fought the good fight for the last two decades on the front of media ownership without much success, as it came face to face with national and transnational capital interests.

A first directive on pluralism, produced by the Commission in 1996 initiated by the EP, was badly defeated and the Commission was forced to withdraw it hastily. The arguments against any form of regulation, often repeated by scholars and analysts, derive largely from the objections of industrial lobbies to the measurement of concentration. It was argued that ownership concentration would be impossible to measure, as *concentration* for one country may be *just* ownership for another. The different (market) size of nation-states and the organization of media systems were also presented as major problems for the definition of 'concentration' and therefore the definition of the problem and its solution. Although market sizes and particularities in the organizational cultures of media systems might be part of the difficulty in constructing a prescriptive and detailed policy, the lack of any substantial control has only helped existing players (with considerable access to national political elites) to expand their operations. An exmple of this is the Antenna Group, owned by a Greek media mogul who controls 40 per cent of Greek television audience, owns radio stations in Greece and has expanded to Cyprus and Bulgaria. Although Kyriakou (the owner of Antenna, who also owns its own journalism school in Greece) is not in the same financial league as Murdoch, he is nevertheless the owner of a regional transnational media company and very close to the newly elected conservative government in Greece. Similarly, other European companies are using the TVWF not only to transmit audiovisual goods and services but also to acquire shares in national media. There emerges within the very space of Europe a situation of internal media imperialism, alongside the much-debated American media or cultural imperialism (Sarikakis 2005). Exemplified by the development of media technologies, the consequences of the absence of restrictive regulation are noted anew by the European Parliament which is trying to bring back onto the agenda the subject of 'pluralism'. But even the calls made by the sixth European Parliament for regulation are unlikely to lead the Commission to introduce a directive that can bring any changes. The question of pluralism and diversity seems to be addressed in a rather limited way in the form of 'diversity of production' under the recent proposals for the amendment of *Television without Frontiers*, as drafted by the European Commission in December 2005. Whether a future pluralism directive will succeed in identifying the boundaries of media and even media services (content) ownership is to be seen, although one cannot be particularly optimistic, given the fact that, despite repeated calls by the EP, the importance of the issue has not been forcefully addressed in the directive. For now, the clause on European content ('where practicable') remains in the new directive, but has been expanded to cover all non-linear media services, such as those where the consumer decides whether or not to receive content (EC 2005). According to this proposal, non-linear media service providers have the obligation to promote European cultural content 'where practicable' and to take into account the effective users' consumption of such works.

The question of the cultural domination of American (US) values and narratives over domestic ones has remained a powerful discourse in international politics. This discourse not only represents genuine fears and real conditions of underrepresentation and market saturation but also represents the interests of capital not yet able to achieve transnational and global mobility. This is particularly the case with small entrepreneurs, and expands well beyond the confines of the broadcasting industry to print and electronic media other than broadcasting. On the cultural front and in particular in the production of films, it is hardly ever the case that national markets, with the exception of a few strong national producers, can support film production.[11] The problem is even more acute when films are not designed for easy consumption. This means that cultural production requires the support of the state, which comes in the form of subsidies, restriction on the entry of foreign (and most importantly Hollywood) films, the application of quotas and other forms of financial or in-kind support. The EU, having opened its trade borders internally as an exchange to the Marshall plan (Pauwels and Loisen 2003:293) becomes a more 'manageable' space of national, therefore decentralized, markets. Entry to one of these markets allows free mobility to the totality of EU market and regional space. This is particularly useful to the US film and television industry that now needs only to deal with the same set of rules across Europe, making significant savings in resources and time.

As cultural expression and the cultural industry as a whole are of particular significance in more ways than simply the economic, the protection and support of the sector is still a very sensitive issue for a number of political and social actors. These tensions between the US audiovisual lobby and the US government, on the one hand, and the reaction to the liberalization of cultural goods represented by most countries, on the other, have formed the level of negotiations at the WTO and GATT rounds for the last fifty years. In the 1947 GATT negotiations and again in 1960s, the US asked that Europeans should remove quota restrictions from their film and later television imports. In both cases strong objections were made by European countries (and in particular the French whose cultural industry is rather important for national economy and identity). And while the argument that culture is unlike other commercial products was easier to accept forty years ago, in the 1980s the argument for deregulation was moved to include services (Pauwels and Loisen 2003). At the time, deregulation became particularly felt as it started expanding to state functions and 'services'. The Uruguay Round became the terrain of tension between those asking for the full liberalization of audiovisual services and those voicing strong opposition on the grounds of 'cultural exception'. As Pauwels and Loisen (2003) argue, the Free Trade Agreement between Canada and the US included a cultural exception clause which helped the rhetorical and discursive battle in favour of cultural exclusion.

In the meantime, as we discussed in the previous chapter, telecommunications services had already been completely liberalized. Furthermore, with the convergence of technologies, certain questions regarding the circulation and distribution of cultural goods and services through liberalized telecommunications and other information technologies remain unanswered. The tendency will be to frame the arguments for liberalization of digital content based on the rationale that it constitutes part of the new information economy. The US has already made proposals for the liberalization of the audiovisual sector in the WTO rounds that were expected to conclude at the end of 2004 but have been extended at least for a year. Section II of the US proposal refers to the 'new' audiovisual sector and the new conditions of cultural production and consumption created by the new technologies. The argument is based on the availability of an increased number of media outlets as enabled by digital technologies that provide increased opportunity for cultural expression to reach audiences. Thus, there can be no argument of Hollywood dominance among the few broadcasters (and the media generally) as has been argued in the Uruguay Rounds (USA Communication 2000). The US government has not simply submitted the proposals for 'negotiation' at the WTO rounds, however, it has also moved towards bilateral free-trade agreements with a number of countries, creating thereby a de facto situation in the acceptance of the liberalization of e-commerce, which includes audiovisual and cultural products in a digital form. Agreements with Chile (2002), Singapore and the Central American States (2003), and Australia and Morocco (2004), all include the liberalization of audiovisual content for e-commerce and via e-communications. Apart from some particularities because of the specificities of each country, the overall policy aims to remove trade barriers that may be harmful to the US motion pictures industry (Bernier 2004). Moreover, the consequences of such policies will be made more visible once the proposed plans find their application through trade in the very near future. The hype of the symbolic economy continues to provide a powerful argumentative edge in international agreements, especially since the plethora of digital outlets points to a theoretically unlimited choice for consumers. Therefore the arguments in favour of protection of national industries vis-a-vis Hollywood appear obsolete. In other words, according to the US audiovisual industry and government policy preferences, there is enough space for all cultures on the screens of our hypermedia. The insistence of the US in ensuring that digital media services are included, without exceptions, in the liberalized agenda is based on the definition of audiovisual content as 'digital content'.

> The digital trade agenda is thus tailored to the free trade of so-called digital products like music, software or movies that derive their value from "content" produced by the information technology (IT) and entertainment industries, and that were previously – in the offline world – delivered on physical carrier media like CDs. (Wunsch-Vincent 2003: 8–9)

This coordinated action of the US is enabled by the introduction of a new law that gives authority to concluding major trade agreements with other parties through a simplified congressional vote on the agreement (and no parts of it). Enacted in 2002, it was the US government's response to the representations made on behalf of the most powerful IT and content industries, by their respective associations, such as the Information Technology Industry Council and Motion Picture Association of America (Wunsch-Vincent 2003). In a way, the recent revision process of the European TVWF seems to present an oxymoron, with its drive to extend regulation to the digital and online services, such as the forthcoming Internet Protocol Television, while at the same time the USA is pulling digital services towards complete deregulation. It is possible that EU policy-makers, anticipating a further deregulation of the (online/digital or multi-) media, are attempting to take a proactive step to maintain minimum principles in the converged media environment, such as minimum, albeit rhetorical, protection of cultural content. Despite the strongest of reactions from industry and PSBs alike the European Commission targeted the regulation of the Internet, even with a rather light touch, as part of the provision for non-linear services. The proposed new directive, however, largely aims to ensure a pan-European legal framework rather than facilitating decisive changes in the Internet and media landscape. What we are now witnessing can be compared to the changing communications environment in the late 1980s and it is reasonable to expect it to constitute a second wave of liberalization of communications, this time including the complete liberalization of content and goods that can be transferred and therefore distributed through digital means. The financial motives behind this new regulatory wave of reregulation are to be found in the profits generated by intellectual rights on conventional and digital content.

Cultural content and public broadcasting: Quo vadis?

As we can see, the redefinition of cultural content and the role of public service broadcasting have been two of the most significant areas of negotiation and opposition in the field of international broadcasting policy. These traits can be found across countries with strong PSB traditions, while those without face greater difficulty in their efforts to develop a public broadcasting system. National PSBs have been under growing pressures from telecommunications and media transnationals in their march to conquer new and emerging markets. The degree of the ability to protect and indeed autonomously develop a new identity has depended largely on the negotiating power of individual states with the forces of market integration and globalization. In the case of the EU, the traditions of identifying national identity with a present PSB have brought the debate over the future of PSBs to the parliamentarian plenaries and consequently to the negotiating table of the EU. The matter has been of such significance that it has been one of the legislative fields that contributed not only to the definition of the EP as a co-legislator (with unique institutional power in global politics in comparison to other representational institutions) but also affected the direction of the EU and added an unusual note to international agreements.

As the decline of PSBs in many parts of the world and the failure to establish such forms of public communication spaces signals the need for better designed policy and participation, it is evident that the issues of recognition gain a central position in the global arena of macro-economic integration and institutional change. Again, legitimating discourses of this era, technological determinism with its variation of technological nationalism (Young 2000) and neoliberalism, seek to underwrite global and local media markets. Resisting ideas and counter policies – often originating from subordinate actors and, in the case of the EU, together with their political representatives – put firmly on the agenda demands for redistribution but also for recognition.[12] Fraser's definition of recognition is careful to address the 'status' rather than 'perception' of recognition and dispels the assumed purity of stability of culture and identity. Policies at the EU level have only partially succeeded in addressing the question of recognition (and redistribution) at the supranational level, as they have failed to turn their attention quickly and sufficiently enough to patterns of internal domination (Sarikakis 2005), among national and intra-national constituencies, among women and men in their access to cultural expression and policy-making and among EU citizens and incoming or existing peoples without official status. From the available global institutions, however, the EU as an international actor and the EP as the first international institution to enjoy full legitimacy through its direct relation to the European citizen have exerted significant resistance to the assault of the integration of tele/communications markets.

However the questions associated with the broadcasting industry, and especially the question of recognition of cultures and their rights to sufficient communicative space and audiences, are not resolved. Instead, we are currently witnessing a sophisticated attempt by powerful states such as the US to elude questions of cultural diversity and protection of non-commercial cultural goods through a new set of discourses and the regulatory opportunity these offer. These discourses maintain their technological deterministic tones, as they frame more and more policy questions within the context of the 'information society' and the 'knowledge economy'. As digital content becomes steadily –but quietly – a firm component of the liberalized list of services among bilateral agreements it will almost automatically constitute part of (liberalized) e-commerce. It is significant to note that the review of the TVWF directive currently underway in the EU has caused strong reactions from Internet Service Providers and the pornography industry by its proposals to expand protection of cultural content and control of content to digital services (EC 2005a; 2005b). Similarly, the latest decision of the EU not to support a US-based administration of the Internet through the private entity ICANN, irrespective of the outcome that saw the US maintaining its position, signals a new turn in EU politics. For one, the assumption that traditional media and the Information Society media can be dealt with separately seems to lose ground, as the concerns expressed in the public consultation procedure indicate. Through the integration of Internet and television, through the Internet Protocol TV, and the system of multiplex, it becomes difficult for policy-makers and states to proceed to any proactive measure that can guarantee a minimum standard of public service mission in the private media. The question of a minimum available supply of audiovisual material that derives from independent productions is one that will remain on the agenda for some time. The following chapter addresses the contexts, myths, and pressures for these Information Society policies that expand to the whole range of the global field of communications policy.

Notes

1. Routinely, claims for 'cultural purity' are utilized to maintain sexist and racist practices across many domains of public and private life throughout the world. Examples are found in elite and everyday politics, in the programmatic statements of (legal) British (British National Party), French (Le Front National), German (Nationaldemokratische Partei Deutschlands) and other political parties in the West, concerned with cultural and racial 'purity' (Jeffries 2002). Examples are: the reports and critique in alternative presses and scholarly research about the Taliban in Afghanistan; Muslim fundamentalists who defend the 'purity' of Islam and Muslim culture when applying gender segregation (Appleton 2001; Hélie-Lucas 2001); patriarchal societies defending the murder of women and young girls as 'restoring the family honour' in 'honour killings'; or even the question of 'autonomy' and independent 'choice' for body mutilation in the form of plastic surgery fiercely defended by the beauty industry in the West.
2. One of the most recent examples was the 2004 distribution of radio frequencies to commercial radio stations in the Netherlands that drove out of the frequencies long-standing Dutch pirate radios. See for example http://www.kuro5hin.org/story/2004/2/27/115517/137. Also see the call from the National Union of Journalists in the UK for a reorganization of the radio spectrum to allow pirate and community radio stations to continue transmissions http://www.nuj.org.uk/inner.php?docid=304. For a thorough discussion of the role of pirate radio see, for example, Soley (1999) or Grant (1990).
3. One can recall the example of US public and commercial broadcasters offering up airtime to government propaganda for the building of patriotism and nationalism, with the rewriting of scripts to suit such visions in World War Two. Other examples would refer to the pressures exercised by the UK government upon the BBC during the Falkland War or in contrast the role of the French ORTF as de Gaulle's spokesman. (We thank David Hutchison for alerting us to this point.)
4. Time AOL Warner, Murdoch's News Corporation, General Electric (see, for example, Sarikakis 2004b for British media ownership patterns) are some of the greatest media conglomerates.
5. It is beyond the purpose of this chapter to provide a full and detailed account of the history of broadcasting policies in the EU. For that see Collins 1998; Hartcourt 2005; Sarikakis 2004c. It is widely accepted that some of the EU institutions are closer to the ideas of PSB and the protection of cultural production, such as the majority of the European Parliament and the Directorate General for Audiovisual,

than others, such as the Director General (DG) responsible for budgets, competition and telecommunications. It is also of interest that institutional arrangements in the EU 'coincide' with particular dominant ideas about the organization of the political economy of the union, whereby, weak (non-central in significance) committees such as the Committee on Culture, deal with 'soft' policies while more powerful actors, such as the DG for telecoms or competition, enjoy more weight in its jurisdiction. Here, the very *raison d'être* of the EU is reflected in the segregation of constituencies.

6. For a detailed discussion on the complex process that led to the Amsterdam protocol see Sarikakis 2004c.
7. Tom Streeter (1996) offers a nuanced and historical account of the rise of commercial and public broadcasting policy in the US, focusing on the limits and possibilities of the discourse of corporate liberalism. For more on the state of US public broadcasting after the 1996 reforms: see McChesney 1999; and Aufderheide 2000. For an activist perspective see: http://www.cipbonline.org/
8. As Young (2000) discusses the document Instant World (1971) was one of the first to address the idea of convergence, followed from 1983 onwards by a new national broadcasting policy that effectively furthered the project of liberalization of the Canadian broadcasting landscape (Raboy 1990).
9. One of the authors (KS) would like to thank one of the academic consultants of the report, Marc Raboy, for offering his invaluable comments about the state of broadcasting policy in Canada and time for discussing them during KS's research leave in Montreal in winter 2004. Thanks also go to Mr Francis Scarpaleggia, Member of Parliament Lac St. Louis, Quebec, for making the report available in the speediest of times.
10. For a detailed account of the politics of cultural exception and the position of the European Parliament see Sarikakis 2004c.
11. Notable exceptions here are Bollywood and the Chinese film industry. Whether these strong film markets are able to or interested in supporting alternative (non-mainstream) film production is a question pointing to the availability of a number of structural and cultural factors, such as access to and involvement in education, funding, skills, distribution etc.
12. Claims for recognition are made by women, aboriginal groups and 'visible' minority immigrant groups in Canada. In Europe, similarly claims around citizenship, language, sexual equality and national identity are reflected in some of the positions of the European Parliament.

Part Three

Policy paradigms

5 Policies for a new world or the emperor's new clothes? The Information Society

Third-generation mobile phones, broadband connections, wireless applications, cybercommunities, cyberwars, cybersex, e-commerce, e-democracy, e-learning: this is some of the language that has come to describe the era of accelerated tele/communications and transactions. These terms have not escaped from a science fiction movie, although some of them have their origins in science fiction novels, but from the consultative papers of 'think tanks' and government policy documents. They have become part of everyday advertising, policy, newspeak and even casual conversation, in global cities across the North–South divide. These are the terms of a particular form of capitalist economic organization of social relations that adheres to two overarching qualities of the new Information Age: *speed* and *universality*. CEO of Microsoft, Bill Gates's *Business @ the Speed of Thought* (1999) not only embodies the ideas and policies that characterize the era of the Information Society and the Knowledge Economy, it also constitutes a manual for the direction of future technological development, policy, economic organization and even social relations. Speed, instant capital transaction across geographic nodes that would have taken hours and days to cross through physical means, almost 'cancels' the concept of time as an obstacle or expense for transnational companies. Spatial universality is also a new achievement for the global enterprises of the twenty-first century. Telecommunications have enabled those connected to premium translocal networks the liquidation of time/space. The beneficiaries of the transcendence of time/space are to be found among transnational corporations that can do business literally around the clock across the globe. This 'transcendence' has adverse consequences for the labourers of the new Information Society whose labour hours – once regulated and largely defined – spill over into the private sphere and invade leisure time. The wonders of technology that would liberate desk-chained analysts and mothers engaged in paid work are overshadowed by a series of intrusive practices, from the toxic production of microchips by young Asian and Latina women in Asia and the Americas to the 'flexible' office that does not cease to work when 'out of office'. Gates's informationist manifesto calls for the literal and metaphorical reform of the human organism to fit the technologized business of the new millennium. What are the characteristics of this new organization of social relations? What does it mean to live and work in the Information Society? How knowledgeable is the Knowledge Economy and most importantly, in which ways has communications policy sought to address the new demands for structural and cultural adjustment, nationally and transnationally?

This chapter explores the nexus of the myth-policy of the Information Society (IS). It maps the trends in designing policy for the Information Age by concentrating on the visions of IS developed in the EU and the USA. It examines the dominant (often partially competing) institutional visions of the IS on the world stage in the last 20 years, and the ways in which they have fallen short of addressing pressing questions of redistributive justice. As we shall see, 'deviating' versions of a socially conscientious IS vision, deriving from different political geographies, clash with more deterministic ones. Social aims seem to lose ground constantly, when economic aims are present. Once again, we are approaching questions of policy through the examination of the struggle for symbolic as well as material hegemony. The legitimacy of the IS visions rests on the articulation of ideas and the construction or apprehension of 'facts' by the various institutional actors engaged in the practice of shaping policy. We will analyse major policy concerns by situating them within the context of their conceptualization, justification and implementation. For that, we turn our attention to the symbiotic relationship between state actors and corporate actors and the role of the market in 'liberating' consumers from the state through IT technology. As the powerful discourse of 'deregulation' or the reality of reregulation of neoliberal trade takes the helm, it produces the discursive conditions for the reregulation of neoliberal subjects as we discussed in Chapter 1. The market discourse subsumes both the state and civil society in an attuned process of legitimating market-led development.

A telematic history of civilization – and its policies

> The benefits of the NII [National Information Infrastructure] for the nation are immense. An advanced information infrastructure will enable U.S. firms to compete and win in the global economy, generating

> good jobs for the American people and economic growth for the nation. As importantly, the NII can transform the lives of the American people – ameliorating the constraints of geography, disability, and economic status – giving all Americans a fair opportunity to go as far as their talents and ambitions will take them. (NII 1993)

> [The European Parliament] considers that the new information technologies may create even greater regional and social disparities in the European Union than at present and considers that in order to obviate this risk, the use of information highways should focus on correcting existing imbalances and discrepancies between regions of the European Union in terms of economic and social development, and social and regional problems . . . (European Parliament 1998 para. 23)

> Transforming digital information into economic and social value is the basis of the new economy, creating new industries, changing others and profoundly affecting citizens' lives. (Commission of the European Communities 2000a: 4)

> Proactive policies are needed to respond to the fundamental changes in technology. Digital convergence requires **policy convergence** and a willingness to adapt regulatory frameworks where needed so they are consistent with the emerging digital economy. (Commission of the European Communities 2005b: 3)

These quotes capture the spirit (and time) of the 'new' informational age and exemplify the directions of national and supranational policy in Europe and the USA. Quite significant in their positioning, the declarations made in Gore's *National Information Infrastructure* (NII) and the European Commission's two major policy documents *eEurope: an Information Society for All* (2000a) and the 'mature' *IS plan for i2010 – a European Information Society for Growth and Employment* (2005b) convey the expectations of policy-makers and in general the rhetoric of a new and therefore promising era for revived economies and an end to poverty. They also clearly convey an almost dogmatic definition of policy which adheres to technological determinism and the 'free' market. Among these celebratory intents, the voice of the European Parliament emerges as an unannounced visitor, the voice of caution and urgency pointing to the vast gap between fairy tales and reality. One of the interesting traits of the development of IS policies is that the boundaries between 'national' and 'global' policy, 'Fordist' and 'post-Fordist' modes of production, conventional and 'new' media are continuously shifting – they coexist and affect societies ripped by divisions old and new. But before we examine the more specific IS policy directions and their effects, it is necessary that the concept of the IS is identified and appropriately defined.

Despite its popularization, the term 'Information Society' is rather ill defined. For some scholars, it represents only an ideology, rather than a concept deriving from the findings of empirical observation of contemporary capitalism. In contrast to Castells's (1996) formulation of 'network society', Garnham (2000) rejects the statement that the social or economic organization of contemporary society is 'transformed' into an 'Information Society'. He asserts that the term, 'rather than serving to enhance our understanding of the world in which we live, is used to elicit uncritical assent to whatever dubious proposition is being put forward beneath its protective umbrella' (2000: 140). Garnham seems to be arguing that the lack of any empirical data to point to 'the real world phenomena' (2000: 141) that can 'prove' the existence of an Information Society is stronger as evidence of the *ideology* of IS than its validity in describing a particular societal transformation. Webster too in *Theories of the Information Society* (2002) discusses at some length the problems with identifying the exact meaning and location of the term in real life, in ways that can be observed not necessarily exclusively quantitatively. Therefore although the 'measuring' of such a 'society' might be desirable in offering a picture of the trends and directions in employment, production, trade and distribution, it is not the only way to define the standards that will prove or disprove the new society. Webster generally maps the criteria applied by theorists to determine the emergence of IS in technological, cultural, economic, spatial and occupational categories. According to this taxonomy of 'criteria', the advent of the information or knowledge society tends to be identified with technological innovation and in particular the use of computer-mediated communication systems in the same way that previous eras have been characterized as transformed by their own technological innovations, such as the Steam Age or the Age of the Automobile.

In economic terms, IS is characterized by the transformation of information into a commodity and by the increasing value of information as the basis of economic activity. Again, here information takes the place of technology in determining the new conditions of social change, implying a concentration of the economy upon those sectors that are separate from the manufacturing sector and the crafts. This shift in the organization of employment is also regarded as indicative of the new form of society which is based on information as its raw material. In that respect as a service-based economy has replaced manufacturing, the organization of labour is based on skills involving the use and analysis of information. The occupational shift characterizes another set of criteria as to whether we are now living the IS. The spatial interconnections also become a criterion for the ultimate 'measurement' of the IS. It is true that information technologies and networks shift not only geographical boundaries but also the boundaries of time and a combination of both. Transactions take place at almost an instant and across previously long distances. The impact of this redefinition of space upon labour patterns can be seen in our everyday lives where, in their simplest forms, mobile telephony and portable communication technologies provide a direct and constant link to the 'office'. Last on Webster's list is the cultural – and the least measurable – criterion to identify an emerging IS. The cultural criterion is rather understood as the information available in the social domain and the use of information in everyday life, from fashion to storytelling. The argument is that the IS is a media-laden society dominated by a complex set (networks) of information about every aspect of public and private life.

As Webster also discusses, this neat categorization of criteria 'proving' the existence of the new society at-work is rather problematic, as no one criterion can determine with certainty the characteristics that are sufficient to define a society as a knowledge or Information Society. Nevertheless, what is probably more important than a clear definition of what constitutes the IS, would be to acknowledge that, even in the case of a social organization with novel characteristics, it is more likely that these coexist with older forms of social and economic and technological organization rather than implement a radical break with the past. For Braman, the IS goes back to the mid-nineeteenth century, starting from 'electrification and globalization', moving on to 'massification and professionalization' until the 1960s, followed by the convergence of technologies and 'awareness of qualitative social changes' between 1960 and 1990, to reach the current forth phase characterized by the 'harmonization of information systems across national boundaries with each other and with other types of social systems' (Braman 1998: 80). This account of the genesis of the IS provides us with a chronology of processes surrounding the development and impact of information technology on society, and it builds historical continuity and social change within the net of explorations of the role of technology.

If an inseparable part of the IS, however, is its post-industrial character, then claims for the existence of the latter have been made long before Bell's much-cited work on the replacement of an industrial society by a service economy (1973). In his genealogical study of the IS, Mattelart (2001) traces such discourses back to the beginning of the twentieth century with the utopian 'neotechnical era' of 'mutual aid' that would surpass the barbaric alienation brought about by the industrial society. This was Kropotkin's, the Russian philosopher's, vision of the use and potential of the new source of energy, electricity (Mattelart 2001: 43–4). It would signal an era where social relations, translated into non-hierarchical networks of support, would be brought forth through the qualities of flexibility and ubiquity inherent in electricity (Mattelart 2001: 43–4). Around the same time, Indian scholar Ananda K. Coomaraswamy expressed the term of 'post-industrial'/ism as the development of a society that would move away from the hierarchical and oppressive organization of industrialism towards a decentralized, culturally diverse second renaissance (Mattelart 2001: 43–4). The 'redistribution' of cultural wealth, specifically understood as High Culture, was also Lloyd Wright's architectural philosophy that would bridge social units of the polis (after the ancient Greek definition of *polis* (city), as the space where *polites* (citizens) gather and interact), through the use of modern technology, in an organic web of networks, therefore promoting a new form of sociability, a new form of decentralization (Mattelart 2001: 46). It is rather significant that the question of culture, whether perceived as High Culture or as 'ways of life', keeps returning to the quest for human liberation through technological advancement. These technocentric accounts of the political and the social dimensions of the cultural occupy the mind of futurists and early utopians, who see the political possibility of decentralized networks in the technological capability of electricity, later broadcasting and currently computers. Braman's (1998) correlation of questions of cultural identity and expression as inherent in the development of the stages of the IS can be seen through this particular but largely agreeable strand of thought that traces such questions to the almost unavoidable 'dismantling' of the shackles of industrial force.

Nevertheless, the socialist-utopian metaphors of 'organic spaces' and decentralized democracies have almost been capitulated by mercantile, mass production, mass-culture-driven informational capitalism. Although a very strong strand of intellectual workers has continued to draw parallels between the decentralizing and anonymizing capabilities of information and communications technologies and the freedom acquired through these qualities, an equally strong web of pre-positioned constraints prove to hurdle this transition. Modern-day believers in the emancipatory capacities of technology, among them feminist thinkers such as Dale Spender (1995) and Donna Haraway (1991), extend the liberational attributes of incorporeal interaction to gender dynamics. For these theorists, computer-mediated communications allow the building of networks among marginalized voices and the integration of the previously marginalized into the web of social relations free from the chains of gender. Time and again, the visions of liberation maintain their power to capture the best political and cultural manifestos,[1] regardless of their phrasing, across the years. Without them of course, it would be difficult to imagine other scenarios of possible world(s); they also succeed in describing moments of social and individual cooperation, while at the same time providing sets of standards to counteract a monolithic market centred and militarized circular logic.

Japan is probably the first case of a society taking proactive measures to define a future IS, the policy for achieving an IS derived from the Ministry of Trade and Industry to 'foster synergies between research and development, and between the public sector and major private firms' (Mattelart 2002: 100). A concept of the early 1970s, the plan envisaged a completely computerized central 'administration', the 'Computeropolis'. That would be a city equipped with specially programmed systems to manage traffic, hypermarkets, financial services, training facilities, transportation and distance-controlled medical systems (Mattelart 2002: 100). The vision of this IS was of gradual development towards the ultimate liberation of human beings from need. The discourse blended with this vision spoke of a society in which 'intellectual creativity would supplant the desire for material consumption' (Mattelart 2002: 101). The prophet of this new world was futurist Yoneji Masuda.

Because of the attention paid to education and computer technologies by the Japanese long-term IS policy, Mattelart argues, Japan is likely to be one of the few places in the world where educational channels have a popular national audience. In its initial stage, the US vision of an IS also made strong references to the aims of surpassing social inequalities and achieving the complete amalgamation of the separate realms of 'home' and 'school', as a policy that would bring access to education to every child who is unable to attend school. That would be accomplished with the help of computers. US state policy discourse tried to build on the momentum of technological awe, after the moon landing in 1969. Through a series of decentralized initiatives for research support and implementation, the research arm of universities together with the military drove computer communications through a series of technological 'breakthroughs' that would project the supremacy of US-based corporations and the military onto world markets. The 'children' of this revolution were IBM, which at one point controlled three out of four computers in the US market (Mattelart 2003), and the Strategic Defense Initiative or, as they are commonly known, *Star Wars* (launched in 1983). Well into the first decade of the twenty-first century, computer access and use for educational purposes, especially within the context of primary education, had yet to achieve the goals envisioned thirty years ago. In particular, schools in urban centres as well as remote rural areas, with higher rates of minority African American, Latino and Native American students, struggle to keep up with technology and make meaningful use of computer-mediated communication, because of structural and organizational constraints (Seiter 2005). For example, although the number of pupils per instructional computer at schools has fallen from twelve in 1998 to five in 2002, more than half of the country's pupils (55 per cent) do not use a computer for their coursework. Furthermore, although the vast majority of teachers working at schools with computer and internet access has been given support to integrate computers in their teaching, poor funding for schools in low-income neighbourhoods, failing technologies, lack of time and general overload of work for teachers, and policy reforms designed around market-based incentives and penalties for educators constrain or prohibit the use of ICTs (see OECD 2004; Seiter 2005; Virnoche and Lessem 2006).

From history to a 'New World' future: the dominance of market visions

In the US, the IS vision grew as an extension of shifts in telecommunications policy discourse that led to the deregulation of the industry in 1984 followed by liberalization in 1996. As examined in Chapter 3, telecommunications constitute the backbone of the IS, the infrastructure upon which the more symbolic, 'ethereal' world of cybercommunication is based. Mattelart (2001) claims that anti-trust efforts against AT&T's private monopoly prepared the way for the gradual withdrawal of public accountability over the private communications infrastructure. As we have argued in the previous chapter, regulatory shifts originating in the US in the 1980s undermined the 'modern infrastructure ideal' associated with public ownership or oversight of transport, energy and telecommunications (Graham and Marvin 2001). At the same time, however, IBM's monopoly came out of these changes unharmed, as this (computer and technology production) was a field where the government did not see the need to regulate. In 1991, the achievements of militarized IS technologies found a testing ground with the first Gulf War (and second phase later in 1993). Star Wars that had been temporarily suspended were again revived by President of the USA George W. Bush in 2001. Indeed, the direction for the militarization of much of the IS project is a criticism echoed by NGOs and grassroots organizations at the World Summit on Information Society (WSIS Civil Society 2003). Initially, the NII programmatic conceptions of the Clinton era Democratic Party included strong references to the potential of using telematics for social purposes in the early 1990s. Telemedicine and educational and training centres became for a brief period part of the comprehensive agenda of a 'New World Information

Order' where economic benefits and social interests were close partners. Soon after the election of the Democrats in 1991, these social dimensions were defeated in the Congress as part of the growing domestic assault on the redistributive components of the battered American welfare state. This process intensified as the newly elected Republican majority realized that it could work together with the fiscally conservative Clinton administration on welfare 'reform', ostensibly dismantling the limited safety net for women, children and the unemployed (Gordon 1994). In this setting, the same administration that had introduced these limited means for public regulation of technological goods and infrastructure in the international arena retreated defensively from the label of 'big government'. The wave of deregulatory policies in the field of telecommunications and transportation, in particular aerospace, but also other economic sectors was not accompanied by a counterbalancing, 'protective' set of actions for a more balanced distribution of wealth.

As we discussed in Chapter 3 the deregulation of US telecommunications was followed by the privatization of British Telecom (BT) the same year. The EU has also been a global player devoted to a series of policies that in essence promoted the neoliberal communications reform agenda. In the late 1980s, the Green Paper on Telecommunications proposed the same 'liberalization' policies for the European telecoms sector as was followed in the US. After all, the EU is an important market for the US-based tele/communications industry and without 'friendlier' policies, *trade in this space would have maintained its costs*. This is not to suggest that the visions of EU and USA policies were identical but rather to emphasize the fact that harmonization of national policy is a crucial component of increased trade integration in world regions, coupled with the construction of a so-called 'flexible' regulatory environment, as evident in the telecommunications sector. The Bangemann Report[2] 'urged' the European Commission to embrace a series of policies that would direct liberalization across Europe. The same year, Al Gore's proposal for the building of a Global Information Infrastructure (GII) prepared the ground for further liberalization and market integration among separate sectors of the economy: the virtual or 'seamless' network and the 'real' business, such as sales of videos, distribution of AV works, telephony and others. The four basic principles of the US version of a GII were the promotion of competition, open access, 'flexible regulatory environment' and universal service[3] (NTIA 1994).

In the 1990s, successive EU policies promoted the liberalization of services and focused on the introduction of new technologies in businesses and education. The predictions expressed in the 'vision'-defining documents such as the 1993 *Growth, Competitiveness, Employment: Challenges* *and Ways Forward into the 21st Century* White Paper, the 1997 report on living and working in the IS and the 1999 public consultations about the convergence of new media, tend to emphasize the positive effects of ICTs and new technologies in general. The lack of any serious investigation into the impact of inequality, deterioration of work conditions, the casualization of work, the withdrawal of the welfare state and the decline in pensions and health provision, as well as the costs of directing public funds towards the mainstreaming of ICTs without at the same time correcting social and economic ills were some of the weak points of EU policy in that period. Especially for the non-'core' economies of the EU, the rate of technological adoption has proved to make these issues visible (Sarikakis and Terzis 2000).

Despite their overt concentration on the marketability of ICTs, the communications policies surrounding the European and American models of IS are not identical. Venturelli (2002) suggests that there are fundamental political philosophic differences between the ways in which the EU and USA approach their analysis of the role of the individual and therefore of the marketplace and of the role of the state, and therefore the very functioning of democracy. These differences can be largely located in the hierarchical arrangement of importance between citizenship and democracy and market. In the European political philosophical tradition, the 'polis' – as the space to which citizens have access to and may participate within the life of their communities – is a notion interconnected with the principles of universal access and with the public service model of regulation. As Venturelli asserts, it is in the constitutional backbone of the EU and the national member states where we find public interest clauses particularly emphasized, such as universal access, protection of privacy, content regulation and public investment in research and innovation among others (2002: 77). Nevertheless, these philosophical differences have not proven unsurpassable: EU policy continues to make strong references to social and cultural goals with a rather systematic – albeit very modest – network of initiatives that aims to foster cultural production and protection of private data, but the course of liberalization is unmistakeable. The most recent EU policy addresses the 'maturing' of the IS in the European space, but with a very clear mandate for market-oriented regulations. These are the integration of the 'European Information Space' which involves the convergence of communications policies (a parallel initiative to the current revision of TVWF as we discussed in the previous chapter); more technological research and an emphasis on security (which takes a number of forms from security of software to that of private data). Social aims involve the quality of life in the EU with three priorities: 'the needs of the ageing society, safe and clean transport and cultural diversity'

(EC 2005b: 11). The EU is largely more focused on the social impact of IS and the future of the public service ethos. This can be understood as an ideological and political tradition related to the historical development of nation-states and the role of governments in the European space, but also the role of cultural contexts and diversity of these political traditions for the EU project. Increasingly, the pressures of transnational capital may appear to win ground over the social argument but the institutional arrangement of the EU is such that can maintain the space for the development of debates resistant to the pan-market argument. This takes place at both national levels (as political representatives also make national cases) and at the supranational (EU) level as the European Parliament with its role in the constitutional and legislative processes of the EU and its presence in the international arena strengthens the infrastructure of counter-policies. As the French Régulation School (FRS) also suggests, it becomes clear that the integration of markets at a global scale does not exclude 'individual' or 'national' approaches as long as these do not fundamentally interfere with the neoliberalist project. At the same time, the spaces for resistance, but also paradoxically the structures that will legitimize and allow market integration, depend on institutional arrangements. The availability of resources and means for the participation of citizens, whether as protesting forces or within the planning of policies, are crucial elements for maintaining resistance. The IS is characterized by new geographies of power exemplified by the construction of market powers across spaces and products. At the same time a new constellation of financial and economic 'hubs' or 'nodes' is accompanied by global institutional structures that provide the necessary institutional hegemony. The emergence of translocal urban spaces in the e-economy energizes the lifeblood of another level of social relations dis/empowered by the position of social groups in the digital web of networks that produce and distribute resources. Importantly, these resources constitute not only the framework of the digital economy or concern the domain of virtual consumption but are also directly linked to the materiality of labour, hardware and time as well as the impact upon the norms of recognition of 'valuable' social groups and their symbolic and material existence. We discuss these implications of structure and policy further in the following pages.

The myth goes global: the Global Information Society

At the G7 Information Society summit in Brussels of 1995, a set of principles was identified and became known as the 'Brussels Principles'. According to these policy principles, the pursuit of market liberalization and the support of private enterprise in the Global Information Society

Table 5.1 G7 Summit 'Information Society' (1995)

<table>
<tr>
<td>• promoting dynamic competition
• encouraging private investment
• providing open access to networks
• defining an adaptable. regulatory framework</td>
<td>• ensuring universal provision of and access to services
• promoting equality of opportunity to the citizen
• promoting diversity of content; including cultural and linguistic diversity
• recognising the necessity of worldwide cooperation with particular attention to less developed countries
• recognising the necessity of worldwide cooperation with particular attention to less developed countries</td>
<td>• promotion of interconnectivity and interoperability – developing global markets for networks, services and applications – ensuring privacy and data security – protecting intellectual property rights – cooperating in R&D and in the development of new applications
• monitoring of the social and societal implications of the information society</td>
</tr>
<tr>
<td>principles</td>
<td>'while'</td>
<td>'by the means of'</td>
</tr>
</table>

(GIS) become paramount, although some social and political goals are also included as part of the action plan to construe a world infrastructure system based on the priority given to the private sector's aims. The principles of a GIS are provided in the first column of Table 5.1. The second column lists a parallel – or secondary, depending on one's reading – set of goals while the third column provides a list of the means by which the first two lists will be achieved.

Despite the fact that this document is now over a decade old, and ultimately the heir of a neoliberal political era of the 1980s, the key stipulations for a global policy framework have remained remarkably the same and have been reinforced through the G8 in Okinawa in 1998, through the Charter on the Information Society and through to the World Summit on Information Society in 2003–5. The role of transnational corporations in the designing of a global media policy cannot be underestimated. The pressures to liberalize the communications fields – audiovisual networks, telecommunications – and transportations have succeeded in determining the 'waves' of liberalization in Europe in the late 1980s and across the "developing" world, through the auspices of the World Bank. These policy directions have been thoroughly represented in policy recommendation papers and consultation meetings between representatives of the industries and representatives at the highest ranks of the state. The core message of these policies was then to be applied at the national level. Analysing the structural changes in Canada with an agenda of harmonization of policies, Abramson and Raboy comment that they correspond to the 'new' version of IS that was to be 'taken home' (1999: 781).

One of these new organizations (but not with any 'new' actors) emerged in 1998 to influence the direction of policy with regards to the global framework of e-commerce: the Global Business Dialogue on electronic commerce (GBD). It consists of some of the most powerful transnational corporations in the field of electronics and telecommunications, such as Deutsche Telecom, France Telecom, Hewlett Packard, Siemens, NEC Corporations and Toshiba, among others. According to GBD, representatives of the organization have been in constant consultations with the governments of Europe, the USA, Canada, Japan (largely the G8) since 1998. It is interesting to note that since its foundation, representatives of the organization have been in official consultations with these governments on a *monthly* basis. The philosophy of GBD and indeed of the corporate world is neither hidden nor modest:

> The private-sector – with its detailed day-to-day involvement in a multinational operating environment – is in a unique position to play an important role in shepherding the world through a sensitive period of globalization. (GBD 2004: 1)

This is the opening statement of GBD's major policy recommendations document in the executive summary of 2004 – a position represented at national, regional and international fora, such as the World Summit 2005. Recommendations cover not only issues of technical standards or issues directly related to electronic commerce, but also on electronic governance, health and information. They also cover issues of surveillance and domestic policy. Again the – oversimplistic – philosophy of the recommendations is spelled out on page 18:

> In point of fact, if the words 'speaker', 'contributor', and 'voter' are replaced by 'consumer', 'purchaser', and 'statements' and/or the words 'contributions' and 'opinions' are substituted with 'inquiries' and 'orders' of products and services, it is readily seen that the very same environment is necessary for e-commerce. Citizens and businesses making requests or opinions to Government are no different than consumers who make similar requests to shops or companies. (GBD 2004: 18)

Following this logic of reducing social and political questions to a market terminology, suggestions include the control of cyberspace (which for marketing reasons is heralded as a 'freedom' space) through surveillance tactics, including digital passports, the withdrawal of regulation from e-commerce, the controlled consuming of purchased items so that intellectual property rights can be controlled and the need to *persuade* consumers to pay for services and information available online. Although not in so many words, the recommendations identify as problems the fact that consumers are unwilling to pay for content online and invite governments to help consumers better understand the benefits of broadband and online services (p. 31).

Effectively, the suggestions offered by the private sector aim at calling upon the subsidization of aspects of e-commerce, especially those that are costly or risky for businesses. However, at the same time, they present state regulation as a barrier to business. Therefore, the role of the state in the IS, according to these recommendations, is not that of a leader but rather of a facilitator of conditions favourable to transnational capital. Among the consequences of facilitating an environment predominantly beneficial to corporations, other liberties and regulations that have until now been taken for granted will need to be revised. Civil liberties, and in particular the use of communications with a degree of anonymity, are now seen as in need of overhaul, with GBD suggesting that electronic ID certification becomes a prerequisite for the use of the Internet. Some governments have proceeded in adopting such policies with potential benefits for private enterprise, while opening the gates to the possibility of controlling access and increasing surveillance by both state and private agencies of the Internet and other electronic activities. Anonymity in media consumption and use is one of the keys to independent and critical use of the media – in the same way that there is no passport or ID required for purchasing a newspaper or watching the news, there should be some guarantee of similar conditions for the use of online services. Furthermore, an attempt to proceed to the criminalization of private behaviour evident in cases of consumption of electronic material becomes similarly evident in the policy directions suggested by the World Intellectual Property Organization (WIPO) and transnational media companies (Sarikakis 2004a). In other words, we are witnessing not simply the claim to change a few rules to accommodate a new technological environment but to alter the contexts of receiving and imparting information and to modify significantly the use of communications technology so that it enables even more precise surveillance of individual habits and communicative actions. The idea is not to restrict personal freedom per se but to 'modify' the conditions of personal freedoms as to comply with the new demands of the market.

Materiality disperses virtuality: the many faces of mobility and poverty

> It is questionable if all the mechanical inventions yet made have lightened the day's toil of any human being. (John Stuart Mill)

The concerns discussed in the previous section represent those of powerful multinationals based largely in the triad regions of Asia, Europe and North America, where national governments with more international clout push for the importance of ICTs to create new markets. These changes in the nation-state's relationship with the transnational ICT industries reflect the changing logic of industrial and post-industrial expansion. For example, the agricultural sector in Europe has decreased significantly in the last twenty years but this has not created any famine crisis, since the productivity of the sector and the availability of food per person have actually increased.[4] Figures 5.1 to 5.4 offer a 'world' view on the rate of Internet and PC use across five continents. If one of the most significant criterion to measure the degree to which a society has become an Information Society is the diffusion and use of ICTs, evident through the use of personal computers and connectivity to the world network of computers through the Internet, then it becomes obvious that the story of a 'global village' is necessarily deeply fractured and uneven.

As the figures show, according to the best estimations, only 10 per cent of the world's population are 'networked' today. The new inequalities reinforce previous colonial divides, with half of the current 10 per cent

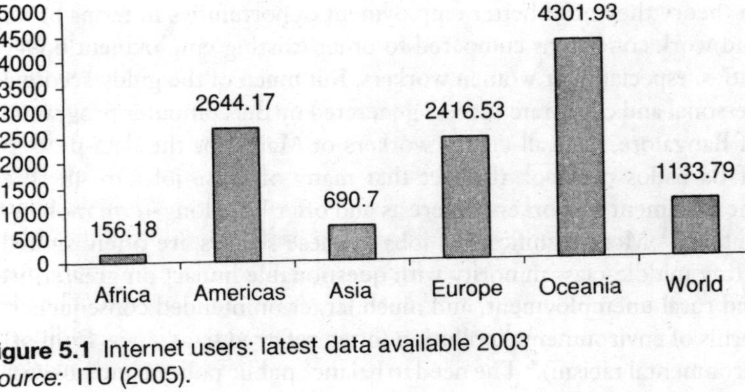

Figure 5.1 Internet users: latest data available 2003
Source: ITU (2005).

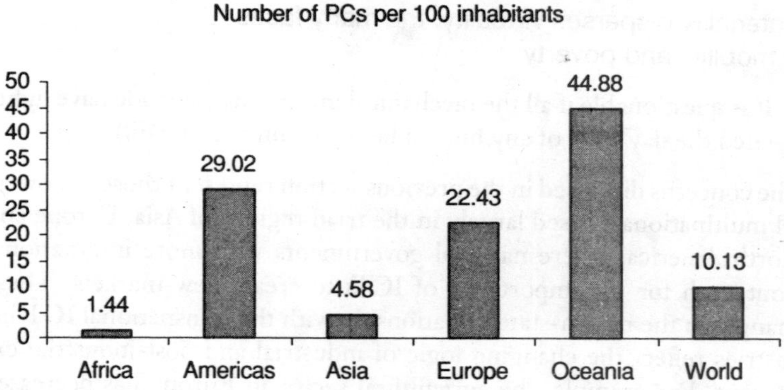

Figure 5.2 Number of PCs: latest data available 2003
Source: ITU (2005).

located in the EU and the USA. However, the 'networked' capacity of Japan, the Asian Newly Industrialized Countries (NICS), along with the enormous expansion in large 'emerging economies' like China, India and Brazil, reveals new kinds of divisions that criss-cross national boundaries. Looking at the national scenario we find that while seven more countries, including Japan, South Korea and China, form 38 per cent of the world's users another 160 countries make up the remaining 6 per cent. The promise of jobs and the high-tech hopes of 'leapfrogging' development associated with ICTs is certainly a powerful vision in the global cities of the South, where local and regional administrations compete to attract foreign firms with the most promising terms of investment and access to a skilled but 'affordable' labour force. Generating new employment is vitally important to nations in the South, and the expansion of ICT-based pink-collar and white-collar jobs are appealing precisely because in theory they offer better employment opportunities in terms of wages and work conditions compared to other existing employment opportunities, especially for women workers. But much of the giddy accounts of personal and corporate success generated by the computer programmers of Bangalore, the call-centre workers of Manila or the data-processors of Barbados overlook the fact that many of these jobs are flexible to the detriment of workers' interests and offer little long-term mobility or stability.[5] More significantly, jobs in these sectors are often limited to a tiny middle-class minority with questionable impact on greater urban and rural unemployment, and much larger unintended consequences in terms of environmental pollution (often referred to as a new form of environmental racism).[6] The need to balance public policy concerns around

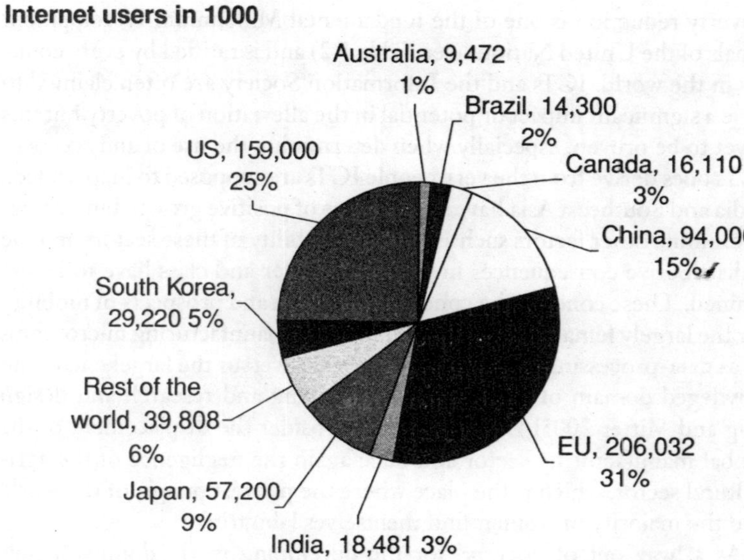

Figure 5.3 Proportion of sum of Internet users, world data
Source: adapted from CIA (2005).

employment generation with broader social concerns about the environment and labour regulations raises the need for greater research in this area and more attention to these issues from the perspective of citizens and workers in the South (Kabeer 2002).

For much of the world's population, especially those living in rural areas, ICTs can only serve as complementary tools for sectors that are of vital importance for the alleviation of poverty. In this regard, the emphasis on ICTs and the neglect of the agricultural sector in terms of policy and regulation at the international level has resulted in stagnation in food productivity in sub-Saharan Africa and growing of food insecurity across rural South and Southeast Asia and rural expanses of much of Latin America (ILO 2005; Shiva 2000). As the International Labour Office World Employment Report states:

> [R]ural development and the agricultural sector in many developing countries fell victim to an era of policy neglect in the 1990s. The neglect, moreover, has occurred both at the national policy level as well as within the multilateral system. While the point cannot be unequivocally made, it is perhaps no mere coincidence that the decade of rural policy neglect of the 1990s also witnessed a pronounced slowdown in the rate of poverty reduction in the developing world. (ILO 2005: 15)

Poverty reduction is one of the fundamental Millennium Development Goals of the United Nations (see Table 5.2) and is ratified by every country in the world. ICTs and the Information Society are often claimed to have a significant impact or potential in the alleviation of poverty but this is yet to be proven, especially when determining the use of and access to ICTs does derive from the very people ICTs are supposed to help. Indeed India and Southeast Asia have shown signs of positive growth but one has to examine other factors such as the sustainability of these sectors and the redistributive consequences in terms of gender and class have to be examined. These concern the conditions of work and prospects of mobility for the largely female workforce employed in manufacturing micro-chips or as data-processing and call-centre workers versus the largely male and privileged domain of computer programming and research and design (Ng and Mitter 2005b). We also must consider the displacement of the global manufacturing sector and once again the negligence of the agricultural sector, which is the place where the poorest people of the world and the majority of women find themselves labouring.

As a 'way out of poverty' for the developing world dominant policy claims, largely inspired by transnational lobbies, bring attention to e-commerce and generally to the commercial potential of ICTs. Apart from the fact that one 'sector' alone would not be enough to provide decent salaries and working conditions in a country, the potential for economic recovery would depend on a number of factors, such as whether ICTs are used by communities to export crafts and goods that would then subsidize agriculture, education and health care; whether craftspeople and other labourers would be able to determine their creative expression or have control over the production process; and whether welfare nets and mechanisms are in place to maintain social cohesion. According to the OECD (2004), computers and ICT/IT employment is at its strongest in the service sector and much lower in the manufacturing and other similar sectors. IT employment, however, includes not only analysts and programmers but also users of computer software for retailing or data input (travel) as well as jobs that are normally classified as manual or generally non-IT such as installers of equipment. IT employment and use density also seem to be on the low side for the EU and the USA in the retail sectors, although the USA has slightly higher rates. These are examples from those regions of the world whose economies tend to benefit most from ICTs. The potential of the IT sector in general to generate wealth for the global South – and not for small elites – depends on the terms and conditions specific to individual regions.

Table 5.2 United Nations Millennium Development Goals

Goal 1. Eradicate extreme poverty and hunger
Target 1. Halve, between 1990 and 2015, the proportion of people whose income is less than one dollar a day
Target 2. Halve, between 1990 and 2015, the proportion of people who suffer from hunger

Goal 2. Achieve universal primary education
Target 3. Ensure that, by 2015, children everywhere, boys and girls alike, will be able to complete a full course of primary schooling

Goal 3. Promote gender equality and empower women
Target 4. Eliminate gender disparity in primary and secondary education, preferably by 2005, and in all levels of education no later than 2015

Goal 4. Reduce child mortality
Target 5. Reduce by two-thirds, between 1990 and 2015, the under-five mortality rate

Goal 5. Improve maternal health
Target 6. Reduce by three-quarters, between 1990 and 2015, the maternal mortality ratio

Goal 6. Combat HIV/AIDS, malaria and other diseases
Target 7. Have halted by 2015 and begun to reverse the spread of HIV/AIDS
Target 8. Have halted by 2015 and begun to reverse the incidence of malaria and other major diseases

Goal 7. Ensure environmental sustainability
Target 9. Integrate the principles of sustainable development into country policies and programmes and reverse the loss of environmental resources
Target 10. Halve, by 2015, the proportion of people without sustainable access to safe drinking water and sanitation
Target 11. By 2020, to have achieved a significant improvement in the lives of at least 100 million slum dwellers

Goal 8. Develop a global partnership for development
Target 12. Develop further an open, rule-based, predictable, non-discriminatory trading and financial system.

Source: http://www.un.org/millenniumgoals

Global policy hegemony and local tension: the pressure for privatization

Scholars have already pointed out that the lead in international information society policy is taken in the e-commerce sector by the global conglomerates (for example, Abramson and Raboy 1999; Cogburn 2003). They see this emphasis on e-commerce as the outcome of a USA-imposed 'free-flow' argument as well as the clear superiority of companies in identifying policy priorities (less regulation). Cogburn goes on to assert that despite a number of international institutions involved, the leading organization in the new international regime of the GIS remains the WTO. The neoliberal sentiments of the WTO are widely declared as a series of meetings has shown; one of the major tasks of WTO in general is the harmonization of regulatory frameworks across the world and the continuation of the liberalization process for industries.

There are differences among the participating countries as to the extent and degree of liberalization, especially with regards to health and education but also culture industries. The United National Economic Commission for Africa has developed a Green Paper to deal with the impact of liberalization, the South Africa Green Paper that particularly deals with the conditions of ecommerce harmonization, according to the international framework as set out by the Global Information Society (GIS) and WTO. In particular, the development of e-commerce would demand the necessary infrastructure and regulation in line with the international 'regime' and to accept the WTO's agreement to liberalize and privatize its telecommunications.

Audenhove et al. (1999) argue that this regulatory framework is based on two assumptions, the ability of new entertainment services to provide revenue to subsidize the building of the infrastructure and the willingness of consumers to pay for new services. Therefore, competition is seen as a paramount policy that encompasses growth and the lowering of prices. Again, as in the case of broadcasters, national operators are seen as hindering development and market growth. It is reasonable to assume that tight control of private enterprise by the state, like the tight control of private and public spheres by the state, can border loss of freedom, especially in regimes or in conditions where democratic standards are rather theoretical than practical.[7] When broadcasting is controlled by the state then not only economic but also social aspects/indicators are lower than those countries with a vibrant public and non-state sector. Venturelli (2002) argues that excessive control of the state in East Asian economies has failed to promote the drive for competition in the telecoms sector. Similarly, it has also failed to promote a vibrant culture production sector that is vital to the production of content in the IS and a weak but emerging civil society sector which suggests a fundamental shift in social and cultural dynamics. Although this is probably generally the case, the opposite, the lack of control over entrepreneurship, does not guarantee freedom of speech or critical expression.

Nevertheless, the dominant argument of 'prosperity' and the opportunity for the diversity of 'cultural expression' continue to rank high in the list of assumed benefits of the liberalization process. Audenhove et al. identify the same arguments in the development of a GIS framework that is imposed upon national policies and across the developing world with only a few exceptions in the *degree* of liberalization. At the national level, and in particular in countries with weak infrastructure such as the African continent, the pressure for privatization is felt more strongly. First, as Audenhove et al. argue, the very 'quality' of national companies and infrastructure – and especially telecommunications – does not correspond to investors' criteria, which is something that makes the position of negotiation of even countries such as South Africa, with probably the best telecoms in the continent, problematic. At the time of writing, the best rate of Internet use in the African continent belongs to the Seychelles with nearly 15 per cent of Internet use and South Africa with 7 per cent (ITU 2005) compared to the USA with 55 per cent and Australia with 56 per cent (ITU 2005). Figure 5.6 provides a comparative listing of the situation in African countries in 2003 regarding Internet use and availability of PCs. As the reader will immediately become aware, even the wealthiest economies are far behind any conceivable approximation to the rates and pace of Internet access and ICT use of the post-industrialized world. Within the African context, at the lowest end of the scale, Ethiopia, Niger, the Central African Republic and Sierra Leone are reporting between 10 and 14 Internet users per 10,000 inhabitants while countries like Egypt, Botswana and Tunisia have between 2 and 4 personal computers per 100 people.

Many African nations continue to negotiate crippling debts which reduce state autonomy to intervene through social policy as well as the legacies of colonial division that have fostered civil war, genocide and discrimination. Under external pressures, these governments have used privatization of their national sectors as a 'symbolic' gesture, a 'positive signal to private local and foreign investors' (Nulens and Van Audenhove 1999: 397–8). They have also tried to reduce other debts through the sale of what effectively is or has been regarded as national or public property. As we have argued previously, telecommunications and other infrastructural industries like air transportation have been at the centre of this liberalization wave because of their role in allowing access to markets and, in particular, linking production to distribution sites in the North. Any policy for 'development' should take into account the voices of these nation-states and their citizens. Instead, global policies are drafted within closed consultative contexts and limited scope. Writing about the Digital Opportunity Task Force (DOT), a policy with the principal aim to expand the domain of e-commerce, Shade argues that this, as do other top-down policies, adheres to the modernization paradigm. She notes 'the legitimization of global capitalism as a natural and vaunted state of affairs needs to be questioned, particularly when the discourse of the

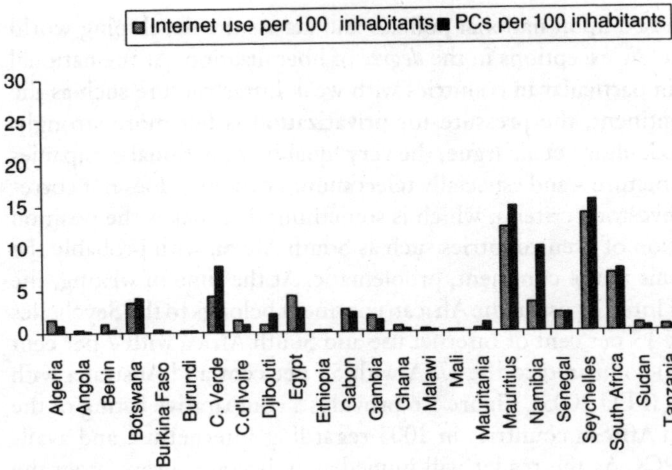

Figure 5.4 Comparative data on African countries in Internet and PC use; latest data 2003
Source: adapted from ITU (2005).

DOT Force posits that citizenship and human development entails participating in a global commercial system' (Shade 2003: 118).

The pressure for privatization is not only relevant to the developing world, however, but also to smaller economies in Europe and across the privileged North, economies which are more vulnerable to international global trade and the negotiating power of transnational telecommunications and content-provider giants. Greece and Portugal, as small EU countries, have also followed the liberalization 'trend', albeit in a more gradual manner than the stronger economies of Germany and the UK. Greece finds itself under pressure to privatize vital sectors of geopolitical significance for the country, such as electricity and water, not only from the EU but also from international organizations. The wide-scale pressure against public resources is profound. OECD (2001) advises the breaking up of national sectors such as water into a network of companies. Experience from other countries such as the UK, however, has shown that the effects of such privatization are not necessarily positive, as vital 'backbone' sectors, railways, electricity and water services have witnessed a decline in service quality while prices in some cases have not followed the predicted fall.[8]

Responding to what World Bank insiders themselves prescribed in the mid-1990s as the 'Post-Washington Consensus' (Stigltiz 1998), the Bank increasingly focuses on social issues despite the fact that its mandate is 'limited' to economic policy (Nulens and Van Audenhove 1999). It does not do so, by trying to direct policies towards the solution of social problems but calls upon governments to deal with them, while at the same time together with the IMF imposing economic policies upon countries with the Structural Adjustment Programs (SAP). Its overall philosophy leans closer to liberalization and the market than the development of national state or communitarian-driven policies for IS, more favourable to the private sector and market mechanisms covering the 'wishes' of consumers with the public sector forming 'partnerships' with the private sector in order to cover those areas that the market will not be able to address, especially in the first years. World Bank policies concentrate on prioritizing private enterprises, restricting the role of the state and directing pressure for the state to improve its capabilities where its role is still regarded as necessary. As a consequence of the hyper-liberalization process, increasingly the state in the developing world is losing its 'jurisdiction' and negotiating power to determine the pace and nature of domestic markets, and this necessarily will take the form of increased demands to correct social inequalities with less means in the hands of public authorities.

Owing to its previous attention to the socioeconomic dimensions of telecommunications the ITU was criticized by the USA as being too politicized, a similar argument exercised against UNESCO when the organization tried to launch a platform of socially responsible policies, as we discussed in chapters 2 and 3, with the effect that the USA withdrew its membership from UNESCO. In the ITU case, the USA and other countries withdrew their funding with the consequence that the ITU sought private funds to support its activities. This situation is evident today during the World Summit on Information Society, one of the most significant events for the implementation of policy globally, as we discuss below. The ITU's African Green Paper brought the institution back to a more prominent position in international policy next to the World Bank. The document 'admitted' the limited success of state-owned telecommunications and was therefore seen to move away from its 'political' support of state control over post, telecoms and transport. Despite this more favourable approach to liberalization, the ITU paper proposes a 'modified' version of liberalization where independent national agencies have the power and the means to oversee the operation of private and public telecoms operators as well as function as arbiters between these operators and the consumers (ITU 1996).

In the same year, the United Nations' Economic Commission for Africa (ECA) designed a charter of policy principles for the developing world, encapsulated in the African Information Society Initiative (AISI). AISI identifies a set of policy issues that are not identical to those

Table 5.3 Major International organizations involved in policy-making for the Information Society in the African continent

ECA	United Nations Economic Commission for Africa
G7/8	Group of Seven / Group of Eight
GBD	Global Business Dialogue on electronic commerce
GIIC	Global Information Infrastructure Commission
ICANN	The Internet Corporation for Assigned Names and Numbers
IMF	International Monetary Fund
ITU	International Telecommunications Union
OECD	Organization for Economic Cooperation and Development
UNESCO	United Nations Educational Scientific and Cultural Organization
WB	World Bank
WEF	World Economic Forum
WIPO	World Intellectual Property Organization
WTO	World Trade Organization

identified by the North, such as agriculture and food security, education and training, culture and tourism, gender and development (ECA 2003). They point to the need for carefully planned policies in ICTs with the aim of defining a course of action that is most suitable to the socioeconomic reality of African countries. However, Urey (1995) suggests that ITU is facing 'competition' from a more liberal global player such as the World Bank, and has had to follow this path in its own discourse and to modify its position over accepting the 'solution' of liberalization. Nulens and Audenhove (1999) conclude that there is a merging of discourses among international organizations that propose and make policy for an 'African' version of the IS (1999: 468) despite the differences in the attention they give to sociocultural and political contexts. We can expand the domain of their conclusion beyond the developing countries and their economies. Indeed it appears that the recipe for the IS of the future is based on the same ingredients for every part of the planet and it involves a dominant position of corporations, in particular transnational corporations, the so-called new form of 'public–private' partnerships and the withdrawal of the state as an active 'compensator' for market failure but as a shock absorber for companies.

The clash of capitalisms? The World Summit on the Information Society

As global governmental actors try to ensure favourable environments for business investments in national territories, often, social goals are subsumed in a market-focused agenda that expands across several sectors of social and private life. Global telecommunications and electronics companies seek to direct the use and development of technologies, in ways that can construct new markets, geographically and in terms of demand. Technological development in the electronics sector, as is, for example, the case of digital radio or television, as well as the development of new computer software and hardware requires the constant updating of workers' technological skills. The control over the use of technologies, as is the case on control over conditions of e-commerce, is pursued by the private sector through policy suggestions for surveillance practices as well as control over the way in which products are consumed, whether in public or private, shared or selectively. Thus, certain conditions must be met at a national and local level to ensure a predictable environment for the function of 'informational' capitalism. Traditional institutions play a very important role in providing a cultural and political economic framework, through training and education, socialization and the legal system and providing the cultural frameworks of human communication and cultural expression.[9] Emerging traits of this international system are:[10]

1. a culture of so-called 'lifelong learning' or continuous deskilling and reskilling of workers and the subsequent production of new forms of socioeconomic inequalities based around the possession or lack thereof of skills associated with the use of ICTs and access to means of production
2. a gradual process of criminalization of previously 'legitimate' forms of private consumer behaviour, such as the private consumption of music or other AV products and their reproduction through technology
3. a culture of surveillance, translated into increased surveillance and control over civil liberties but also consumer behaviour, which is not only limited to market interaction but allows the commercial use of private data and invasion of privacy
4. a paramount emphasis on technological consumption and use of means of communication for a limited range of purposes and the neglect of other sectors of primary importance to human survival, such as the agricultural sector, especially in developing countries
5. a shift in state discourses and policies tackling social inequalities towards a direction that specifies poverty and inequality predominantly in terms and in relation to the consumption of ICT-generated goods and services.

In this global environment, where international organizations attain a more significant role than those the world was accustomed to, the ones deriving from the Bretton Woods agreements, social, political and economic questions become of common concern across cultures and societies. It is not the case that issues of freedom of expression, human dignity, poverty and the environment have not been of significance across the world. However, at this particular phase of market integration and the process of a perceived 'globalization', these issues enter a different political arena. This is also the case because of the change in military and power dynamics in the world after the end of the Cold War, perhaps not so much by changing the dominant actors in the 'game' of international relations, but rather because the context of and points of reference for this game have changed. As we have seen, the technology has been identified as the definite criterion for the governing of communications in the late twentieth and early twenty-first century. As such, the coordination of an international effort to address relevant issues, as we have discussed in this chapter, has been directed towards the designing of the Information Society or a certain version thereof. Again under the auspices of the United Nations, but this time under the ITU and not UNESCO, a meeting of international actors has been organized throughout the period 2003–5. The World Summit on the Information Society is organized into two phases of official meetings between participating governments, including contributions from civil society and the private sector.

The significance of this summit is seen by some parts of the academic and larger civil society as unique owing to the official inclusion of national and international NGOs in the course of these meetings. The first phase of the WSIS took place in Geneva (10–12 December 2003) and concluded with the adoption of the Declaration of Principles and Plan of Action outlining the participants' 'Common Vision of the Information Society' to 'build a people-centred, inclusive and development-oriented Information Society' (Clause 1). Nevertheless, and despite the 'unitarian' language of these first declarations that were presented as common visions and statements by a tripartite alliance – governments, civil society and private sector – there has been a not insignificant delineation of the *difference* in 'visions' between actors of civil society and those represented by states and companies. The result was a separate and markedly differentiated statement issued by civil society that reemphasizes the social and political aspects of any future 'society'. Notably, the *Civil Society Declaration* issued after the end of Phase 1 states that its vision is information *societies* and that it aims to create a *communication society*, where 'every person must have access to the means of communication and must be able to exercise their right to freedom of opinion and expression' (*Civil Society Declaration* at WSIS-I). Although this declaration is the outcome of a compromise on several early drafts among actors of the Civil Society, the separate statement was created out of a sense of frustration with the policy process and the sense of decisions being made behind closed doors as well as its first output. The most apparent difference between stakeholders' positions is the fact that the former tends to view ICTs and equitable access to them as an end in itself, while the latter views it as a means to achieving global equity. Previous, unsuccessful attempts for an international communications policy with a progressive agenda, such as the NWICO, left UNESCO in a weak negotiating position. At the elite political level, it also marginalized international demands for social justice expressed through UNESCO, as these were discredited as 'political' positions that have no place in the 'neutral' zone of technology and policy. As we have seen throughout our discussion of the developments in international systems of communication, technology is still presented as a 'neutral' good and policy is still promoted as an apolitical activity.

The socially conscious tone promoted in the set of principles that defines the agenda at the first phase of the WSIS is in direct contrast to the policy pursued by the most dominant parties of the 'partnership' between stakeholders with its emphasis on the creation of markets for ICT use and the expansion of e-commerce. Reflecting on this first phase summit, Zhao (2004) and Hamelink (2004) observe a lack of political economic context to the discourse of the WSIS. WSIS was initially perceived by the civil society sector as an unique opportunity to provide space for the debate related to long-standing claims for communication rights protected as human rights. The priorities given by the WSIS are clearly stated in the Declaration of Principles:

> b) The commitment of the private sector is important in developing and diffusing information and communication technologies (ICTs), for infrastructure, content and applications. The private sector is not only a market player but also plays a role in a wider sustainable development context.
>
> c) The commitment and involvement of civil society is equally important in creating an equitable Information Society, and in implementing ICT–related initiatives for development. (Declaration of Principles; World Summit on the Information Society 2003)

Although the aim of this discussion is not to emphasize semantics over praxis, it is important to be attuned to the role of language and presentation in legitimizing policy normative frameworks. Although the role of the actors within civil society seems enhanced in this particular summit, the role 'officially' recognized for civil society appears to be that of a secondary, assisting agent, behind the private sector upon which the whole project of IS rests. The WSIS principles echo the decisions made at the

Okinawa meeting of the G8, where once again the role of civil society is appreciated as being secondary to that of the private sector. Here, again, the issue of technology is offered as a catalyst for policy towards a certain direction, but at the same time is heralded as neutral:

> The private sector plays a leading role in the development of information and communications networks in the information society . . . It is important to avoid undue regulatory interventions that would hinder productive private-sector initiatives in creating an IT-friendly environment. We should ensure that IT-related rules and practices are responsive to revolutionary changes in economic transactions, while taking into account the principles of effective public–private sector partnership, transparency and technological neutrality. (The Okinawa Charter on Global Information Society, G8 Summit 2000)

It is worth noting that the main directions of policy for a future 'Information Society' currently debated at the WSIS meetings (preparatory meeting as well as the summit itself) have been set at a very early stage in meetings among the most powerful countries in the world, the G7/G8, and can be found in the statements made as summaries of their negotiations. Table 5.4 shows the main principles governing the visions of IS as expressed through these global organizations. In particular, the ideas of a neutral technology and the prominence of the private sector are paramount in both sets of statements.

Much of the WSIS agenda is dedicated to pursuing the fulfilment of the minimal requirements of social cohesion objectives that conform to the transnational circulation of electronic goods and services, the opening up of public property to private management and the establishment of an international regime of corporatism in electronic communications. Within this implicit agenda, civil-society actors participate from a point of reference of pursuing social objectives that are often characterized by policy preferences with a restorative social justice disposition – a destatization of governance as discussed in Chapter 2. Despite the differences among NGOs and other civil-society actors regarding the radicalism of their political agendas, the institutional category of civil society occupies an increasingly prominent role in transnational and local politics through a number of functions. Some of them are the closeness to citizens and in particular marginalized groups, their role in implementing policy at the grassroots level and their role in legitimizing processes of decision-making at a transnational level (Moll and Shade 2001). Research on transnational civil society organizations in global policy-making environments highlights the limitations of specific NGO intervention on social policy (e.g. Keck and Sikkink 1998; Korzeniewicz and Smith 2001).

Table 5.4 Information Society policy statements of the Okinawa Charter and WSIS Declaration of Principles compared

OKINAWA CHARTER 1998	WSIS DECLARATION OF PRINCIPLES 2003
Its revolutionary impact affects the way people live, learn and work and the way government interacts with civil society. *IT* is fast becoming a vital engine of growth for the world economy. (1)*	It has restructured the way the world conducts economic and business practices, runs governments and engages politically.
[Foster] appropriate policy and regulatory environment to stimulate competition and innovation, ensure economic and financial stability, advance stakeholder collaboration to optimise global networks, fight abuses that undermine the integrity of the network, bridge the digital divide, invest in people, and promote global access and participation. (4)	Policies that create a favourable climate for stability, predictability and fair competition at all levels should be developed and implemented in a manner that not only attracts more private investment for ICT infrastructure development but also enables universal service obligations to be met in areas where traditional market conditions fail to work. (23)
Development of human resources capable of responding to the demands of the information age through education and lifelong learning and addressing the rising demand for *IT* professionals in many sectors of our economy (6d)	Continuous and adult education, retraining, life-long learning, distance-learning and other special services, such as telemedicine, can make an essential contribution to employability and help people benefit from the new opportunities offered by ICTs for traditional jobs, self-employment and new professions. (31)
Development of effective and meaningful privacy protection for consumers, as well as protection of privacy in processing personal data, while safeguarding the free flow of information (7)	Within this global culture of cyber-security, it is important to enhance security and to ensure the protection of data and privacy, while enhancing access and trade. (35)

*refers to paragraph

Despite their multifaceted roles, civil society actors seem to be less able to direct or shape the agenda of negotiations, at least at the level of WSIS, as the dominant institutional actors – nation-states and transnational corporations. The first WSIS phase of negotiation led to a largely technocratic focus on a single issue: the question of Internet Governance. This has mainly focused around the political and administrative nature – and future – of ICANN. Some scholars seem to agree that ICANN represents a first democratic experiment in global electronic governance, an institutional realm outside the framework of national legitimacy bound with the nation-state that demands a global democratic 'plan of governance'. Its foundational origins as a not-for-profit private (and therefore not state) organization with more open participatory structures is considered a *cause célèbre* for some scholars (Kleinwächter 2004a; Klein and Mueller 2005). Nevertheless attempts to broaden the base of decision-making, such as the ICANN-at-large, has not resulted in any significant progress, as we shall see in the following chapter. The ICANN experiment attracts the favourable attention of industry, some governments and scholars – probably for different reasons – but it also attracts criticisms by many, largely because of its elitist organization, its close affiliation with the USA government and industry in particular and its lack of accountability.[11] Deriving from the WSIS process, proposed changes to the governance of the internet echo those offered by the dominant WSIS discourse based on the allegory of 'competition': here the competition is proposed on the political and institutional level whereby internet users can choose their 'preferred' alternate governing system (see, for example, Klein and Mueller 2005). Obviously the questions over legitimacy, control and jurisdiction over the names and domains and the nervous system of the electronic age become technical in definition, as technology takes its toll of these debates, with the effect that large parts of civil society become alienated from the debate. Furthermore, although the technicology of the largely political question 'who owns' the Internet discourages those actors with less technical expertise and functions as a filter of participants and agendas, Internet Governance, in effect, although significant, has become the focal point for the energies and resources of civil society to a large extent, with the result that policy issues that do not fit directly under the 'umbrella' of internet governance enjoy less attention.

In the following chapter we examine the role of civil society in more detail as well as the shortcomings of treating technology as a neutral factor in the determining of future global socioeconomic developments for ICTs, communication and cultural rights. We approach this issue by adopting a view from the social margins, the minoritized majorities, as we specifically examine a vision of the IS from a feminist perspective, exposing the violence of gender-neutral assumptions in current policy formulations. In this discussion the recurrent questions of redistribution and recognition take centre stage to guide us towards a normative framework that will help explain the plurality of visions for an electronic global 'commons' and offer a guiding principle for the design of an emancipatory public policy.

Notes

1. From Huxley's (1932) perhaps sarcastic *Brave New World* to *The Cyborg Manifesto* (Haraway 1991) the envisioning of the liberation of human beings from all that binds them to the limitations of material need, corporeal existence and the effects of social inequality, such as alienation, poverty, hunger and imprisonment, has given rise to the most exciting scholarly but also fictional works. Although it is not within the remits of this work to provide an adequate account of such works and their most important representations, we consider such a body of works as a vital element of the counter-visions of the so-called Information Society.
2. As the report by the Members of the High-Level Group on the Information Society (1994), *Recommendations to the European Council: Europe and the Global Information Society*, became known. Accessible at http://europa.eu.int/ISPO/infosoc/backg/bangeman.html
3. Compare the GII and the GIS agendas and the ways in which they infiltrate and define the Okinawa Charter and the WSIS programmatic declarations in Tables 5.1 and 5.4.
4. ILO 2005. This is not to suggest that the quality of food that Europe's poor consume is good or that the intensification of food production has born only good results, as we now know about the detrimental effects that genetically modified crops and pesticides among other things have on human health and the environment.
5. Focusing on gender, Swasti Mitter has led a comprehensive study, in terms of studies on ICTs and employment, that shows both the limits of high-tech development strategies adopted by a number of countries in South and Southeast Asia (including an extensive study on India where IT-related exports comprise the fastest growing sector of the national economy) as well as means of possible progressive intervention. For more see: Mitter 2000.
6. This issue is increasingly being explored by both researchers and NGOs in both the North and South. For more on this issue in Silicon Valley, see Pellow and Park (2002); for more on this in the South, see Nair 2005.
7. The questions of democratic governance are not limited to the situation in many authoritarian state regimes in the world but they also concern the long-standing liberal democracies of the West. One

example is the constant state of alert for the UK, US and increasingly other Western countries in the face of terrorism (perceived or real). Under such circumstances, the first victim seems to be civil liberties.

8. For example, telecoms liberalization in Greece has not resulted in a decrease of phone calls costs, as all companies have set their tariffs within specific limits, currently at 0.24–0.26 Euro /minute (EETT 2003).
9. Several studies have addressed the role of formal education in accommodating the needs of the private sector and more generally abiding by the requirements of capitalism. The effects of the corporatization of the university for the 'production' of knowledge, equity in academic and communication professions, the scope of learning and teaching in Higher Education, potential for civic involvement and active citizenship are some of the spheres severely influenced by the nature and *raison d'être* of universities (see, for example, Byerly 2004; Hides 2006).
10. For a detailed analysis see Sarikakis and Terzis 2000 and Sarikakis 2004a.
11. See for example the ICANN-at-large website http://alac.icann.org/

6 Civil society and social justice: the limits and possibilities of global governance

Global Communication Policy regime: insert 'public' – press 'Enter'

In the previous chapter we examined the competing logics behind the normative framework of the emerging information society as produced through alliances between private and public social actors representing interests in both the US and the EU. Although we identified two competing visions of IS, we showed how one coherent dominant discourse of the neoliberal IS emerged by the close of the twentieth century. We demonstrated the profound shortcomings of the dominant neoliberal IS policy discourse by highlighting the unevenness of access and narrowness of vision. We showed how civil society organizations have led the charge for equity in this process and have proposed a competing and democratic vision for change embodied in the WSIS Civil Society declaration (Civil Society Statement 2005). In this chapter, we explore the role of civil society as a new social actor in the shifting field of global communication policy, by taking a closer look at the novel institutional context of the WSIS. The space for civil society participation – however limited – allows new social actors outside state and corporate interests to raise claims about redistribution and recognition while negotiating the issue of legitimate representation. This chapter examines both the institutional constraints as well as the discursive parameters of this process.

We focus on civil society because of its expanded symbolic power to shape normative debates in the field of communication policy. One of the gains for civil society organizations at the first summit in Geneva in 2003 was the introduction of the language of 'multistakeholderism' in the negotiating process, which led some participants to observe that global governance is 'no longer the sole domain of governments' but rather 'a laboratory which develops innovative models and mechanisms for a new global diplomacy' (Kleinwächter 2004b). Today, multilateral institutions are increasingly expanding formal and informal modes of participation for civil society organizations (CSOs),[1] often with the expectation that these groups representing the interests of citizens will raise humanitarian and welfare concerns, thereby acting as a check on the balance of power held firmly by state and corporate actors. This trend is in many ways a response by multilateral institutions to the legitimacy crisis of the 'governance of governance' (Keohane 2002), when the WTO, the World Bank and the IMF, as well as the ITU and WIPO face opposition from multiple publics across the North–South divide. In mounting these challenges, access to new communications technologies, most obviously the Internet, is now seen as playing a pivotal role in sustaining effective transnational mobilizations, fostering novel modes of community and identity that support new theories of collective action (Castells 2003). The presence of a wide range of civil society representatives has become a prominent feature of international summitry since the 1990s, with the practice of parallel independent civil society forums often serving as a moral check to the official process of meetings by state officials.[2]

The 'post-Washington Consensus' thus follows two decades of sustained opposition, challenging austerity programmes in the South, responding to mass mobilization against trade agreements in the North and attempts to create coherence amidst the complex alliances that make up a sense of 'globalization from below' through transnational political experiments such as the World Social Forum (WSF). Despite these signs of opposition to the dominant discourse of neoliberal trade, the concept of a global civil society is in practice a murkier and much more contradictory category than the 'purist' counter-hegemonic picture of local social movements effectively and legitimately challenging from below the forces of global capitalism from above (Chandhoke 2001; Keane 2003: 57). Critics also caution against the overly optimistic reading of ICTs as transformative of the substance of political engagement by civil society (Sassen 2002: 3). Feminist analysts have been particularly vigilant about the complexities of transnational social movements and networks, pointing out that there is significant heterogeneity under the umbrella of global civil society. They vary in terms of structure and organizational form, depending on funding, scope of activity and access to institutional power and embody differences in political objectives between nationally based social movements and international non-governmental organizations (INGOs) and transnational advocacy networks (Keck and Sikkink 1998; Naples and Desai 2002). The political orientations of civil society groups are diverse and range from conservative think-tanks, corporate charities and development NGOs, to organizations representing ethnic or religious chauvinists as well as progressive post-industrial social movements – environmental and feminist movements, immigrant human rights organizations, social movement unionism – usually associated with 'globalization from below' (Kaldor 2003).

The relationship between civil society actors and state and market institutions is a matter of ongoing debate between scholars of social movements and democratic theory (Cohen and Arato 1993; Kaviraj 2001; Keane 2003). For our purposes, it is useful to historicize the concept of civil society, which for Gramsci was always a contradictory category in relation to the state as described by Michael Burawoy:

> Civil society refers to the growth of trade unions, political parties, mass education and other voluntary associations and interest groups, all of which proliferated in Europe and the United States at the end of the nineteenth century. At the same time, new forms of transportation (automobiles and railroads) and communication (postal service and newspapers) and regulation (police) connected people to each other and the state. On the one hand, civil society collaborates with the state to contain class struggle, and on the other hand its autonomy from the state can promote class struggle. (Burawoy 2003: 198)

The contradictory position of civil society in today's global order remains a constant. Moreover, this grounded and nuanced definition reminds us to pay attention to politics and history in ways that are often taken for granted in discussions about the role of civil society in shaping policy outcomes. In the contemporary field of global communication policy, groups within civil society span the traditional Left–Right spectrum.

Instead of a singular axis of politics defined by class and state autonomy, we have argued that post-Fordist claims for justice are multifaceted along at least three recognizable, interrelated dimensions of *redistribution* (claims around economic equality) and *recognition* (claims around cultural difference) and *representation* (claims for democratic accountability). As discussed in Chapter 2, the scale of contest and the terrain of political claims has expanded beyond class and the sovereign nation-state as we have moved from the era of NWICO to that of the WSIS. Chapters 3, 4 and 5 examined how the negotiation of communication as public policy has shifted beyond the exclusive domain of the nation-state, while the publics at stake define interest through class, gender, race and ethnicity, nationality and other markers of difference. As we seek to elaborate on the larger political stakes of what remains a narrow and for the most part technical debate about the future of the Information Society, feminist analysis offers insights into the normative dimensions of global social justice after more than two decades of theory and praxis around transnational social movements and the challenges of deliberation through difference.

In this chapter we begin our discussion about the role of civil society in shaping the normative debates around global communication policy by examining the institutional context of the WSIS process. We trace how NGOs, based and funded primarily in the North, have to some effect replaced the predominant role of non-aligned Third World nation-states of the cold-War era, as the most vocal advocates of a social justice platform countering the dominant vision of the neoliberal information society. Taking into account the organizational limitations and the historical specificity of the concept of civil society, we consider the reasons why weak claims for redistribution have been overshadowed by narrow claims for recognition. In the final section of the chapter, we draw from feminist critiques to interrogate the discourse of civil society and social justice in the field of global communication governance.

Taming civil society at the World Summit on the Information Society (WSIS)

> NWICO-UNESCO + ICANN = WSIS? (Selian and Cukier 2003: 137)

The call for a New World Information and Communication Order (NWICO) was a collective response to the machinations of the Cold War and the structural biases of development in the Fordist era by national leaders from the non-aligned nations demanding redistribution of communication resources and emphasizing national cultural sovereignty and diversity. Charges of 'politicization' of global communication policy during the NWICO era was followed by a stealth campaign by transnational corporate lobbyists and First World state delegations to 'depoliticize' the debate – shifting the object of regulation away from questions of structural imbalance between nation-states, for example, or incendiary claims about 'cultural imperialism', towards the seemingly more neutral realm of creating regulatory conditions that would 'harmonize free trade' and accelerate technological convergence. As discussed earlier, the site of policy debates also changed most notably with the emergence of the WTO, shifting policy emphasis almost exclusively around trade-related areas of governance.

We have seen a variety of social movements that challenge the neoliberal mandates of global communication governance in the last two decades. Based on our discussions thus far, we can point to the mass mobilizations by trade unions against the liberalization of national telecommunications monopolies and the role of marginalized racial, ethnic and/or religious minorities – making claims for recognition through the redistribution of public-media resources. The last decade has also seen successful social movements of small farmers, health workers, women's and sexual rights activists and indigenous rights activists effectively mounting challenges to the implementation of the WTO's Trade Related Property Rights (TRIPs) (Erni 2004; Escobar 1998; Shiva 1998). As well, transnational alliances between urban community and media activists have launched widespread alternative participatory media networks – from Indymedia to open-source and tactical media movements (Downing 2001; Lovink and Schneider 2002).

On a parallel front in the policy arena, Calabrese (1999) has argued that the failures of the UNESCO debates spurred a next generation of activism through a series of international MacBride Roundtables held since 1989. Complementing these meetings, the Cultural Environmental Movement based in the US and the Centre for Communication and Human Rights, based in the Netherlands, initiated the Platform for Communication Rights and the People's Communication Charter with the overlapping objectives of democratizing media access and formulating the basis of a 'humanitarian agenda' to challenge the neoliberal policy framework focused on enhancing trade.[3] Building on this momentum, in 1999 several NGOs involved in media-based activism launched a global civil society initiative entitled Voices 21 (A Global Movement for People's Voices in Media and Communications in the 21st century), which laid out the basic objectives for the new movement targeting the institutions of communication governance.[4] The principle CSOs involved in this effort were the World Association of Community Radio Broadcasters (AMARC), the World Association for Christian Communication (WACC) based in the UK and the Association for Progressive Communication (APC), initially a civil society networking initiative that began in the US and UK. In 2001, these organizations became involved in shaping the terms of civil society participation in the WSIS process by establishing the Communication Rights in the Information Society (CRIS) Campaign (Raboy 2004: 228–9).

The NWICO debates were carried out primarily by national state actors with the objective of transforming the rules of multilateral governance within the United Nations. Social justice claims focused on the redistribution of international communications resources, and claims about recognition were mediated through an exclusively national cultural frame – with national state representatives defining what counted as 'national' and 'local' culture. We have argued earlier that the issue of national sovereignty cloaked 'internal' injustices within Third World societies, just as the Fordist social contract failed to distinguish gender and racial discrimination. In both the North and the South, feminist groups along with a variety of 'new' and transformed social movements have challenged the role of states to represent what is accepted as public interest. In the field of global communication policy, we see that as the majority of Southern states were signing on to the new terms of the neoliberal information economy in the 1990s, it was Northern-based civil society organizations that began to formulate an oppositional humanitarian agenda.

Calabrese has argued that the 'legacy' of the MacBride Commission has engaged 'people's' movements in order to 'stimulate support for a new global constitutionalism aimed at establishing social and cultural policies that would parallel the already well-developed efforts to constitutionalise global market principles' (Calabrese 1999: 272). The CRIS campaign, which has coordinated an official civil society voice in the WSIS process, reinforced the right to communicate as a foundation for debates about social justice:

> Our vision of the Information Society is grounded in the Right to Communicate, as a means to enhance human rights and to strengthen the social, economic and cultural lives of people and communities. The information society that interests us is one that is based on principles of transparency, diversity, participation and social and economic justice, and inspired by equitable gender, cultural and regional perspectives. (http://www.crisinfo.org/content/view/full/79)

This statement clarifies the continuities and ruptures from the social justice vision of the earlier NWICO era. The redistributive focus emphasizes open public communication and equitable access, while the claims for recognition displaces the earlier emphasis on the role of the nation-state, and instead focuses on the cultural autonomy of communities and the human right to communicate.

Calabrese has argued that at the 'core' of the 'movement lies the widespread recognition that the media are profoundly essential to the fulfilment of human needs and the realization of human dignity in the modern world' (Calabrese 2004). Advocates of the CRIS campaign have argued that their more expansive articulation of the human right to communicate attempts to overcome the narrow and legalistic rendering of the individual right to the freedom of information (Hamelink 2003). In practice, however, we argue that the 'transcultural resonance' (Keck and Sikkink 1998) of the narrower claims for recognition without redistribution would prevail in the WSIS process, in some ways serving as a mirror opposite to the earlier NWICO era of redistribution without recognition.

The influence of civil society organizations like CRIS was significantly constrained given the institutional limitations of the ITU, as opposed to UN bodies like UNESCO. The ITU, which served as the institutional base for the WSIS meetings, has a feeble history in terms of its relationship to civil society. The dominant actors involved in WSIS through the ITU were its 191 member states and the over 650 corporate actors represented by the ominously named 'Coordinating Committee of Business Interlocutors' (CBBI).[5] Scholars associated with the 'MacBride legacy' like Siochrú (2004) and Hamelink (2004) have repeatedly raised concerns about the limits of the ITU as an institutional venue capable of fostering dialogue and deliberation through meaningful participation in civil society. The WSIS process was preceded by the three PrepComs (preparatory committee) meetings as well as regional meetings facilitated by UNESCO, leading to the first summit in Geneva in December 2003. In contrast to corporate and state representatives who followed already established protocols within the ITU, the new procedural terms of engagement dominated discussions amongst civil society groups in this first phase. In the end, only recognized organizations registered through the intergovernmental ITU and, coordinated by the Civil Society Bureau (CSB), would count as civil society delegates.[6]

Cammaerts and Carpentier (2005) have documented the participation of the hundreds of CSOs from both the North and the South involved in the three PrepComs (preparatory communication) meetings , as well as the thousands of participants involved in regional meetings facilitated by UNESCO, all of which led to the first WSIS meeting in Geneva in December 2003. In addition, CSOs along with corporate 'stakeholders,' were encouraged to submit written contributions to the ITU, and CSOs themselves mobilized through a variety of online efforts collecting information, networking between organizations and providing information leading up to the first meeting in Geneva, and then again to the second meeting in Tunis (in November 2005).[7] The active participation of CSOs in the global governance process is seen by many academic experts as positive in and of itself by creating informal networks, contacts and expertise (Siochrú 2004; Padovani 2004), as well as by expanding the basis for a 'coordinated voice' within civil society (Klenwächter 2004: 1).

The cautious optimism leading up to and around the WSIS gave way to the realization that at most the first stage of the summit served to enhance networks and expertise of civil society actors, and at worst there was minimal impact on policy outcomes to change incorporating broader objectives for social justice. As documented by many participants in the summit,[8] the lack of freedom of information within the first WSIS meeting was reinforced by the intimidating 'architecture of the event' (Selian and Cukier 2004), which physically separated state and corporate actors from civil society representatives. In addition, the prohibitive costs of accessing the paid wireless internet services at the event, the intense surveillance of civil society groups entering official buildings, and the arrest of protesters for threatening security,[9] cast a dark shadow on a summit meant to highlight the benefits of a global information society (Hamelink 2004; Sreberny 2005).

The limited influence of CSOs on policy outcome in the Geneva stage of the Summit was restricted to the areas of communication rights and Internet Governance. Specifically, the WSIS Declaration of Principles (2003) reaffirms the right to the freedom of expression, a right that virtually all CSOs, private-sector actors and a vast majority of nation-states, most importantly Northern nations like the US, supported. In the area of Internet Governance, CSOs called for greater democratization of ICANN, with the US and some of its Northern allies and the private sector arguing strongly in support of the status quo as a non-profit organization based in the US.

As discussed in Chapter 5, the Civil Society Declaration shows that there were other areas of disagreement between civil society and its more powerful 'partners' in negotiation. These found little resolution or more importantly, discussion in this first stage of the Summit. The two most significant include the area of norms over intellectual property rights (IPRs) and financing the 'bridge' to the digital divide. In the area of Intellectual Property, Northern states have been largely successful at reinforcing existing IPRs and keeping meaningful negotiation off the WSIS agenda, despite the fact that Southern nations like Argentina, Brazil, China, South Africa and others have argued persistently for the need to rethink the redistributive and developmental impact of laws that favour Northern nations and private firms (Shashikant 2005). On the second issue, the Senegalese delegation proposed a 'Digital Solidarity Fund' (DSF) to redistribute resources from the North to the South in order to finance the expansion of ICTs in the face of strong opposition from the US, the EU and Japan. The US proposed a counter 'Digital Freedom Initiative' (DFI) that essentially promoted a pre-existing US Agency for International development (USAID) programme 'enabling environments' for the 'creation of US corporate interests in Africa' (Accuosto and Johnson 2005: 13–14). Coordinated opposition by Northern state actors and the private sector against establishing such a financing mechanism rendered the Digital Solidarity Fund weak and dependent on nominal voluntary contributions as opposed to a tax on users or firms.

The lack of emphasis and meaningful intervention on redistributive claims should be seen as a problem of representation. In fact, as these Northern-based CSOs have gained technical competence to challenge dominant state and corporate interests, a variety of analysts at the WSIS argued that delegates from civil society based in the South were underrepresented and often did not have the requisite 'expertise' in technical areas of intellectual property (IP) regulation or the intricacies of Internet governance (Sreberny 2005; Kleinwächter 2004a). Overall, participation by civil society was highly 'Eurocentric', with experts arguing that European CSOs dominated discussions. Southern CSOs were seen to lack 'human, financial and technical resources' (Dany 2004), coupled with the fact that CSOs from Africa were deemed relatively 'young organizations' (Cammaerts and Carpentier 2005). Although active in the preparatory process, African groups were not 'active participants' in the summit in Geneva. Active participation in this context is defined by 'securing access to all official documents, to the negotiation process and by participation rights (e.g. the right to observe or to vote)' (Dany 2004). Similarly, experts cite the high cost of attendance and reliance on European languages to account for the low turn-out of Southern CSOs more generally, and point to the negative impact of authoritarian regimes to account for the underrepresentation of Asian organizations.[10]

The second phase of the summit followed another series of PrepCom and regional meetings in 2004 and 2005, with civil society deliberations 'characterized by difference, division, and questions of identity and representation' (Banks 2005). Key figures from the groups centrally involved in the WSIS process like Seán Ó Siochrú (2004) from the CRIS campaign and Karen Banks (2005) from APC pointed out that questions about the legitimacy of civil society were increasingly raised by US-backed conservative groups challenging the social justice platform on issues like intellectual property rights. Although this is no doubt a disturbing trend, organizations and individuals from the South also raised the opposite set of concerns, about the lack of focus on more expansive claims for both recognition and redistribution.

The CRIS campaign and others most involved in the Civil Society Bureau focused on the fact that Tunisia – an authoritarian state with an inexcusable record on freedom of information – was to host the second summit. The Tunisian state's decision to ban the planned parallel Citizen's Summit heightened concerns raised about freedom of expression and human rights. At the summit, some 150 people attended a demonstration to support a hunger strike organized by the Tunisian Human Rights League protesting against the censorship of the human rights issue within Tunisia. The cruel irony of Tunisia hosting a summit on the Global

Information Society was not lost on individuals and organizations who raised their concerns, once again, with the narrow definition of rights in these discussions, as the US State Department voiced official 'concern about Tunisia's restrictions on the broadcast media' (http://usinfo.state.gov/gi/Archive/2005/Nov/19-134756.html). The US position on the issue of human rights seems especially galling given the Bush administration's blatant evasion if not violation of universal standards applied to other nations and peoples.

The Tunis phase of the summit did not see any changes in the way that civil society participated in the multistakeholder process, leading to a growing sense of disappointment amongst activists from the South over the lack of confrontation, much less intervention, over redistributive claims (ITEM 2005). Many CSOs participating in Tunis felt that a substantial victory was evident in the area of Internet Governance against corporate interests, and US dominance in establishing the multistakeholder Internet Governance Forum (IGF) to act as a check on ICANN. Hans Klein, a civil society expert in the Working Group on Internet Governance (WGIG), has argued that the Tunis outcome should be seen as a victory for civil society because ICANN is the 'same but different' thanks to intense pressures from CSOs that led the EU to alter its position against the US's unilateral control over the Domain Name System (DNS) which directs the flow of data on the Internet. Given the clear limits of the change, the extent of meaningful intervention by civil society in this area is being questioned by researchers and activists alike (Gurnstein 2005; McLaughlin and Pickard 2005).

Meanwhile, the Tunis Summit saw little progress in the area of financing access to ICTs, which was meant to be the second main focus of discussion (alongside Internet Governance). Accusoto and Johnson have argued that the participation of CSOs in the multistakeholder Taskforce on Financing led only to the 'inclusion of some timid language into the official documents' (Accusoto and Johnson 2005: 24). The Digital Solidarity Fund remained sidelined, dependent on voluntary contributions from the North. This 'charity' model of development is also prevalent in the new emphasis on 'public-private-partnerships' (PPPs) between companies like Cisco, Microsoft and Hewlett Packard and national governments as well as UN bodies which run the risk of 'imposing technological solutions that transform Southern societies into captive markets' (Accusoto and Johnson 2005: 43). Alternative proposals based on a Global Public Goods model of regulation based on taxation of the manufacture of microchips or other methods of raising funds did not make inroads leading up to the Tunis Summit. Moreover, the Tunis Summit saw even less discussion of the issue of Intellectual Property Rights than at its Geneva counterpart, with the private sector and Northern states effective in displacing the crucial issue of access to content and technology transfer almost completely from the official deliberations. In Geneva, open-source software was recognized as important if not preferential from the perspective of development by most Southern nations. Partially in response to this trend, IP Watch has reported how Microsoft became an official sponsor of the WSIS Tunis Summit, gaining its own 'speaking slot' to reinforce the importance of the 'strict protection of intellectual property', expanded its participation in WSIS by bringing 70 representatives to Tunis versus some 6 to Geneva and played a disproportionate role in drafting the official WSIS documents (Ermert 2005). If civil society engaged primarily in the areas of human rights and Internet Governance, the Tunis Summit showed how the private sector had mastered the discourse of sustainable and multicultural info-development. In Tunis, the 'trade fair' look of the event was played down by corporate representatives who pointed out that their booths were not manned by salespeople but rather 'community affairs' or 'public sector managers'. Representatives from Sun Microsytems, Microsoft, Nokia, among others, argued that they were 'selling success stories' and the growing presence of the private sector in the development arena was explained as a 'win–win' proposition. As the Managing Director for Africa of Hewlett-Packard Co. exclaimed, 'Investors are not doing business only for charity . . . Business must be sustainable. And funds could be cycled to local communities' (Toros 2005). This logic strongly opposes any mention of tax-based solutions or the Global Public Goods model of regulation as proposed by CSOs from the South, as evident in the official documents produced in Tunis (see: http://www.itu.int/wsis/).

While progressive Southern-based NGOs supported the communications rights agenda of holding authoritarian states in the South accountable, the separation of recognition-based claims targeted at states in the developing world deflects the larger scale of ongoing human rights violations by Northern states like the US and the UK, especially in the context of the egregious violations of human rights resulting in the 'War on Terror'.[11] The civil society priorities that did manage to surface in the content of the WSIS official documents raised only the narrowest of claims for gender advocacy as well as human rights, steering clear of redistributive issues that faced enormous opposition by corporate and Northern state actors (Dany 2004). The civil society outcry against the violation of communication rights by Southern states therefore served to displace, however unintentionally, a focus on redistributive claims. As we have seen, the Civil Society Declaration critiques the technological determinism of the dominant policy framework and promotes instead a communication rights approach that attempts to balance claims for recognition (freedom of expression, right to communicate and pluralistic media) with claims for redistribution (promoting community/citizen's ownership and control of media and communication resources).

We are arguing that the institutional limits of the WSIS explain why a narrow set of claims for recognition displaced wider claims for both recognition and redistribution as outlined in the Civil Society Declaration. Specifically, claims to protect communication rights and freedom of expression succeeded in securing 'transcultural resonance' as the issue positioned civil society *against* Southern states – in this case with the support of many Northern states. Once again, we return to the issue of representation and accountability of civil society to citizens. Beatriz Busaniche (2005), a Free Software activist from Argentina argued that the centralization of the Civil Society Bureau (CSB) and its focus on a coherent but ultimately watered-down voice in presenting an *Alternate Civil Society Declaration* diminished the capacity of delegates to intervene in politically charged negotiations with dominant stakeholders (49). Busaniche (2005) argues that participating CSOs 'should not pretend to represent anyone except their own organizations' and that 'citizenry should be the basis of participation' (51). Echoing these sentiments, a number of international activists and researchers involved in and at the margins of the WSIS process formed the innovative Incommunicado Project in 2005 – 'refusing to allow an organizational incorporation of grassroots or subaltern agendas into the managed consensus being built around the dynamic of an "international civil (information) society"' (see: http://incommunicado.info/conference).

This line of criticism challenges the arguments made earlier about the lack of expertise and resources alone explaining the relative absence of civil society voices from the South. It becomes important in this context to consider the conceptual and historical role of civil society organizations – especially in the form of NGOs in the South since the 1980s. Table 6.1 provides a vivid picture of some of the new inconsistencies of 'splintered urbanism' that makes up the new geography of globalization. In this case, we see that network practices of NGOs sometimes in line, but often out of synch with the integration of cities in the global economy (as measured by the presence of TNCs).[12] The table shows that the density of transnational NGO presence is actually higher in the South as compared to the North.

If we take into account the fact that Nairobi, New Delhi, Manila, Mexico City and Beijing (among other Third World cities) make up the top twenty-five rankings of the highest NGO-networked global cities, then we must reconceptualize the relationship between democratic

Table 6.1 Top 25 NGO Cities by Network Connectivities*

NGO Network Connectivity		Global Network Connectivity		
Level	**Rank**	**City**	**Rank**	**Difference**
3729	1	Nairobi	99	98
3408	2	Brussels	15	13
3378	3	Bangkok	28	29
3211	4	London	1	−3
3209	5	New Delhi	52	47
3109	6	Manila	46	40
3181	7	Washington	37	30
2999	8	Harare	132	124
2796	9	Geneva	67	58
2779	10	Moscow	34	24
2758	11	New York	2	−9
2626	12	Mexico City	18	6
2624	13	Jakarta	22	9
2616	14	Tokyo	5	−9
2599	15	Accra	150	135
2569	16	Cairo	59	43
2562	17	Dhaka	152	135
2560	18	Rome	53	35
2433	19	Dakar	206	187
2408	20	Santiago	57	37
2326	21	Abidjan	131	110
2320	22	Buenos Aires	23	1
2256	23	Dar es Salam	196	173
2256	24	Copenhagen	44	20
2251	25	Beijing	36	11

*The first two columns measure 'global cities' according to the presence of global NGO networks while the second two columns measure the presence of transnational corporate networks. For more on method see Taylor 2004.
Source: Taylor (2004).

accountability and the generic category of civil society as assumed in the above discussion of the WSIS.

The dramatic expansion of the number and influence of NGOs in the South is part and parcel of neoliberal regulatory reform, with over two decades of multilateral agencies and aid organizations based in the North advising developing countries to promote the 'democracy sector' by funding groups within civil society. There is a clear political objective with this version of civil society from above, as described by Jenkins:

> While the preservation of individual liberties is deemed by most agencies to be a good in itself, it is the contribution of individual rights to engendering and maintaining democracy and promoting sound

> government policy and economic performance that primarily animates aid policy. By funding organized groups within developing countries, aid agencies seek to create a virtuous cycle in which rights to free association beget sound government policies, human development, and (ultimately) a more conducive environment for the protection of individual liberties. (Jenkins 2001: 253)

The influence of multilateral bodies like the World Bank and bilateral aid agencies like USAID have created a 'sanitized' version of civil society where NGOs serve as 'public-spirited watchdogs quarantined from political society' (Jenkins 2001: 261).[13]

Political society includes social movements that are often at odds with the narrow development agendas of NGOs, publics that may be outside formal channels of participation and a variety of state actors that have sometimes productive relationships to different sectors of what counts as 'civil society'. In practice, civil society should be historically situated in relation to the nation-state and the complex trajectories of modern capitalism. It is vital, therefore, to question assumptions about the universality of civil society such that more training and resources to local NGOs in the area of ICTs will inevitably lead to greater public-interest intervention following models established in the North. In fact, as Anita Gurumurty and Parminder Jeet Singh (2005), Directors of IT for Change, have argued, there is a need to reinforce the centrality of the role of the state in discussions about ICTs and development – as the only institutional actor capable of funding and coordinating development on this scale. In the case of India, they call for pressures on the state to reprioritize ICTs as a sustainable development priority. In this vein Carlos Afonso (2005), the Director of RITS (Third Sector Information Network) argues that the reason that civil society has had more impact on debates over Brazil's position on Internet Governance is because 'The Brazilian government continues to seek a national consensus proposal regarding the future of global Internet governance' (131).

In this chapter we have so far argued that the fact that CSOs within the WSIS were able to make claims about freedom of information but were unable to make progress on redistributive claims forces us to pay attention to the structural limitations of multistakeholderism, as well as the limitations of civil society as a universal category. In contrast to the North, where CSOs have emerged in public-policy debates over communication and information policy as 'public interest' or 'consumer rights' groups, in postcolonial societies we must pay attention to the murky lines which divide state institutions from civil society, as well as those between civil society and political society. As we discussed at the end of Chapter 2, this dilemma reflects the structural inequality embedded in institutions of global governance, where the transcultural resonance of claims associated with negative freedoms – in this case the freedom of information *from* state control for example – displaces claims associated with inequality. The dilemma of displacement is inextricably linked to the third political dimension of social justice: representation. The last section of the chapter examines the vexing question of representation by expanding on feminist critiques, which help us interrogate the discourse of civil society and social justice in the field of global communication governance.

Gender, power and place

In this section, we argue that despite the limitations imposed by the ITU's multistakeholder structure, the Gender Caucus within the WSIS allowed for the articulation of more expansive claims for recognition and redistribution as well as greater emphasis on the issue of representation. We contend that this is a reflection of decades of volatile and invariably productive discussion about how to formulate campaigns for global social justice while paying attention to difference. If Northern CSOs most actively engaged in the WSIS process can trace their origins to the legacy of the MacBride Commission, then the gender justice advocates who took part in WSIS have a separate trajectory from the 1985 and 1995 UN-sponsored Summit on Women in Nairobi and Beijing which set the stage for two decades of transnational advocacy and fierce debate over women's empowerment, gender equality and norms of modernization. The individuals and organizations that became involved in the WSIS process through the establishment of the multistakeholder Gender Caucus in 2002 in Mali brought a wealth of experience in transnational mobilization grounded in broader social concerns than most activists and policy-makers in the relatively narrow world of ICT governance.

One of the problems facing gender advocates in WSIS is the 'fragmentation' of policy generally combined with the approach that gender is an issue that can be dealt with *after* the basic working structures or problems have been solved. In other words, gender is seen as a secondary rather than an organizing factor, an 'added' element in the policy agenda that is dealt with after the 'urgent' business is attended to. It is also treated as a 'subcategory' in selected policy 'sections'. It was only in 1998 that the ITU set up a taskforce on 'gender issues,' producing gender awareness guidelines for policy-making and regulatory agencies only in 2001. In 2002, the multistakeholder Gender Caucus was formed at a regional preparatory meeting in Mali with funding from development agencies within several Nordic states and UNIFEM, in contrast to the other caucuses within the 'civil society family' (Jensen 2005). The structural organization of the Gender Caucus thus allowed for regional meetings with local organizations and individuals, with an emphasis on incorporating perspectives from the South especially leading up to the second phase of the summit. The brief appearance of 'gender' in matters of primary or basic education in the proposed topics and outcome of the WSIS, directly related to the UN Millennium Declaration and UN Millennium Development Goals, was thanks to intense lobbying by the Gender Caucus of the WSIS. Here we see the formulation of political claims around both redistribution and recognition, offering a novel perspective on framing development goals that were unsurprisingly seen as restrictive or too 'limiting' by the US delegation.[14]

Feminist activists argued from the beginning that a sense of technological determinism, insensitivity to gender inequalities and the dominance of male 'experts' was rampant across all three multistakeholder bodies, including civil society organizations that promoted 'gender-blind and hence male-centered' policy interventions (Jensen 2005).

Feminist groups within the Gender Caucus raised the issue of the human rights of girls, women and marginalized communities in the context of the Global War on Terror; 'We cannot hope for an information society that promotes the highest values of humankind if we do not address meaningfully the ways in which information and communications channels including the media can be harnessed in the service of peace, and in strong opposition to all illegal wars' (George 2003). Gender justice advocates argued for greater 'gender sensitive infrastructure development', affordable universal access and sustainable and appropriate technologies, prioritization of free and open software and attention to gender biases in educational and employment opportunities associated with ICTs, among other areas.

ICTs as a policy concern constitute a complex combination of education and educational cultures for the training of specialists: organizational and working structures and cultures for the further research and development but also use of technology; structures for access and determination of such use according to needs; the political economic and cultural context within which individuals and groups can participate in this development and use it on equal terms; and the chances for participating in decision-making structures that influence the future of ICTs and the mechanisms that would promote free and emancipatory expression through such technological means. We have argued throughout that gender is a fundamental factor of social organization, inherent in any aspect of social and economic life, from education to the labour market but also from the media images promoting the sales or adaptation of these technologies to the quality and degree of use in everyday life. Studies have shown the segregation of almost all spheres of social life starting from educational systems and reaching the very top echelons of transnational business or state governments. In the 'developed' world alone, the number of women training and working in IT industries has dropped, that of enrolled female students in science degrees has decreased, the ratio of women and men in mass communications education and industry has hit a low threshold for the last three decades, and employment in the communication sector and especially ICTs consists predominantly of part-time, low-paid, temporary contracts without adequate labour conditions (Adam 2000; Etzkowitz et al. 1994; Millar and Jagger 2001; NOP World 2001; Rush et al. 2004).

Feminist advocates have also argued that, within policy debates, there is a false division between developers (scientists/specialists) and the users, as two separate groups. The process of production, direction, development and redevelopment of technology is therefore seen as cut off from the social relations defining the direction of this process. The dominant policy discussions do not seem to ask the question to what degree the segregation of 'techies' and users affect not only the degree of acceptance and use of new technologies but also the rate and spectrum of distribution, application, relation to users, impact on economies and politics. Limiting the debate over the sociality of ICT technologies to the conditions of usage and access to technology and information is fragmented. The 'world's inhabitants' and citizens are treated almost as passive receivers of technology. This line of reasoning suggests that the opening up of technology to many more receivers is enough to guarantee commercial success and high rates of adaptability. It is only under this limiting agenda that gender appears in policy considerations.

According to the WSIS agenda and proposed themes, three areas are important in the discussions of the Information Society: *Vision* which refers to the shared visions, if any, of the international community; the use of ICTs for development; and steps to the reduction of impediments to cross-border e-commerce. A significant body of research has shown that girls and women perform better in all-women environments than mixed-sex classes. In science, where the number of female students is falling steadily in Western nations, the symbolic separation of the 'expert' and the 'user' further exclude women from the development processes of technology (see Clegg 2001). The marginal proportion of women in the 'new media' industries is evident throughout: women represent a small minority of workers employed in the Australian IT sector with only 17 per cent of the Computer Society members being female (Sinclair 2002). Women remain marginalized users at clerical 'pink-collar jobs', low paid with less chances of job mobility, a continuation of the career trajectory as witnessed by teachers at school and in science courses at universities (Clegg 2001).

Gender-blind policies can worsen the situation of women, as they can reinforce gender segregation by placing technologies and their control away from women's reach. In contrast, gender justice advocates that, if policies are to correct power and resource imbalances, they have to depart at the point of the most disadvantaged, in a bottom-up process, where the definition of policy problems as well as the range of responses to these problems is designed with the concept of accountability in mind. This is not a formula for reifying local communities or taking for granted essential qualities that define 'women's experience' as Gurumurthy explains:

> This cannot be left unarticulated or relegated as a task for 'local communities'. The policy process will have failed the goal of women's equality unless it consciously pushes for the expansion of choices for women, for new spaces that promote women's capacity, self-determination and autonomy. Equal access needs thus to be understood as a political notion – it means equal stakes in the gains from technology for the most marginalized women, within a given cultural context. (Gurumurthy 2005a)

Like other CSOs, gender justice advocates had limited influence in shaping policy outcomes, beyond a disputed paragraph on women's empowerment and gender equality through access to ICTs in the *Geneva Declaration of Principles* as well as in the *Tunis Commitment* and a pledge to establish 'gender-sensitive indicators' for 'ICT uses and needs'. These limited gains have to be weighed against the insights from the regional activities that will continue to draw from the priorities and experiences of activists and researchers and their role in following up and monitoring the implementation of WSIS priorities (Jensen 2005). In between the two summits, activists voiced concerns about differences in priorities between CSOs in the North and South and the lack of community or citizen participation in the WSIS deliberative process at the regional meetings organized by the Gender Caucus (Mundkur and Kochar 2005). In these ways, feminist advocates within the WSIS are the most consistent advocates for the need to connect the narrow policy debates to wider discussions about social and economic development and political transformation. This strategy of broadening our understanding of the politics of communication policy runs counter to the assumptions by many Northern-based CSOs that argue that citizens, particularly citizens in the developing world without civil society organizations in the area of communication, require greater education and awareness about the issues at stake. Feminist critics within the WSIS process argue that social actors engaged in the policy-making field often fail to recognize the reality of the politics of communication policy, especially in the case of the developing world where the stakes of the IS debate are perhaps the highest and civil society participation the weakest.

The slippery slope in most postcolonial societies between the state and civil society has to be taken into account when we consider the MacBride legacy and the issue of representation in multilateral governance. Instead, as discussions in the Gender Caucus advocate most strongly, there is a need to reconsider policy priorities based on social practice. This means that instead of finding or funding CSOs based in the South to carry out policies meant to close the 'digital divide', there is a need to learn from how civil society organizations, state bodies and even informal networks that have less institutional power, approach claims arising from communication concerns.

As we saw in Chapter 5, technology is projected as a determining factor in debates about the IS, as neutral. A driving force in policy-making but also an object and objective, it serves as the normative framing of political economic decisions, it bears the 'metadata' for the redefinition of social problems – such as the renaming of inequalities into 'digital divide'. Communication policy tends to celebrate the 'changing' effect that technology has upon the social world, but it largely concentrates on a limited range of questions. In terms of the digital divide, the questions have focused almost exclusively on ICTs and skills to enable access and use (or consumption) of ICTs and related products but they tend to avoid the structural dimensions of poverty and prioritization of uses of technologies or political and cultural practices that perpetuate structural and symbolic inequity. These latter concerns are often seen by the majority of policy-makers as outside the legitimate scope of communication policy.

In stark contrast, feminist activists have been some of the loudest critics within the WSIS process of the 'market fundamentalism' inherent in global and national ICT policy where 'pro-poor' interventions can only be justified through 'pro-market' solutions (Gurumurthy 2005b). Feminist advocates from the South argued persistently for the need to prioritize productive capacities of ICTs over the consumption of ICT services in the developing world, especially because of the impact that they might have on marginalized communities.

On the issue of ICTs, globalization and the feminization of work, feminist scholarship has emphasized that any policy debate must include the perspective of actual and potential workers from the South as opposed to the predominant focus on experiences of displaced white-collar workers in the North (Chakravartty 2005; Ng and Mitter 2005a; Freeman 2000).

Feminist economists such as Swasti Mitter and Celia Ng have conducted extensive empirical research on employment in ICT-based industries in the South to argue for greater state intervention to improve the 'quality and quantity' of jobs for women workers fostering sustainable as opposed to export-led development.[15]

Deliberation through difference: lessons for transnational public interest advocates

Feminist advocacy within the WSIS process shows the ways in which redistributive claims over appropriate technology and basic ICT access are deeply entangled in claims for recognition marked by gender, class, race and nationality, among other differences. We have argued that two decades of debates over representation within transnational civil society have given advocates for gender justice a wider perspective on how to challenge the Eurocentric claims of human rights without abandoning an emancipatory vision of social justice. The notion that *both* states and corporations need to be held accountable to universal principles of social justice is an indisputably positive outcome of the 'MacBride legacy'. We have argued that building on this legacy, we must recognize the need for a normative framework of social justice that incorporates recognition, redistribution and representation as linking issues of 'development' with concerns about individual and community 'rights'.

If we consider the issue of Intellectual Property Rights (IPRs), for instance, we can see how expansive redistributive claims coupled with claims for recognition based on community rights can successfully challenge IS discourse and practice. Relevant to this discussion is the fact that civil society organizations have worked with state actors, specifically states where there are vibrant social movements engaged in policy-making more broadly – in this case Argentina, Brazil, India and South Africa, among others. Since the 1986 signing of the controversial TRIPS Agreement in the GATT strongly advocated by the US and its Northern allies, Southern nation-states have formed alliances among themselves and also with civil society organizations to oppose the implementation of free-trade norms, especially in the area of agricultural seeds and medicine. Northern nations and TNCs have meanwhile pushed for patenting of plants and other living organisms against arguments for community use of resources and the need for affordable transfer of technologies to promote economic and technological development (Shashikanth 2005). The battle over TRIPs has taken place at the WTO and more recently at WIPO, where Argentina, Bolivia and Brazil were successful in 2004 of convincing the general assembly to adopt a resolution that established a

'Development Agenda' in contrast to its previous mandate that had singularly favoured the rights of owners of intellectual property over the creators and the publics or users.[16] In this context, civil society organizations along with state representatives have been able to legitimately challenge the terms of trade along social justice principles.

In this chapter, we have traced the origins of civil society participation in debates on the global information society. We have shown that the NWICO era's legacy of redistribution at the expense of recognition has been reversed in the WSIS era when civil society participation has become bureaucratized and centralized within the field of global communication policy. Drawing from the experiences of the Gender Caucus, we have argued that there is a need to combine claims for recognition and redistribution in the field of global communication policy which would mean that concerns about the digital divide should centrally address institutional sexism, as well as racism and marginalization faced by minority and immigrant communities in the North. Similarly, while redistributive claims over appropriate technology and basic ICT access in the South are crucial, they are in much of the world deeply enmeshed in claims for recognition by marginalized communities marked by difference – whether gender, class, race (ethnicity), religion or sexuality. Research that incorporates the experiences and voices of women from the South, show the heterogeneity of needs, while at the same time highlighting the importance of income generation and employment opportunities for both individual women, and the families and communities that increasingly rely on them. The institutional limits placed on civil society actors in shaping the outcome of the WSIS process thus far reveals some of the problems associated with balancing claims for recognition and redistribution, and reinforces the importance of representation as a crucial dimension of struggles for social justice.

Notes

1. As we have discussed earlier, formal mechanisms for NGO participation increased within the UN and other multilateral organizations and has been promoted as a central component of development aid since the 1980s. Studies of organizational structure reveal that UNESCO has historically had the most formal channels for NGO participation in its deliberation of cultural and educational policy in contrast to the WTO which has been criticized for its secrecy and lack of transparency with NGOs' participation limited to 'information exchange and briefings'. The WIPO and ICANN, although structurally very different, clearly give preference to corporations

and industrial associations in lieu of civil society organizations representing some form of 'community' or 'public' interest (Kleinwächter 2004a; Siochrú 2003). We will discuss the role of civil society within the ITU in greater detail below.

2. Cammaerts and Carpentier very usefully point out that the Conference on Environment and Development in Rio de Janeiro in 1992 featured the participation of some 2,400 people and 1,400 accredited NGOs within the formal process, with some 17,000 people participating in the parallel NGO forum. Similarly, during the Fourth World conference in Beijing, 5,000 people participated in the official process representing 2,100 accredited NGOs, with an additional 30,000 people participating in the parallel NGO forum. More recently, at the World Conference against Racism, Racial Discrimination, Xenophobia and Related Intolerance in Durban in 2001, there were 1,300 accredited NGOs participating in the forum with another 8,000 people involved in a parallel NGO forum. See: Cammaerts and Carpetier (2005): 3.
3. This alternate vision includes defining the IS on the following critical terms:
   1. Access to communications resources for citizens as opposed to consumers.
   2. Knowledge understood as a public good as opposed to a commodity.
   3. Advertising regulated on the basis of the ecological implications of consumer society as opposed to promoting the commercialization of space and peoples.
   4. Promoting individual privacy as opposed to mining of personal data.
   5. Protecting the Intellectual Property Rights of communities as opposed to the protection of the rights of transnational corporations.
   6. Exempting trade in culture by promoting the right to protect cultural autonomy and promote public spaces.
   7. Regulating concentration of ownership on the basis of promoting plurality of perspectives.
   8. Promoting the ideals of the 'commons' – protecting public property and public accountability as opposed to the private exploitation of common assets. (Summarized from Hamelink 2002: 252–3).
4. The Voices 21 initiative identified four areas of action: (1) Access and Accessibility; (2) Right to Communicate; (3) Diversity of Expression; (4) Security and Privacy; (5) Cultural Environment (promoting a culture of peace, solidarity and environmental awareness). For more details see: http://www.comunica.org/v21/statement.htm

5. The CBBI website clarifies the 'business community's' objectives in maintaining a neoliberal vision of an IS as discussed in Chapter 5. For more see: http://businessatwsis.net/realindex.php
6. According to the Civil Society Meeting Point website, accredited members participating in the WSIS process includes: 'representatives from "professional" and grassroots NGOs, the trade union movement, community media activists, mainstream and traditional media interest groups, parliamentarians and local government officials, the scientific and academic community, educators, librarians, volunteers, the disability movement, youth activists, indigenous peoples, "think-tanks", philanthropic institutions, gender advocates and human and communication rights advocates'. http://www.wsis-cs.org/wsis-intro.html
7. See: www.wsis-cs.org, choike., etc.
8. A variety of NGO and CSO participants to the Geneva Summit discuss lack of access at the conference site itself, for more see: http://cyber.law.harvard.edu/wsis/home
9. In addition to the parallel civil society meetings, a group of about fifty 'dissident' CSOs – mostly social movements and NGOs based in Western Europe – took part in alternative events and actions protesting the logic of the summit itself, under the collective banner of 'WSIS: WE SEIZE'. Although only one of these events was a small public protest, the activists were immediately arrested and disbanded. For more see: Cammaerts and Carpentier 2004: 21.
10. The relatively low presence of Latin American CSOs is not explicitly addressed in their piece, but the number of 'active' CSOs from Latin America makes up 7 per cent versus 6 per cent from Asia. See Cammaerts and Carpentier 2004: 15–16.
11. See Human Rights Watch on civil liberties and human right violations after 11 September: http://www.hrw.org/campaigns/september11/
12. Taylor uses his findings to forward an argument about the emancipatory potential for civil society in the Global South. He argues that the 'potential diffusion of power consequent upon the network of practices of NGOs is what our results are showing. The Global South is not represented in any sense through NGOs but their global activities are providing a legitimizing platform for dissent and diverse voices from regions where economic and political power is lacking' (Taylor 2004).
13. Here, the distinction between civil and political society signals the inability of the category of formal associational life to capture the complex realities of political engagement in postcolonial societies. This argument is elaborated by Partha Chatterjee (2004) who distinguishes between official civil society in the form of NGOs and social

movements, both formal and informal (spontaneous), that animate political struggle outside electoral and civic politics. Whether the distinction between political and civil society is as stark as Chaterjee suggests is open to question.

14. The USA representation at the beginning of the summit for example refered to the UN Millenium Development Goals (MDG) as 'too limiting', referring rather to the obligation of countries to eradicate poverty and ensure education for all – see government statements to WSIS at www.ITU.org
15. It is beyond the scope of this chapter to cover this important issue in greater detail. For an excellent cross-national overview of this area, see Mitter 2002: http://gab.wigsat.org/partIII.pdf
16. For more on the development objectives outlined in WIPO's new mandate as well as more details on IP-related issues see: http://www.choike.org/nuevo_eng/informes/2263.html; http://www.ip-watch.org

Conclusion

The three pillars for the construction of information societies are not telecommunications, equipment and software, rather info-ethics, digital education (with an approach on the use and social impact) and real and effective citizen participation in all the phases of the process, from the definition of public policy related to the information society and its impact to its implementation and evaluation.

The promotion of free software implies certain social, educational, scientific, political and economic benefits for the region. Open licensing models are essential for the free exchange of knowledge, which would benefit national development and the production of own local knowledge.

The promotion of the production of technological and organizational knowledge by Southern countries makes them proactive actors in neither the development of information societies and not passive agents nor mere consumers of developed countries' technologies.

We emphasize that the strengthening of democracies and the construction of citizenship is based on the recognition of the role of civil society as a political actor. For this reason, we express our nonconformity with the fact that at the Latin American and Caribbean Ministerial Regional Conference, held in preparation for the second phase of the WSIS, the multistakeholder mechanisms for participation and procedural rules established within the framework of the Summit were not respected. This has hindered the participation of civil society delegates in the discussions and meetings and appropriate access to the documents being discussed.

We express our concern on the formation of the official panels in which the absence of gender, racial, and ethnic diversity is evident. We assume that these have not been deliberate omissions but do feel it is indicative of how much we have left to go in the creation of inclusive information societies. We pledge our continued support to the development of social systems based on justice and equity within a framework [of] continental solidarity.

> Olinca Marino, on behalf of various Latin American-based civil society organizations. *Statement Submitted to the Regional Preparatory Ministerial Conference of Latin America and the Caribbean for the second phase of the World Summit on the Information Society* (10 June 2005) http://wsispapers.choike.org/cs_intervention_10_06.pdf

This statement captures the nexus between redistributive and recognition-based claims made in the context of the WSIS as articulated by a significant section of civil-society delegates from Africa, Asia and Latin America. The emphasis here is not on the negative freedoms associated with individual liberty, but rather the positive freedoms ensuring relevance and access of ICTs and the need for meaningful participation to rectify the structural inequities of policy design and outcome. As we discussed in the previous chapter, NGOs have played a prominent role in the process of socioeconomic development in the post-Fordist era. These largely bureaucratized, development-based organizations have a separate trajectory from grassroots social movements with a history of involvement in civil and community rights, movements representing the landless and small farmers, movements that have mobilized marginalized ethnic, religious, caste-based or racial minorities, and a variety of other oppositional movements. Although there are overlaps between development-based NGOs and oppositional social movements, it is usually the latter that in the context of the South have reinforced the notion that civil society is a 'political actor' that 'strengthens democracy and citizenship', the point being that, in practice, the universality and normative function of 'civil society' as the institutional body accountable to public interest in the field of global communication policy must be re-examined.

We began this book with our premise that the changing role of the state in the global field of communications and media policy has to be assessed against a longer history of the modern nation-state and the shifting modes of accumulation and regulation/regularization. In subsequent chapters, we have traced the legitimacy of the policy-making process and its outcomes both within the institutional framework and in terms of how it is negotiated within given political cultural contexts. We have aimed to provide a comprehensive account of issues that are central within this field, but we deliberately focused our attentions beyond the 'specifics' of regulation, by examining policy areas that have proved to be of common concern for societies across different socioeconomic realities situated in the uneven neoliberal economic order. The logic behind the organization of the book and the choice of empirical examples reflects our unorthodox approach to the study of communication policy. Throughout, we have argued that there is a need to consider the symbolic politics as well as the structural conditions that shape the material outcome of policy practices, combining insights from the French Régulation School, the work of cultural theorists of the state and feminist and poststructuralist theory.

As female scholars in an area that is definitively a male domain, we are daily reminded of the discrepancy between the technical expertise of governance and the wider world of politics and lived experience. Our ecumenical approach to theory and our empirical focus, which is meant to be broad but by no means comprehensive, reflects and limits our own areas of expertise, interest and engagement.[1] We have tried in this book to take the productive insights of critical political economy while paying attention to historical difference. The 'mode of observation and analysis' that we have followed attempts to overcome the taken-for-granted polarities between the international/global policy world and the local/national policy arena. Mattelart has identified the need to reconceptualize international communications precisely because:

> [T]here is a danger of allowing oneself to be enclosed within the 'international,' just as some, at the other end of the spectrum, risk becoming immured in the ghetto of the 'local'. In succumbing to this danger, one risks subscribing to a determinist conception in which the international is converted into the *imperative* – just as, the opposite pole, the exclusive withdrawal into the local perimeter is the shortest way to relativism . . . All these levels of reality, however – international, local, regional, and national – are meaningless unless they are articulated with each other, unless one points out their interactions, and unless one refuses to set up false dilemmas and polarities but instead tries to seek out the connections, mediations, and negotiations operating among these dimensions, without at the same time neglecting the very real existence of power relations among them. (Mattelart 2002: 242. Italics in original text.)

We have argued throughout that discussions of communications policy in the South often 'become immured to the ghetto of the local' both by liberal and Marxist theorists who may become too entangled in their own conceptions of determinism, technological or economic. We argued in Chapter 2 that postcolonial states were already negotiating uneven transnational pressures and domestic policy priorities such as national integration, technological self-reliance and national development as early as in the Fordist era. Tracing the history of the NWICO era from the vantage point of the 'imperfect' postcolonial state allowed us to reconsider the limits of the norms set by powerful Western welfare states and the justification for its undoing in the 1980s and 1990s. The objective here was neither to deny the substantial achievements of the NWICO era nor to underplay the extraordinary influence of media industries and the US and UK in opposing any moves to challenge the development paradigm. Rather, recognizing the legacy of the postcolonial state and historicizing this specific mode of transnational imagining of a coordinated nationalist response to Western cultural dominance exposes the gaps in international communication and media policy debates. When during the NWICO debates political leaders from large sections of Africa and Asia argued that 'democracy was a luxury that could wait for the serious business of development' (Alhassan 2004: 65), the legitimacy of the nation-state to represent public interest was certainly open to question. It is thus without romantic illusions about a more just past that we analyzed the evolution of North–South relations in the post-Fordist regulatory era.

In the same spirit, we considered the limits of the Western welfare-state model of regulation of communications and media industries, which would set the standard for international regulatory norms. Throughout the book, and in particular when examining Western regulatory arenas, we focused on the institutions of policy, norms and objectives and their impact for the publics concerned as these are experienced through internal dichotomies and inequalities, including multisectional, cross-cutting experiences of disadvantage. In the second part of the book we explored the historical and political and cultural contexts of the 'backbones' of infrastructure and culture, through the study of telecommunications and broadcasting policies. In Chapter 3 we began our discussion of telecommunications policy as a fundamental domain as it sets the minimum condition of entry and participation in the 'new information economy'. We pointed out that the global reregulation of telecommunications policy reinforced a 'new geography of inequality' marked by uneven global integration of connected cities and regions, transforming earlier Cold War imaginaries of the developed versus undeveloped worlds. We traced the growing power of transnational corporate actors to shape both domestic and transnational policy outcomes in this period whereby pubic policy priorities came to reflect the welfare of private interests and foreign investment. Once again, we returned to the experiences of states and societies in the South to consider the vantage point of nations that have undergone the most dramatic scale of change in this sector in the past twenty years. Our focus on the experiences of postcolonial states showed us that the lack of legitimacy of the state's failed commitment to redistribution helped mobilize public support for a liberalization paradigm pushed by Northern institutional actors. Considering these internal factors helps account for the legitimacy of these reforms and foregrounds the possibility for contestation of these new rules of governance. In drawing from the experiences of the South, we explored common features of the ways in which postcolonial states negotiated the terms of telecommunications policy. The cases of Brazil, China and India are of importance partially because of their relative economic power as emerging economies and because of the support and opposition by multiple publics about the cost of rapid global integration. We saw that novel forms of policy intervention and contestation are at play in both the area of access to telecommunications infrastructure and in the related area of access to content. Public discontent over corruption linked to the neoliberal development agenda is apparent in demands for accountability from state bodies involved in telecommunications reform as well as transnational and local capital. In all three cases, the state continues to play a central role in mediating redistributive concerns – at times articulated through a nationalist discourse against the growing influence of multilateral institutions, dominant Northern nation-states and TNCs. We have also seen new forms of South–South alliance emerge both contesting the dominant rules of trade in the WTO and establishing a development agenda within WIPO. Similarly, we have seen the emergence of competing alliances and formations such as the India–Brazil–South Africa (IBSA) trilateral initiative and other efforts among Southern nations, in collaborating on a 'social agenda' in trade and technology-related areas. These efforts should not be seen as a panacea to the limits of the neoliberal regulatory regime, but deserve greater research and inquiry. In this spirit, researchers and activists have turned their attention to the Brazilian example in taking the lead through its 'digital inclusion' policies with its state-sponsored initiatives in using and promoting open-source software and how this model may be replicated by states across the North–South divide (Gil 2005). In the specific area of telecommunications reform, the gaps between the information 'haves' and 'have-nots' were not expressed solely in terms of class, but also through urban versus rural divides, gender disparities, caste, race and regional distinctions. Consequently, demands for access bring together 'unpredictable' combinations of social actors. It is in this context, that greater attention must be paid to the institutional and cultural logics of emerging information societies of the South. We feel that there is a pressing need for transolocal and transnational comparative as well as ethnographic research that connects the everyday experience of citizens having access to and being excluded by (tele)communications and ICT services, that can offer new insights into the role institutional actors including state bureaucracies, private firms and civil society across the world. Detailed, process-tracing research is needed to explore the commonality of experience across geographies of exclusion within the privileged 'North' and between and across the North–South divide (Gil 2005).

Claims for fair redistribution, recognition and representation have been present within the very heart of Western capitalism, countries in the EU and the social margins of North America. The questions most posed – and not always heard – revolve around the quest for cultural space and recognition of difference, equity and social justice, as found (or not) in the policies regulating the political economy of cultural industries and, in particular, broadcasting. Our discussion of the public service model of regulation in the context of the EU and Canada showed that pressures of global market integration together with pressures exercised by national capital are diminishing the capacity of national PSBs to serve public interest objectives, just as a broader constituency of publics make claims on these state institutions. The case of broadcasting policy-makes clear the widening gap in the post-Fordist context between national interest and public interest. The transnational reach and regional and translocal appeal of broadcast media require new sets of questions about the relationship between state institutions and public interest. The shifting discourse of public interest in the case of broadcasting policy in the EU is not simply a story of the growing influence of private capital over state bodies, but also the reality of redistributive intervention at the supranational level, sometimes failing to gain national attention and legitimacy, often being absent from international negotiations about the future of communication. Our discussion shows that in the cases where public representation becomes a recognized part of the institutional arrangement of transnational and supranational relations (as in the form of the European Parliament) the inclusion of a public interest focused agenda is possible. This political inclusion should be understood as a necessary element of democratic deliberation at a supranational level. It should not be considered though as the ultimate, adequate and sufficient, form of citizen involvement, but rather as one of the additional spaces where civil society can put forth claims for redistributive justice and recognition of agency. Chapters 4 and 6 both explore the involvement of the 'public' in shaping communication policy agendas: in the EU case, the representational character of the European Parliament lends the EU communication policies legitimacy. In the global arena, as we see in the case of the WSIS, the inclusion of civil society fulfils this function. The quality of this involvement – both in terms of institutionalized political representation and in terms of inclusion of a loose organization of civil society actors in the process of policy-making – has been studied only recently. More empirical research is needed to provide sets of longitudinal data and the qualitative information needed to assess and evaluate the conditions under which framing, representing and advocating policy change corresponds to fluctuations of power within the institutional framework of regional constellations of political systems, similar to the EU, but also on the international level. The lack of public representation in the highest decision-making echelons in the international system renders policies illegitimate in the eyes of the citizenry. Research is needed to explore the consequences of that 'legitimation crisis' as operationalized through communication and cultural policy. Finally, the lack of public involvement in the definition and shaping of what ultimately constitutes the very means of human expression (especially the 'creative' industries) raises a number of questions about the relationship between political and economic systems and the experience of being 'human'. In other words, our understanding about the human condition represented as the content of stories told on national television or in the press, increasingly through converged technological platforms, and as the agency with the force and creativity to shape the future, depends upon the functionality and independence of channels of communication and democratic deliberation.

The last two chapters turn from a focus on specific communication sectors as discrete fields of policy to the meta-policy field of the emerging 'Information Society'. This 'meta-policy' arena is indicative of the tendency of convergence among technological outlets and equipment, communications media and institutional constituencies. Convergence is also actively pursued in the very exercise of policy-making. Here, the discourse of IS echoes the technological determinism that drove earlier visions of international communications policy practice, most notably the early optimism of 'communications for development' associated with US academic and foreign policy interests during the Cold War. Once again, the architects for this deeply ahistorical and technology-led mode of rapid modernization are institutional actors located in the 'developed' world, but this time the geography of 'development' has shifted. The centres of the post-Fordist economy are based as much in Tokyo as in London and New York, but also incorporate cities and regions from across Asia, Eastern Europe, Latin America, the Middle East and, to a lesser extent, Africa. We saw in Chapter 5 how this new form of splintered urbanism fosters uneven global integration within Europe and North America, raising new redistributive questions about ICTs and social policies. These range from education and employment to the environment and affect low-income communities, historically marginalized minority groups and new immigrants, and of course women members of all these communities will experience the burdens of poverty and inequality even more intensely. There are similar sets of concerns emerging in the global cities and regions of the South, but here the promise of the IS is based on the often implicit assumption that reregulating policy objectives to attract foreign investment in ICT industries will in itself lead to educational and employment opportunities for significant numbers of workers, including women targeted by the 'pink-collar' service industries and manufacturing. We argue that, in both the North and the South, there is a compelling need to research such implicit policy questions, balancing the central concerns of employment generation with broader social concerns about the environment and sustainability, and claims for access to the benefits of the 'new economy' by those who have remained at its margins. This requires incorporating perspectives of workers and communities who are linked by industries across national borders, as well as paying attention to those left behind and outside the necessarily limited imagination of the dominant IS vision.

In Chapter 5 we saw how competing but symmetrical visions of the IS as imagined by EU and US state representatives institutionalized the legitimacy of corporate actors to set the parameters of policy design. Northern state actors, especially the US and the UK, have not flinched at capitulating on the new bounds of the 'free flow of information' in the current context of the 'War on Terror'. The militarization of new communication technologies and their use as surveillance machinery is being supported by a transnational industrial complex eager to protect the domain of e-commerce at any cost. Control of communications reflects the political and economic restraints of the market economy, on the one hand, and the 'paradox' of the seeming diffusion of politics and economics through globalization/internationalization with the increase in restrictive civic policies in the local/national territory, on the other. These trends, increased securitization of communication policy, militarization of technology, subjugation of the civic to the 'economic' in matters of communication liberties, are not exclusive of the 'digital' age, but they are exacerbated when contrasting the euphoric proclamations of the potential of ICTs. As with multistakeholderism within the WSIS, civil society organizations are positioned to raise welfare and humanitarian concerns in contrast to state and corporate actors, and their role is often seen as oppositional or at least reformist in multilateral governance.

In Chapter 6, we argued that any humanitarian agenda that seeks to displace the dominant neoliberal vision of the information society must contend with questions of recognition, redistribution and representation. We drew from feminist theory and practice that has grappled with the difficult dilemma of articulating a transnational social justice platform while recognizing the foundational need to acknowledge difference. In this chapter, we traced how the shift from the failed state-centric NWICO vision of social justice was replaced by the institutional ascendancy of CSOs based primarily in the North to define and articulate a social justice alternative within the WSIS process. We argued that despite progress in the area of Internet Governance and the opportunity for CSOs to create new networks of social activism in the ICT area, the real limitations of the heavily centralized and bureaucratized process of civil society engagement in the WSIS must also be acknowledged. Specifically, we focused on the ways in which narrow claims for recognition in the area of freedom of information displaced both more expansive claims for recognition of community rights as well as meaningful claims for redistribution. It is in this light that we must question the legitimacy of CSOs as the representative voice of public interest in the field of global communications policy especially as private capital adeptly masters the discourse of sustainable and multicultural info-development.

The last section of Chapter 6 examined gender advocacy within the WSIS to contend that the Gender Caucus can be seen as a site of progressive institutional engagement, offering some lessons for researchers and activists in the field of global communications policy. First and foremost, feminist advocacy within the WSIS process formulated redistributive claims over appropriate technology and ICT access through claims for recognition marked by difference based primarily but not exclusively on gender. This framing of questions of access around identity resonates with wider publics because it explicitly situates the technocratic terms of the debate in a wider political and cultural context. Secondly, the Gender Caucus, especially through its regional meetings, was a site of open discussions about representation within transnational civil society, and the difficult but necessary need to balance the articulation of universal values like human rights with attention to difference. Within feminist theory and practice, this has not led to the abandonment of core universal values or emancipatory visions for change, but it has led to greater attention to cultural practice and historical difference.

These lessons provide an important template for communications policy scholars and activists engaged in the implementation and follow-up stages of the WSIS process, and well beyond.[2]

Notes

1. One area within the field of global communications policy that deserves much more discussion than has been possible in this text is intellectual property rights regimes and the oppositional social movements around open-source software platforms and alternatives such as creative commons licenses for digital content (Lessig 2004; Vaidyanathan 2001). We feel that our larger conceptual framework offering a historical and culturally grounded critique holds true, while this added empirical focus would open up a variety of new questions for debate

and introduce a range of new actors (activists, for example) in the policy arena.

2. There has been much reflection and analysis of the WSIS process, civil society and the larger institutional and political context. For more see: Special Issue on WSIS in Global Media and Communication 1 (3)(2005): 357–73; Lovink and Soenke (eds) 2005; Raboy and Landry (2005).

Bibliography

Abramson, Bram Dor and Marc Raboy (1999), 'Policy globalization and the "Information Society": a view from Canada', *Telecommunications Policy* 23 (10): 775–91.

Abu-Lugodh, Lila (2004), *Dramas of Nationhood: The Politics of Television in Egypt*. Chicago: University of Chicago Press.

Accusoto, Pablo and Niki Johnson (2005), 'Financing the Information Society in the South: a global public goods perspective', in Instituto del Tercer Mundo (ITeM), *Information Society for the South: Vision or Hallucination? Briefing Papers towards the World Summit on the Information Society*, Montevideo, Uruguay: ITEM, pp. 13–46.

Adam, Alison (2000), 'Gender and computer ethics in the Internet Age', The Computer Professionals for Social Responsibility (CPSR), *Newsletter* 18 (1). http://archive.cpsr.net/publications/newsletters/issues/2000/Winter2000/adam.html (accessed on 1 November 2002).

Agambem, Girogio (2004), *The State of Exception*, Chicago: University of Chicago Press.

Aksoy, Asutosh and Kevin Robbins (2002), 'Banal transnationalism: the difference that television makes', WPTC-02-08, Oxford: ECRC Transantional Communities Programme.

Albelda, Randy and Chris Tilly (1994), 'Towards a broader vision: race, gender, and labor market segmentation in the social structure of accumulation framework', in David M. Kotz, Teresa McDonough and Michael Reich (eds), *Social Structures of Accumulation: The Political Economy of Growth and Crisis*, New York: Cambridge University Press, pp. 172–96.

Alfonso, Carlos (2005), 'Internet Governance: a review in the context of the WSIS process', in Instituto del Tercer Mundo (ITeM), *Information Society for the South: Vision or Hallucination? Briefing Papers towards the World Summit on the Information Society*, Montevideo, Uruguay: ITEM, pp. 129–42.

Alhassan, Amin (2004), 'Communication and the postcolonial nation-state: a new political economic research agenda', in Mehdi Semati (ed.), *New Frontiers in International Communication Theory*, Boulder: Roman & Littlefield, pp. 55–70.

Alston, Richard (1998), 'Government digital television bill passes Senate', Media Release 130/98, 3 July, Parliament House, Canberra [Online]. Available: http://www.dcita.gov.au/graphics_welcome.html

Alvarez, Sonia, Evalina Dagnino and Arturo Escobar (eds)(1998), *Culture of Politics, Politics of Cultures: Re-Visioning Latin American Social Movements*, Boulder, CO: Westview Press.

Amsden, Alice (1989), *Asia's Next Giant: South Korea and Late Industrialization*, Oxford: Oxford University Press.

Anand, Anita and Mahesh Uppal (2002), 'Engendering management and regulation of ICTs: narrowing the digital divide for women'. At UN/INSTRAW Virtual Seminar series on Gender and ICTs, seminar 1: 'Are ICTs gender neutral?' 1–12 July 2002. http://www.un-instraw.org/en/ (accessed on 19 July 2002).

Anderson, Benedict (1991), *Imagined Communities: Reflections on the Origins and Spread of Nationalism*, New York: Verso.

Appadurai, Arjun (1996), *Modernity at Large: Cultural Dimensions of Globalization*, Minneapolis: University of Minnesota Press.

Appleton, Josie (2001), *Lifting the Veil*, 30 October, Spiked-Politics http://www.spiked-online.com/articles/00000002D2A0.htm

Association for Progressive Communications (APC), *Women: Gender Evaluation Methodology (GEM) for Internet and ICTs*. http://www.apcwomen.org/gem (accessed on 14 June 2004).

Audenhove, Leo van, Jean-Claude Burgelman, Gert Nulens and Bart Cammaerts (1999), 'Information society policy in the developing world: a critical assessment', Third World Quarterly 20 (2): 387–404.

Aufderheide, Patricia (1999), *Communication Policy and Public Interest: The Telecommunications Act of 1996*, New York: Guildford Press.

Aufderheide, Patricia (2000), *The Daily Planet: A Critic on the Capitalist Culture Beat*, Minneapolis: University of Minnesota Press.

Baiocchi, Gianpaolo (2005), *Militants and Citizens: The Politics of Participatory Democracy in Porto Alegre*, Palo Alto, CA: Stanford University Press.

Baldoz, Rick, Charles Koelbler and Philip Kraft (eds)(2001), *The Critical Study of Work: Labour, Technology and Global Production*, Philadelphia: Temple University Press.

Bandow, Doug (1994), 'The IMF: a record of addiction and failure', in Doug Bandow and Ian Vasquez (eds), *Perpetuating Poverty: The World Bank, the IMF, and the Developing World*, Washington DC: The CATO Institute, pp. 15–36.

Banks, Karen (2005), 'Summitry and strategies', Eurozine. http://www.eurozine.com/articles/2005-10-19-banks-en.html (accessed on 1 December 2005).

Bauermann, Susanne (2000), 'Frauen und Technik: die unsichtbaren Mauern des Kapitalismus', *Marxistische Blaetter*, 38 (2 February): 17–21.

Beale, Alison (1999), 'From "Sophie's Choice" to consumer choice: framing gender in cultural policy', *Media, Culture and Society* 21 (4): 435–58.

Beale, Alison (2002), 'Gender and transversal cultural policies', in M. Raboy (ed.), *Global Media Policy in the New Millennium*, Luton: Luton University Press, pp. 199–214.

Bell, Daniel (1973), *The Coming of the Post-Industrial Society*, New York: Basic Books.

Belson, Ken (2005), 'Dial M for merger', *New York Times* (28 January): C1.

Benhabib, Seyla (2004), *Claims of Culture: Equality and Diversity in the Global Era*, Princeton: Princeton University Press.

Berizen, Mabel (1999), 'Politics and belonging: emotion, nation, and identity in facist Italy', in George Steinmentz (ed.), *State/Culture State-Formation after the Cultural Turn*, Ithaca: Cornell University Press, pp. 355–77.

Bernard, Elaine (1982), *The Long Distance Feeling: A History of the Telecommunications Workers Union*, Toronto: New Star Books.

Bernard, Elaine and Sid Schnaid (1998), 'Fighting neoliberalism in Canadian telecommunications', in Robert McChesney, Ellen Mieksens Woods and John Bellamy Foster (eds), *Capitalism and the Information Age: The Political Economy of the Global Communication Revolution*, New York: Monthly Review Press, pp. 140–68.

Bernier, Ivan (2004), 'The Recent Free Trade Agreements of the United States as Illustration of Their New Strategy Regarding the Audiovisual Sector', *Media Trade Monitor*. http://www.mediatrademonitor.org/taxonomy/page/or/36 (accessed on 22 November 2004).

Bobrow, Davis B., Heinz Beulau, Martin Landau, Charles O. Jones and Robert Axelrod (1977), 'The place of policy analysis in political science: five perspectives', *American Journal of Political Science* 21 (2): 415–33.

Born, Georgina (2003), 'Strategy, positioning and projection in digital television: Channel Four and the commercialization of public service broadcasting in the UK', *Media Culture and Society* 25 (6): 774–99.

Bourdieu, Pierre (1999), 'Rethinking the state: genesis and structure of the bureaucratic field', in George Steinmentz (ed.), *State/Culture State-Formation after the Cultural Turn*. Ithaca: Cornell University Press, pp. 53–75.

Bourdieu, Pierre and Alain Accardo (eds)(1999), *The Weight of the World: Social Suffering in Contemporary Society*, Palo Alto: Stanford University Press.

Bourdieu, Pierre and Loïc J. D. Waquant (1992), *An Invitation to Reflexive Sociology*, Chicago : University of Chicago Press.

Bovens, Mark (2002), 'Information rights: citizenship in the Information Society', *The Journal of Political Philosophy* 10 (3): 317–41.

Braman, Sandra (1991), 'The impact of confidence-building measures on information policy', in Kaarle Nordenstreng and Wolfgang Kleinwächter (eds), *Confidence-building in the Non-military Field*, Tampere, Finland: University of Tampere, pp. 47–58.

Braman, Sandra (1998), 'The right to create, *Cultural Policy in the Fourth Stage of the Information Society Gazette*, 60 (1): 77–91.

Braman, Sandra (1999), 'The telecommunications infrastructure and invention, innovation, and diffusion processes', in Stuart MacDonald and Gary Madden (eds), *Telecommunications and Socio-economic Development*, Amsterdam: North-Holland, pp. 13–24.

Brown, Allan (2002), 'Different paths: a comparison of the introduction of digital terrestrial television in Australia and Finland', *The International Journal on Media Management*, 4 (4): 277–86.

Burawoy, Michael (2003), 'For a sociological Marxism: the complementary convergence of Antonio Gramsci and Karl Polanyi', *Politics and Society*, 31 (2): 193–261.

Burchell, Graham, Colin Gordon and Peter Miller (eds)(1991), *The Foucault Effect : Studies in Governmentality*, London: Harvester Wheatsheaf.

Burgelman, Jean-Claude and Peter Perceval (1996), 'Belgium: the politics of public broadcasting', in M. Raboy, Public Broadcasting for the 21st Century, Whitstable, Kent: John Libbey Media/University of Luton.

Busaniche, Beatriz (2005), 'Civil society in the carousel: who wins, who loses and who is forgotten by the multistakeholder approach?', *Visions in Process II The World Summit on the Information Society*, Berlin: Heinrich Boll Foundation, pp. 46–52.

Butler, Judith (2004), *Precarious Life: The Power of Mourning and Violence*, New York: Verso.

Byerly, Carolyn (2004), 'Women and the concentration of media ownership', in R. R. Rush, C. Oukrup and P. Creedon (eds), *Women in Journalism and Mass Communication*, Mahwah, NJ: Lawrence Erlbaum Associates.

Calabrese, Andrew (1999), 'The welfare state, the Information Society, and the ambivalence of social movements', in Andrew Calabrese and Jean-Claude Burgelman (eds), *Communication, Citizenship, and Social Policy: Rethinking the Limits of the Welfare State*, Boulder: Rowan & Littlefield Publishers Inc., pp. 259–77.

Calabrese, Andrew (2004), 'The promise of civil society: a global movement for communication rights', *Continuum: Journal of Media and Cultural Studies* 18 (3): 317–29.

Cammaerts, Bart and Nico Carpentier (2005), 'The unbearable lightness of full participation in a global context: WSIS and civil society participation', in J. Servaes and N. Carpentier (eds), *Deconstructing WSIS: Towards a Sustainable Agenda for the Future Information Society*, Bristol: Intellect, pp. 17–49.

Castells, Manuel (1996), *The Rise of the Network Society (Volume I)*, Cambridge, MA: Blackwell.

Castells, Manuel (2003) The Internet Galaxy: Reflections on the Internet, Business and Society. Oxford: Oxford University Press.

Chadha, Kalyani and Anandam Kavoori (2000), 'Media imperialism revisited: some findings from the Asian case', *Media, Culture & Society* 22: 415–32.

Chakrabarty, Dipesh (2000), *Provincialising Europe: Postcolonial Thought and Historical Difference*, Princeton, NJ: Princeton University Press.

Chakravartty, Paula (2001a), 'Flexible citizens and the Internet: the global politics of local high-tech development in India', *Emergences: Journal for the Study of Media and Composite Cultures* 11 (1): 69–88.

Chakravartty, Paula (2001b), 'Laboring to be a citizen: trade unions, cyberpopulism and public interest in India', in M. Pendakur (ed.), *Citizens at the*

Crossroads: Whose Information Economy?, Ottawa: Government of Canada, pp. 65–78.

Chakravartty, Paula (2004), 'Telecommunications, development and the state: a post-colonial critique', *Media, Culture and Society* 26 (2): 227–49.

Chakravartty, Paula (2005), 'Weak winners of globalizations: Indian H-1B workers in the American information economy', *Asian American Policy Index (AAPI) Nexus*, 3 (2): 59–84.

Chakravartty, Paula and Yuezhi Zhao (eds), (forthcoming 2007), *Global Communication: Toward a Transcultural Political Economy*, Boulder, CO: Rowan and Littlefield.

Chalaby, Jean K. and Glen Segell (1999), 'The broadcasting media in the age of risk: the advent of digital television', *New Media and Society* 1 (3): 351–68.

Chandhoke, Neera (2001), 'The limits of global civil society', in Helmut Anheier, Marlies Glasius and Mary Kaldor (eds), *Global Civil Society*, Oxford: Oxford University Press, pp. 79–101.

Chandhoke, Neera (2005), 'Revisiting the crisis of representation thesis: the Indian context', *Democratization* 12 (3): 308–30.

Chatterjee, Partha (1993), *The Nation and Its Fragments: Colonial and Postcolonial Histories*, Princeton, NJ: Princeton University Press.

Chatterjee, Partha (2004), *The Politics of the Governed: Reflections on Popular Politics in Most of the World*, New York: Columbia University Press.

Chatterjee, Piya (2001), *A Time for Tea: Women, Labor, and Post/Colonial Politics on an Indian Plantation*, Chappel Hill, NC: Duke University Press.

CIA (2005), *The World Factbook*. http://www.odci.gov/cia/publications/factbook/rankorder/2153rank.html (accessed on 3 April 2005).

Civil Society Statement (2005), *Much More Could Have Been Achieved: Civil Society Statement on the World Summit on the Information Society*. 18 December 2005. http://www.worldsummit2003.de/download_en/WSIS-CS-summit-statement-rev1-23-12-2005-en.pdf (accessed on 10 January 2006).

Clegg, Sue (2001), 'Theorising the machine: gender, education and computing', *Gender and Education* 13 (3): 307–24.

Cockburn, Cynthia (1998), 'Technology, production and power', in Gill Kirkup and Laurie Smith Keller, *Inventing Women: Science Technology and Gender*, Cambridge: Polity/Oxford University Press, pp. 196–211.

Cockburn, Cynthia and Susan Ormrod (1993), *Gender and Technology in the Making*, London: Sage.

Cogburn, D. L. (2003), 'Governing global information and communications policy: emergent regime formation and the impact on Africa', *Telecommunications Policy* 27: 135–53.

Cohen, Jean and Andrew Arato (1992), *Civil Society and Political Theory*, Cambridge, MA: MIT Press.

Collins, Richard (1994), *Broadcasting and Audio-visual Policy in the European Single Market*, London: Libbey.

Collins, Richard (1998), *From Satellite to Single Market*, London: LSE Books/Routledge.

Collins, Richard (2003), 'Enter the Grecian horse? Regulation of foreign ownership of the media in the UK', *Policy Studies* 24 (1): 17–31.

Commission of the European Communities (1993), *Growth, Competitiveness, Employment: Challenges and Ways forward into the 21st Century*, White Paper, COM (93) 700 final/A and B, 5 December 1993. Bulletin of the European Communities, Supplement 6/93.

Commission of the European Communities (2000a), *eEurope: An Information Society for All Communication on a Commission Initiative for the Special European Council of Lisbon, 23 and 24 March 2000*. http://www.e-europestandards.org/Docs/eeurope_initiative.pdf

Commission of the European Communities (2000b), *IS Plan for i2010 – a European Information Society for Growth and Employment.*

Commission of the European Communities (2006), Communication from the Commission to the European Parliament, the European Economic and Social Committee and the Committee of the Regions: i2010 – a European Information Society for Growth and Employment, Brussels 1.6.2005 COM(2005) 229 final.

Council (1989), 'Council Directive 89/552/EEC of 3 October 1989 on the coordination of certain provisions laid down by law, regulation or administrative action in Member States concerning the pursuit of television broadcasting activities', *Official Journal L 298 17/10/1989 P. 0023–0030.*

Cowhey, Peter and Mikhail M. Klimenko (1999), *The WTO Agreement and Telecommunication Policy Reforms*, Washington DC: World Bank. www.worldbank.org/trade (accessed on 15 January 2004).

Crow, Barbara and Michael Longford (2004), *Digital Activism in Canada*, Canadian Research Alliance for Community Innovation and Networking (CRACIN), in http://www.fis.utoronto.ca/research/iprp/cracin/publications/final.htm

Cuilenburg, Jan van and Dennis McQuail (2003), 'Media policy paradigm shifts: towards a new communications paradigm, *European Journal of Communication* 18 (2): 181–207.

Dany, Charlotte (2004), Civil Society and Preparations for WSIS 2003: Did Input Lead to Influence?', Heinrich-Böll-Foundation. http://www.worldsummit2003.de/en/web/615.htm (accessed on 5 March 2005).

DCMCS (Department of Media Culture and Sport)(2004), *Review of the BBC's Royal Charter What You Said about the BBC* http://www. bbccharterreview.org.uk/pdf_documents/what_you_said_aboutthe_BBC.pdf

Dicken, Peter (2003), *Global Shift, Fourth Edition: Reshaping the Global Map in the 21st Century*, London: Guilford Press.

Downing, John (2001), *Radical Media: Rebellious Communication and Social Movements*. London: Sage.

Dubb, Steve (1999), *Logics of Resistance: Globalization and Telephone Unionism in Mexico and British Columbia (Transnational Business and Corporate Culture: Problems and Opportunities)*, New York: Garland Publishing.

Dunn, Hopeton (1995), *Globalisation, Communication and Caribbean Identity*, Kingston: Ian Randall Press.

ECA (Economic Commission for Africa)(1996), *African Information Society Initiative (AISI): An Action Framework to Build Africa's Information and Communication Infrastructure*, Addis Ababa: ECA.

ECA (Economic Commission for Africa)(2003), *Briefing Paper towards an Information Society in Africa: The Case for National Policies*, http://www.uneca.org/aisi/docs/AISIBriefingPaperNo1.PDF

EET (2003), *Telecommunications in Greece* http://www.eett.gr/eng_pages/publications/Pepragmena/Pepragmena2003/Telecommunications2.pdf

Eisner Gillett, Sharon (1999), 'Universal service: defining the policy goals in the age of the Internet', *The Information Society* 16 (2): 147–9.

EP and Council (1997), 'Directive 97/36/EC of the European Parliament and of the Council of 30 June 1997 amending Council Directive 89/552/EEC on the coordination of certain provisions laid down by law, regulation or administrative action in Member States concerning the pursuit of television broadcasting activities', *Official Journal L 202, 30/07/1997 P. 0060–0070*.

Ermert, Monika (2005), 'Intellectual property issues kept off WSIS agenda', *IP-Watch*. http://www.ip-watch.org/weblog/wp-trackback.php/158

Erni, John Nguyet (2004), 'Global AIDS, IT, and critical humanisms: reframing international health communication', in Mehdi Semati (ed.), *New Frontiers in International Communication Theory*, Boulder: Roman & Littlefield, pp. 71–88.

Escobar, Arturo (1994), *Encountering Development: The Making and Unmaking of the Third World*, Princeton, NJ: Princeton University Press.

Escobar, Arturo (1998), 'Whose knowledge, whose nature? Biodiversity, conservation, and the political ecology of social', *Journal of Political Ecology*. http://www.ikap-mmsea.com/resource/Escobar.pdf

Etzkowitz, Henry Kemelgor, Carol Neuschatz, Michael Uzzi and Brian Uzzi (1994), 'Barriers to women in academic science and engineering', in Willie Pearson Jr. and Irwin Fechter (eds), *Who Will Do Science? Educating the Next Generation*, Baltimore: Johns Hopkins University Press, pp. 43–67.

European Commission (2000), *Measuring Information Society 2000: A Eurobarometer Survey Carried Out for the European Commission by INRA*, Brussels: European Coordination Office.

European Commission (2001), *Can Gender Equality Reform Science?* http://europa.eu.int/comm/research/press/2001/pr1705en.html (accessed on 24 January 2002).

European Commission (2005a) *Communication from the Commission to the Council, the European Parliament, the European Economic and Social Committee and the Committee of the Regions 'i2010 – a European Information Society for Growth and Employment'*, Brussels 1.6.2005, COM(2005) 229 final.

European Commission (2005b), *i2010: A European Information Society for Growth and Employment*, Communication from the Commission to the Council, the European Parliament, the European Economic and Social Committee and the Committee of the Regions, COM(2005) 229 final, Brussels: European Commission.

European Commission (2005a c), 'Issues paper for the Liverpool Audiovisual Conference, Rules Applicable to Audiovisual Content Services July 2005'. http://europa.eu.int/comm./avpolicy

European Commission (2005d), *Proposal for a Directive of the European Parliament and of the Council Amending Council Directive 89/552/EEC on the Coordination of Certain Provisions Laid Down by Law, Regulation or Administrative Action in Member States concerning the Pursuit of Television Broadcasting Activities*, Brussels 13.12.2005, COM(2005) 646 final.

European Parliament (1998), *Cohesion and Information Society A4-0399/97 Resolution on the Commission Communication on Cohesion and the Information Society*, COM(97)0007-C4-0044/97, Brussels: European Parliament.

Evans, Peter (1979), *Dependent Development: The Alliance of Multinational, State and Local Capital in Brazil*, Princeton, NJ: Princeton University Press.

Evans, Peter (1995), *Embedded Autonomy: States and Industrial Transformation*, Princeton, NJ: Princeton University Press.

Ferguson, Kathy (1984), *The Feminist Case against Bureaucracy*, Philadelphia, PA: Temple University Press.

Flew, Terry (2002), 'Broadcasting and the Social Contract', in Marc Raboy (ed.), *Global Media Policy in the New Millennium*, Luton: University of Luton Press, pp. 113–30.

Fountain, Jane E. (2000), 'Constructing the information society: women, information technology and design', *Technology in Society* 22: 45–62.

Fraser, Nancy (1989), *Unruly Practices: Power, Discourse and Gender in Contemporary Social Theory*, Minneapolis: University of Minnesota Press.

Fraser, Nancy (2001), 'Recognition without ethics?', *Theory Culture and Society* 18 (2–3): 21–42.

Fraser, Nancy and Axel Honneth (2003), *Redistribution or Recognition: A Political-Philosophical Exchange*, New York: Verso.

Fraser, Nancy and Nancy Naples (2004), 'To interpret the world and to change it: an interview with Nancy Fraser', *Signs* 29 (4): 1103–24.

Freeman, Carla (2000), *High-Tech and High Heels in a Global Economy*, Chappel Hill: Duke University Press.

Friedman, Thomas (2005), *The World Is Flat: A Brief History of the Twenty-First Century*, New York: Farrar, Straus and Giroux.

G7 (1997), Conclusions of G7 Summit 'Information Society Conference'. http://europa.eu.int/ISPO/docs/services/docs/1997/doc_95_2_en.doc (accessed on 29 March 2005) DOC/95/2 of 1995-02-26.

G7 Summit 'Information Society' (1995), Conclusions of the G7 Summit 'Information Society Conference'. http://europa.eu.int/ISPO/intcoop/g8/i_g8conference.html

G8 Summit (2000), *The Okinawa Charter on Global Information Society*. http://www.g8.fr/evian/english/navigation/g8_documents/archives_from_previous_summits/okinawa_summit_-_2000/okinawa_charter_on_global_information_society.html (accessed on 10 December 2005).

Galtung, Jon and R. C. Vincent (1993), *Global Glasnost: Toward a New World Information and Communication Order?*, Creskill: Hampton Press.

Garnham, Nicholas (1990), *Capitalism and Communication*, Thousand Oaks, CA: Sage.

Garnham, Nicholas (2000), *Emancipation, the Media and Modernity: Arguments about Media and Social Theory*, Oxford: Oxford University Press.

Garnham, Nicholas and Robin Mansell (1991), *Universal Service and Rate Restructuring in Telecommunications*, OECD/ICCP Report No. 23, Paris: OECD.

Gates, Bill (1999), *Business @ the Speed of Thought: Using a Digital Nervous System*, New York: Warner Books.

GBD (2002), *Fourth Annual Conference of the Global Business Dialogue on Electronic Commerce*. http://www.gbde.org/pdf/BrusselsDeclaration.pdf

GBD (2004), *Executive Summary* http://www.gbde.org/pdf/recommendations/GBDe2004Final.pdf (accessed on 10 March 2005).

George, Susan (1992), *The Debt Boomerang: How Third World Debt Harms Us All*, Boulder CO: Westview.

George, Susanna (2003), 'NGO Gender Strategies Working Group Intervention', *Isis International Manila*. http://www.isiswomen.org/onsite/wsis/ngo-gsw-intervention.html (accessed on 20 November 2005).

Gerbner, George, Hamid Mowlana and Kaarle Nordenstraang (1993), *The Global Media Debate*, Norwood: Ablex.

Gil, Gilberto (2005), Transcript of Speech at NYU 'Voices of Latin American Leaders'. http://www.nyu.edu/voices/rsvp?action=4&projectid=7 (accessed on 10 November 2005).

Gillespie, Judith A. (1998), 'The new civic society in the information age: a comparative analysis of Mongolian models of women's empowerment', *Mongolian Studies* 21: 1–20.

Giroux, Henry A. (2004), *The Terror of Neoliberalism: Authoritarianism and the Eclipse of Democracy*, Boulder/London: Paradigm Publishers.

Golding, Peter (1974), 'The media's role in national development: critique of a theoretical orthodoxy', *Journal of Communication* 24 (3): 39–53.

Goldsmith, Ben Thomas Julian, Tom O'Reagan and Stuart Cunningham (2002), 'Asserting cultural and social regulatory principles in converging media systems', in Marc Raboy (ed.), *Global Media Policy in the New Millennium*, Luton: University of Luton Press, pp. 93–112.

Gordon, Linda (1994), *Pitied But Not Entitled: Single Mothers and the History of Welfare*, Cambridge, MA: Harvard University Press.

Gore, Charles (2000), 'The rise and fall of the Washington consensus as a paradigm for developing countries', *World Development* 28 (5): 789–804.

Gowswami, Rahul (2003), 'This Very Uncivil Society', *Himal*, December, accessed on 29 January 2005. http://www.himalmag.com/2003/december/opinion.htm

Graham, Stephen and Simon Marvin (1996), *Telecommunications and the City: Electronic Spaces, Urban Places*, New York: Routledge.

Graham, Stephen and Simon Marvin (2000), 'Urban planning and the technological future of cities', in J. Wheeler, Y. Aoyama and B. Warf (eds), *Cities in the Telecommunications Age: The Fracturing of Geographies*, New York: Routledge, pp. 71–96.

Graham, Stephen and Simon Marvin (2001), *Splintering Urbanism: Networked Infrastructure, Technological Motilities and the Urban Condition*, New York: Routledge.

Grant, Nigel (1990), *Pirate of the Airwaves: The Story of Radio Free London*. n.p.: ITMA.

Green, Venus (2001), *Race on the Line: Gender, Labor and Technology in the Bell System*, Chappel Hill: Duke University Press.

Gross, Larry and Sasha Costanza-Chock (2004), 'The West and the rest: a drama in two acts and an epilogue', in Peter van der Veer and Shoma Munshi (eds), *Media, War and Terrorism: Responses from the Midddle East and Asia*, New York: Routledge, pp. 22–45.

Gross, P. (2004), 'Between reality and dream: Eastern European media transition, transformation, consolidation, and integration', *East European Politics and Societies* 18 (1): 110–31.

The Guardian (2004), 'Lord Burn's Report at a Glance', Tuesday 21 July. http://media.guardian.co.uk/broadcast/story/0,,1265185,00.html

Gunter, Karen (1994), 'Women and the information revolution: washed ashore by the third wave', *Women Work and Computerisation*, 57: 439–52.

Gupta, Akhil (1997), 'The song of the Non-Aligned World: transnational identities and the reinscription of space in late capitalism', in Akhil Gupta and James Ferguson (eds), *Culture, Power, Place: Explorations in Critical Anthropology*, Durham, NC: Duke University Press, pp. 179–202.

Gurumurthy, Anita (2005a), 'Civil society and feminist engagement in WSIS: some reflections' and 'Cake for the North, crumbs for the South: the political economy of the information society', papers presented at the Gender Perspectives on the Information Society – South Asia Pre-WSIS Seminar 18–19 April 2005. Permisssion to cite from author. http://www.itforchange.net/WSIS/gis/schedule.php (accessed on 15 May 2005).

Gurumurthy, Anita (2005b), 'Tracking the development agenda at WSIS', in Olga Drossou and Heike Jensen (eds), *Visions in Process II: The World Summit on the Information Society*, Berlin: Heinrich Boll Foundation, pp. 90–7.

Gurumurthy, Anita and Parminder Jeet Singh (2005), 'Political economy of the Information Society: a Southern view', in Instituto del Tercer Mundo (ITeM), *Information Society for the South: Vision or Hallucination?*, Montevideo, Uruguay: ITEM, pp. 103–16.

Gurstein, Michael (2005), 'Networking the networked/closing the loop: some notes on WSIS II'. http://incommuincacdo.info/aggregator/sources/42 (accessed on 1 December 2005).

Gustavsson, E. and B. Czarniawska (2004), 'Web woman: the on-line construction of corporate and gender images', *Organization* 11 (5): 651–70.

Habermas, Jürgen (ed.)(2001), *The Postnational Constellation: Political Essays*, Cambridge: Polity.

Hafkin, Nancy J. (2002), 'Are ICTs gender-neutral? A gender analysis of six case studies of multi-donor ICT projects', at UN/INSTRAW Virtual Seminar

Series on Gender and ICTs, seminar one: 'Are ICTs gender neutral?' 1–12 July 2002. http://www.un-instraw.org/en/ (accessed on 19 July 2002).

Hamelink, Cees J. (1994), *The Politics of World Communication*, London: Sage.

Hamelink, Cees J. (1995), *World Communication: Disempowerment & Self-empowerment*, London: Zed Books.

Hamelink, Cees J. (2003) 'CRIS and the Right to Communication: A Brief Response to Article 19'. http://www.crisinfo.org/content/view/full/157 (accessed on 24 November 2005).

Hamelink, Cees J. (2004), 'Did the WSIS achieve anything at all?', *Gazette: The International Journal for Communications Studies*, 66 (3/4): 281–90.

Hamm, Susanne (2001), 'Information communications technologies and violence against women', *Development*, 44 (3): 36–41.

Hansen, Thomas Blom and Finn Stepputat (eds)(2001), *States of Imagination: Ethnographic Explorations of the Postcolonial State*, Durham, NC: Duke University Press.

Hanson, Gordon H. (2001), *Should Countries Promote Direct Foreign Investment?*, UNCTAD G-24 Discussion Paper Series No. 9. http://www.unctad.org/en/docs/pogdsmdpbg24d9.en.pdf

Haraway, Donna J. (1991), *Simians, Cyborgs, and Women: The Reinvention of Nature*, New York: Routledge.

Harcourt, A. (2005), *The European Union and the Regulation of Media Markets*, Manchester: European Policy Research Unit, Manchester University Press.

Harrison, J. L. and L. M. Woods (2001), 'Defining European public service broadcasting', *European Journal of Communication* 16 (4): 477–504.

Harrison, Mark and J. Sinclair (2004), 'Globalization, nation, and television in Asia: the cases of India and China', *Television & New Media* 5 (1): 41–54.

Harvey, David (1989), *The Conditions of Post-Modernity: An Inquiry into the Origins of Cultural Change*, London: Blackwell.

Hay, Colin (2004), 'Common trajectories, variable paces, divergent outcomes? Models of European capitalism under conditions of complex economic interdependence', *Review of International Political Economy* 11 (2): 231–62.

Headrick, Daniel (1981), *The Tools of Empire: Technology and European Imperialism in the Nineteenth Century*, Oxford: Oxford University Press.

Held, David (1997), 'Democracy and Globalization', *Global Governance* 3 (3): 1–28.

Held, David (2002), 'National culture, the globalization of communications and the bounded political community', *Logos* 1 (3): 1–18.

Held, David (2004), *Global Covenant: The Social Democratic Alternative to the Washington Consensus*, London: Polity.

Held, David and Anthony McDrew (2002), *Globalisation Anti/Globalisation*, London: Polity Press.

Helie-Lucas, M. A. (2001), 'What is your tribe? Women's struggles and the construction of Muslimness', at Women Living under Muslim Laws, Dossier 23–24. http://www.wluml.org/english/pubsfulltxt.shtml?cmd%5B87%5D=i-87-2789

Hendy, David (2000), 'A political economy of radio in the digital age', *Journal of Radio Studies*, 7 (1): 213–34.

Herman, Edward S. and Robert W. McChesney (1998), *The Global Media: The New Missionaries of Corporate Capitalism*, London: Cassell.

Hides, Shaun (2006), 'Knowledge/information: an Internet symptomology', in K. Sarikakis and D. Thussu, *Ideologies of the Internet*, Cresskill, NJ: Hampton Press.

High Level Group on the Information Society (1994), *Recommendations to the European Council: Europe and the Global Information*. Accessible at http://europa.eu.int/ISPO/infosoc/backg/bangeman.html

Hills, Jill (1998), 'U.S. rules. OK?: telecommunications since the 1940s', in Robert W. McChesney, Ellen Meiksins Wood and John Bellamy Foster (eds), *Capitalism and the Information Age: The Political Economy of the Global Communication Revolution*, New York: Monthly Review Press, pp. 99–121.

Hirst, Paul and Grahame Thompson (1995), 'Globalization and the future of the nation-state', *Economy and Society* 24 (3): 408–42.

Hirst, Paul and Grahame Thompson (1999), *Globalization in Question: The International Economy and the Possibilities of Governance*, Cambridge: Polity Press.

Hoffmann-Riem, W. (1996), *Regulating Media: The Licensing and Supervision of Broadcasting in Six Countries*, New York: Guilford Press.

Hopkins, A. G. (1973), *An Economic History of West* Africa, Harlow: Longman.

Horwitz, Robert (1989), *The Irony of Regulatory Reform: The Deregulation of American Telecommunications*, New York: Oxford University Press.

Horwitz, Robert (2001), *Communication and Democratic Reform in South Africa*, New York: Cambridge University Press.

Howcroft, Debra (1999), 'The hyperbolic age of information: an empirical study of internet usage', *Information, Communication & Society* 2 (3): 277–99.

Hughes, Robert (2002), *Privatization and Modernization of Telecommunications in Latin America*, Conference Proceedings for the Southwestern Social Science Association. http://www1.appstate.edu/~stefanov/proceedings/hughes.htm (accessed on 6 February 2004).

Humphrey, J., R. Mansell, D. Pare and H. Schmitz (2003), *The Reality of E-commerce with Developing Countries*. http://www.lse.ac.uk/collections/media@lse/pdf/Report.pdf

Humphreys, Peter (1996), *Mass Media and Media Policy in Western Europe*, Manchester: Manchester University Press.

Huntington, Samuel (1968), *Political Order in Changing Societies*, New Haven: Yale University Press.

Huws, Ursula (2003), *The Making of a Cybertariat: Collected Essays*, New York: Monthly Review Press; London: Merlin Press.

Huyer, Sophie and Tatjana Sikoska (2003), *Overcoming the Gender Digital Divide: Understanding ICTs and Their Potential for the Empowerment of Women*, INSTRAW Research Paper Series 1. http://www.un-instraw.org/en/docs/gender_and_ict/Synthesis_Paper.pdf (accessed on 20 April 2005).

Institutio del Tercer Mundo (ITEM) (eds) (2005), *Information Society for the South: Vision of Hallucination*, Montevideo, Uruguay: ITEM.

International Centre for Public Enterprises (ICPE) and International Research and Training Institute for the Advancement of Women (INSTRAW)(1993), 'Social impact assessment of investment/acquisition of technology in developing countries, with particular reference to the position of women', *Public Enterprise* 13 (3–4): 239–56.

International Labour Office (2005), *World Employment Report 2004–2005 Employment, Productivity and Poverty Reduction*, Geneva: International Labour Office.

International Telecommunications Union (ITU) (1996), *The African Green Paper*, Telecommunications for Africa, Geneva: Telecommunications Development Bureau (BDT).

International Telecommunications Union (ITU) (2003), *World Telecommunications Development Report: Access Indicators for the Information Society*, Geneva: ITU.

International Telecommunications Union (ITU) (2005), Statistics and Analysis (various), available on http://www.itu.int/osg/spu/statistics/

Iwabuchi, Koichi (2002), *Recentering Globalization: Popular Culture and Japanese Transnationalism*, Durham, NC: Duke University Press.

Jakubowicz, Karol (1996), 'Poland: Prospects for Public and Civic Broadcasting', in M. Raboy (ed.), *Public Broadcasting for the 21st Century*, Luton: John Libbey Media/University of Luton Press, pp. 175–94.

Jakubowicz, Karol (2004), 'Ideas in our heads: introduction of PSB as part of media system change in Central and Eastern Europe', *European Journal of Communication* 19 (1): 53–74.

Jawara, Fatoumata and Aileen Kwa (2004), *Behind the Scenes at the WTO: The Real World of International Trade Negotiations*, 4th edn, London: Zed Press.

Jeffries, Stuart (2002), 'I am drawn to a racially pure society', *The Guardian*, Wednesday 1 May.

Jenkins, Rob (2001), 'Mistaking "governance" for "politics": foreign aid, democracy and the construction of civil society', in Sudipta Kaviraj and Sunil Khilnani (eds), *Civil Society: History and Possibilities*, Cambridge: Cambridge University Press, pp. 250–68.

Jensen, Heike (2005), 'Gender equality and the multistakeholder approach: WSIS as best practice', in Olga Drossou and Heiki Jensen (eds), *Visions in Process II: The World Summit on the Information Society*, Berlin: Heinrich Boll Foundation, pp. 53–62.

Jessop, Bob (1992), 'Fordism and post-Fordism: critique and reformulation', in A. J. Scott and M. J. Storper (eds), *Pathways to Regionalism and Industrial Development*, London: Routledge, pp. 43–65.

Jessop, Bob (1997), 'The regulation approach', *The Journal of Political Philosophy*, 5 (3): 287–326.

Jessop, Bob (1999), 'Narrating the future of the national economy and the national state: remarks on remapping regulation and reinventing governance', in George Steinmetz (ed.), *State/Culture: State-Formation after the Cultural Turn*, Ithaca, NY: Cornell University Press, pp. 378–406.

Jessop, Bob (2003), 'Regulationist and autopoeticist reflections on Polanyi's account of market economies and the market society', Lancaster: Department of Sociology, Lancaster University. www.comp.lancs.ac.uk/sociology/papers/jessop-regulationist-and-autopoieticist-reflections.pdf

Jhunjhunwala, Ashok, Sudhalakshmi Narasimhan and Anuradha Ramachandran (2004), *Enabling Rural India with Information and Communication Technology Initiatives*, ITU Symposium on Building Digital Bridges, Document BDB/09. http://www.itu.int/osg/spu/ni/digitalbridges/docs/casestudies/India.pdf (accessed on 15 March 2005).

Jorgensen, Rikke Frank and Meyrem Marzouki (2005), 'Human rights: the missing link', in Olga Droussou and Heike Jensen (eds), *Visions in Process II: The World Summit on the Information Society* , Berlin: Heinrich Boll Foundation, pp. 17–23.

Kabeer, Naila (2002), *The Power to Choose: Bangladeshi Women and Labour Market Decisions in London and Dhaka*, London: Verso.

Kabeer, Naila (2003), *Reversed Realities: Gender Hierarchies in Development Thought*, New York: Verso.

Kaldor, Mary (2003), *Global Civil Society: An Answer to War*, London: Polity Press.

Kaplan, Karen, Norma Alarcon and Minoo Moallem (1999), *Between Woman and Nation: Nationalisms, Transnational Feminisms and the State*, Durham, NC: Duke University Press.

Karim, Karim (2002), *Diaspora and Communication: Mapping the Globe*, New York: Routlege.

Kaviraj, Sudipta (2001), 'In search of civil society', in Sudipta Kaviraj and Sunil Khilnani (eds), *Civil Society: History and Possibilities*, Cambridge: Cambridge University Press, pp. 284–324.

Keane, John (2003), *Global Civil Society?*, Cambridge: Cambridge University Press.

Keck, Margaret and Katharine Sikkink (1998), *Activists beyond Borders?*, Princeton, NJ: Princeton University Press.

Keohane, Robert O. (2002), 'Global governance and democratic accountability', in David Held and Mathias Koenig-Archibugi (eds), *Taming Globalization. Frontiers of Governance*, Cambridge: Polity, pp. 130–59.

Kirkup, Gill (1998), 'The social construction of computers: hammers or harpsichords?', in Gill Kirkup and Laurie Smith Keller, *Inventing Women. Science Technology and Gender*. Cambridge: Polity/Oxford University Press, pp. 267–81.

Kirkup, Gill (2002), 'ICT as a tool for enhancing women's education opportunities; and new educational and professional opportunities for women in new technologies', United Nations Division for the Advancement of Women (DAW) Expert Group Meeting on 'Information and communication technologies and their impact on and use as an instrument for the advancement and empowerment of women', Seoul, Republic of Korea 11–14 November 2002. http://157.150.195.47/womenwatch/daw/egm/ict2002/reports/Kirkup%20paperwith%20refs.PDF (accessed on 25 August 2003).

Klein, Hans and Milton Mueller (2005), 'About ICANN: a proposal for structural reform', Concept paper by the Internet Governance Project, 5 April 2005. www.internetgovernance.org (accessed on 15 December 2005).

Klein, Hans (2005), *An Assessment of the WSIS Tunis 05 Outcomes*, 23 November 2005. http://www.ip3.gatech.edu/images/Significance_of_WSIS-II_Tunis-05.pdf

Kleinwächter, Wolfgang (2004a), 'Beyond ICANN Vs ITU? How WSIS tries to enter the new territory of Internet governance', *Gazette: The International Journal for Communication Studies*, 66 (3–4): 233–51.

Kleinwächter, Wolfgang (2004b) 'Multistakeholderism, a new form of interaction in the emerging global diplomacy of the 21st Century'. http://www.crisinfo.org/content/view/full/494 (accessed on 21 November 2005).

Korzeniewicz, Roberto P. and William C. Smith (2001), *Protest and Collaboration: Transnational Civil Society Networks and the Politics of Summitry and Free Trade in the Americas*, Miami: The Dante B. Fascell North–South Centre, University of Miami.

Kraidy, Marwan (2005), *Hybridity or the Cultural Logic of Globalization*, Philadelphia, PA: Temple University Press.

Laclau, Ernesto and Chantal Mouffe, (1985), *Hegemony and Socialist Strategy: Towards a Radical Democratic Politics*, London: Verso.

Lasswell, Harold D. (1951) 'The policy orientation', *The Policy Sciences*, Stanford: Stanford University Press.

Lee, Kelley (1996), *Global Telecommunications Regulation: A Political Economy Perspective*, London: Cassell.

Lerner, Daniel (1958), *The Passing of Traditional Society: Modernizing the Middle East*, New York: McMillan Press.

Lessig, Lawrence (2004), *Free Culture: How Big Media Uses Technology and the Law to Lock Down Culture and Control Creativity*, New York: Penguin.

Lewis, Justin and Toby Miller (2002), *Critical Cultural Policy Studies: A Reader*, Cambridge, MA: Blackwell Publishers.

Lovink, Geert and Florian Schneider (2002), 'A virtual world is possible: from tactical media to digital multitudes', *Nettime Post*. http://www.cyberaxe.org/04/pdf/lovink_schneider.pdf (accessed on 2 August 2005).

Lovink, Geert and Soenke Zehle (eds)(2005), *The Incommunicado Reader: Information Technology for Everybody Else*, Amsterdam: Institute of Network Cultures.

McChesney, Robert (1993), *Telecommunications, Mass Media, and Democracy*, New York: Oxford University Press.

McChesney, Robert (1999), *Rich Media, Poor Democracy*, New York: The New Press.

McChesney, Robert (2004), *The Problem of the Media*, New York: Monthly Review Press.

McChesney, Robert and Dan Schiller (2003), *The Political Economy of International Communications: Foundations for the Emerging Global Debate on Media Ownership and Regulation*, Technology, Business and Society Programme Paper Number 11, New York: United Nations Research Institute for Social Development.

McDowell, Stephen (1997), *Globalization, Liberalization and Policy Change: A Political Economy of India's Communicaitons Sector*, New York: St. Martin's Press.

McGuigan, Jim (1996), *Culture and the Public Sphere*, London: Routledge.

McLaughlin, Lisa (2004), 'Feminism and the political economy of transnational public space', *Sociological Review*, 52 (1): 156–75.

MacLean, Don, David Souter, James Deane and Sarah Lilley (2002), *Louder Voices: Strengthening Developing Country Participation in International ICT Decision-Making*, London: The Commonwealth Telecommunications Organisation.

McMichael, Philip (2003), *Development and Social Change: A Global Perspective*, Thousand Oaks, CA: Pine Forge Press.

Mamdani, Mahmoud (1996), *Citizen and Subject: Contemporary Africa and the Legacy of Late Colonialism*, Princeton, NJ: Princeton University Press.

Mansell, Robin (1994). *The New Telecommunications: A Political Economy of Network Evolution*, London: Sage.

Mansell, Robin (2001), 'Digital opportunities and the missing link for developing countries', *Oxford Journal of Economic Policy* 17 (2): 282–95.

Mansell, Robin (ed.)(2002), *Inside the Communication Revolution: Evolving Patterns of Social and Technical Interaction*, Oxford: Oxford University Press.

Marquette, Heather (2001), 'Corruption, democracy and the World Bank', *Crime, Law and Social Change*, 36: 395–407.

Martin-Barbero, Jesus (1993), *Communication, Culture and Hegemony: From Media to Mediation*, London: Sage.

Mathew, Biju and Jagdish Parikh (1996), 'The web as a marginalising technology: the structure of web-based resources', *South Asia Bulletin of Concerned Asian Scholars* 28 (3–4): 8–14.

Mattelart, Armand (2001), *The Information Society: An Introduction*, London: Sage.

Mattelart, Armand (2002), *Mapping World Communication: War, Progress, Culture*, Minneapolis: University of Minnesota Press.

Mbembe, Achille (2001), *On the Post-Colony*, Berkeley: University of California Press.

Meehan, Eileen R. and Ellen Riordan (eds)(2001), *Sex and Money: Feminism and Political Economy in the Media*, Minneapolis: University of Minnesota Press.

Melkote, Srinivaws and Leslie Steeves (2001), *Communication for Development in the Third World*, Thousand Oaks, CA: Sage.

Melody, William (1991), 'The Information Society: transnational economic context and its implications', in G. Sussman and J. Lent (eds), *Transnational Communications: Wiring the Third World*, London: Sage, pp. 27–41.

Melody, William (ed.) (1997), *Telecom Reform: Principles, Policies and Regulatory Practices*, Denmark: Technical University of Denmark.

Miles, Hugh (2005), *Al Jazeera: How Arab TV News Challenges America*, New York: Grove Press.

Millar, Jane and Nick Jagger (2001), *Women in ITEC Courses and Careers*, London: Department for Education and Skills, Department for Employment, The Women's Unit.

Millar, Melanie Stewart (1998), *Cracking the Gender Code: Who Rules the Wired World?*, Toronto: Second Story Press.

Miller, Toby, Nitin Govil, John McMurria and Richard Maxwell (2001), *Global Hollywood*, London: British Film Institute.

Miller, Toby and George Yudice (2002), *Cultural Policy*, Thousand Oaks, CA: Sage.

Mitchell, Timothy (2002), *Rule of Experts: Egypt, Techno-Politics, Modernity*, Berkeley: University of California Press.

Mitter, Swasti (2000), 'Teleworking and teletrade in India: diverse perspectives and visions', *Economic and Political Weekly* 35 (26): 2241–52.

Mitter, Swasti (2002), 'Globalisation and ICTs: employment opportunities for women', in Sophia Huyer and Swasti Mitter, *ICTs, Globalisation and Poverty Reduction: Gender Dimensions of the Knowledge Society Part I, Poverty Reduction, Gender Equality and the Knowledge Society: Digital Exclusion or Digital Opportunity?*, in http://gab.wigsat.org/partI.pdf

Mitter, Swasti and Shiela Rowbotham (1997), *Women Encounter Technology: Changing Patterns of Employment in the Third World*, New York: Routledge.

Mohanty, Chandra (2003), *Feminism without Borders: Decolonizing Theory, Practicing Solidarity*, Durham, NC: Duke University Press.

Moll, Marita and L. Shade (2001), 'Community networking in Canada: do you believe in magic?', in Marita Moll and L. Shade (eds), *E-Commerce vs. E-Commons: Communications in the Public Interest*, Ottawa: Canadian Centre for Policy Alternatives, pp. 165–81.

Moody, Kim (1988), *An Injury to All: The Decline of American Unionism*, New York: Verso.

Moore, Nick (1997), 'Neoliberal or dirigiste? Policies for an information society', *The Political Quarterly*: 276–83.

Mosco, Vincent (2004), *The Digital Sublime: Power and Cyberspace*, Cambridge, MA: MIT Press.

Mundkur, Anu and Piyoo Kochar (2005), *Mapping Gender in the Information Economy: From Reality to Discourse*, 31 October 2005, Bangkok, Thailand. http://itforchange.net/mambo/content/view/72/32/

Nair, Janaki (2005) *The Promise of the Metropolis: Bangalore's Twentieth Century*, New Delhi: Oxford University Press.

Naples, Nancy A. and Manisha Desai (2002), *Women's Activism and Globalization: Linking Local Struggles and Transnational Politics*, New York: Routledge.

The National Information Infrastructure (1993), *Agenda for Action*. http://www.ibiblio.org/nii/ nii/NII-Executive-Summary

National Telecommunications and Information Administration (NTIA)(1994), *Annual Report*, available on http://www.ntia.doc.gov/ntiahome/annualrpt/94repasc.html

Nauriayal, Bharat and Galal Ahmed (1995), *Regulating Telecommunications in Developing Countries*, World Bank Policy Research Working Paper No. 1520, World Bank, October. http://ssm.com/abstract=569212

Ng, Celia and Swasti Mitter (2005a), *Gender and the Digital Economy: Perspectives from the Developing World*, London: Sage Press.

Ng, Celia and Swasti Mitter (2005b), 'Valuing women's voices', *Gender, Technology and Development* 9 (2): 209–33.

Nicol, Chris (ed.)(2003), *ICT Policy: A Beginner's Handbook*, Montevideo, Uruguay.

Noam, Eli (1992), *Telecommunications in Europe*, Oxford: Oxford University Press.

Noam, Eli (1998), *Telecommunications in Latin America*, London: Oxford University Press.

Noll, Roger D. (1999), 'Telecommunications in developing countries', *AEI Joint Center for Regulatory Studies Working Paper*, No. 99–11. http://ssrn.com/abstract=181030

Noll, Roger D. (2002), 'Telecommunications reform in developing countries', in Anne Kreuger (ed.), *Economic Policy Reform: The Second Stage*, Chicago: University of Chicago Press, pp. 183–215.

NOP World (2001), 'Women in technology: an uncertain future says Deloitte & Touche survey'. http://www.roperasw.com/newsroom/news/n0106002.html (accessed on 13 November 2001).

Nordenstreng, Kaarle (1984), *The Mass Media Declaration of UNESCO*, Norwood, NJ: Ablex.

Nulens G. and L. van Audenhove (1999), 'An information society in Africa? An analysis of the information society policy of the World Bank, ITU and ECA', *Gazette: The International Journal of Communication Studies*, 61 (6): 451–71.

OECD (2001), *Economic Survey of Greece 2001*. http://www.oecd.org/document/18/0,2340,en_2649_34489_1917266_1_1_1_1,00.html (accessed on 29 March 2005).

OECD (2004) *2004 OECD Information Technology Outlook*. http://www.oecd.org/dataoecd/31/53/34238722.pdf (accessed on 29 March 2005).

Ohmae, Kenichi (1990), *The Borderless World: Power and Strategy in the Interlinked Economy*, New York: Harper Business.

Ohmae, Kenichi (1999), *The Borderless World: Power and Strategy in the Interlinked Economy*, rev. edn, New York: Harper Business.

Ong, Aihwa (2001), *Flexible Citizenship: The Cultural Logics of Transnationality*, Chappel Hill: Duke University Press.

Orloff, Anne (1999), 'Motherhood, work and welfare in the United States, Britain, Canada and Australia', in George Steinmetz (ed.), *State/Culture: State-Formation after the Cultural Turn*, Ithaca, NY: Cornell University Press, pp. 321–54.

Padovani, Claudia and Arjuna Tuzzi (2004), 'The WSIS as a world of words: building a common vision of the information society', *Continuum: Journal of Media and Cultural Studies* 18 (3): 360–79.

Page, David and William Crawley (2001), *Satellites over South Asia: Broadcasting, Culture and the Public Interest*, London: Sage.

Papatheodorou, F. and D. Machin (2003), 'The umbilical cord that was never cut: the post-dictatorial intimacy between the political elite and the mass media in Greece and Spain', *European Journal of Communication* 18 (1): 31–54.

Park, Donghyun (2000), 'The dichotomy between Northeast Asian capitalism and Southeast Asian capitalism', *Journal of the Asia Pacific Economy*, 5 (3): 234–54.

Parnis, Deborah (2000), 'Tuning in the future: digital technology and commercial radio broadcasting in Canada', *Journal of Canadian Studies*, 35 (3): 231–50.

Pauwels, Caroline and Jan Loisen (2003), 'The WTO and the audiovisual sector: economic free trade vs. cultural horse trading?', *European Journal of Communication* 18 (3): 219–313.

Pellow, David and Park, Lisa Sun-Hee (2002), Silicon Valley of Dreams: Immigrant Labor, Environmental Injustice, and the High Tech Global Economy, New York: New York University Press.

Petrazzini, Ben (1996a), *Competition in Telecoms: Implications for Universal Service and Employment*, Public Policy for the Private Sector, Note 96, Washington DC: World Bank.

Petrazzini, Ben (1996b), 'Telecommunications policy India: the political underpinnings of reform', *Telecommunications Policy* 20 (1): 39–51.

Pieterse, Jan Nederveen (2002), 'Global inequality: bringing politics back in', *Third World Quarterly* 23 (6): 1023–46.

Pinches, Michael (ed.)(1999), *Culture and Privilege in Capitalist Asia*, New York and London: Routledge.

Pinheiro, Armando Castelar (2003), *Regulatory Reform in Brazilian Infrastructure: Where Do We Stand?*, Institute for Applied Economic Research (IPEA) Paper No. 964. http://papers.ssrn.com/sol3/papers.cfm?abstract_id=482823

Polanyi, Karl (1957), *The Great Transformation: The Political and Economic Origins of Our Times*, Boston: Beacon Press.

Polanyi, Karl (1965), *The Great Transformation: The Political and Economic Origins of Our Time*, Boston: Beacon Press.

Pool, Ithiel de Sola (1983), *Technologies of Freedom*, Cambridge, MA: Belknap Press.

Prakash, Gyan (1999), *Another Reason: Science and Imagination in Modern India*, Princeton: Princeton University Press.

Preston, William Jr., Edward Herman and Herbert I. Schiller (1989), *Hope and Folly: The United States and UNESCO 1948–1985*, Minneapolis: University of Minnesota Press.

Raboy, Marc (1990), *Missed Opportunities: The Story of Canada's Broadcasting Policy*, Montreal/Kingston: McGill-Queen's University Press.

Raboy, Marc (1995), 'The role of public consultation in shaping the Canadian broadcasting system', *Canadian Journal of Political Science* 28 (3): 455–77.

Raboy, Marc (1996), Public Broadcasting for the 21st Century, Whitstable, Kent: John Libbey Media/University of Luton.

Raboy, Marc (2004a), 'WSIS as a political space in global media governance', *Continuum: Journal of Media and Cultural Studies* 18 (3): 345–59.

Raboy, Marc (2004b) 'The World Summit on the Information Society and its legacy for global governance', *Gazette: The International Journal for Communication Studies* 66 (3–4): 225–32.

Raboy, Marc and Normand Landry (2005), *Civil Society, Communication and Global Governance: Issues from the World Summit on the Information Society*, New York: Peter Lang.

Rafael, Vincente (2003), 'The cell phone and the crowd: messianic politics in the contemporary Philippines', *Public Culture* 15 (3): 399–425.

Rajagopal, Arvind (2001), *Politics after Television: Hindu Nationalism and the Reshaping of the Indian Public*, Cambridge: Cambridge University Press.

Roach, Colleen (1990), 'The movement for a new world information and communication order: a second wave?', *Media, Culture and Society* 12 (3): 283–307.

Roach, Colleen (1997), 'The Western world and the NWICO', in Peter Golding and Paul Harris (eds), *Beyond Cultural Imperialism: Globalisation, Communication and the New International Order*, London: Sage, pp. 94–116.

Robles, A. (1994), *French Theories of Regulation and Conceptions of the International Division of Labour*, New York: St. Martin's Press.

Rodino, Michelle (1997), 'Breaking out of binaries: reconceptualizing gender and its relationship to language in computer-mediated communication', *Journal of Computer-Mediated Communication*, 3 (3). http://www.ascusc.org/jcmc/vol3/issue3/rodino.html (accessed on 24 September 2002).

Rogers, Everett M. (1995), *Diffusion of Innovations*, 4th edn, New York: Free Press.

Ross, Andrew (2004), *Low Pay High Profile*, New York: New Press.

Ross, Lex Heerma van (ed.)(2002), *Class and Other Identities: Gender, Religion, and Ethnicity in the Writing of European Labor History*, London: Berghan Books.

Rush, R. R., C. E. Oukrop and P. Creedon (eds)(2004), *Seeking Equity for Women in Journalism and Mass Communication Education: A 30-year Update*, Mahwah, NJ: Lawrence Erlbaum.

Sadeque, Najma (2005), 'Feminist perspectives on gender in the information society: perspectives from Pakistan', paper presented at 'Gender perspectives on the information society': South Asia Pre-WSIS Seminar. http://www.itforchange.net/WSIS/gis/schedule.php (accessed on 15 May 2005).

Samarajiva, Rohan (2001), 'Regulating in an imperfect world: building independence through legitimacy', *Info*, 3 (5): 363–8.

Samarajiva, Rohan (2004), *Telecom Connectivity for the Rural and Urban Poor*, New York: Social Science Research Council. http://www.ssrc.org/programs/itic/publications/ITST_materials/samarajivabrief1.pdf. (accessed on 15 February 2005).

Samarajiva, Rohan and P. Shields (1990), 'Integration, telecommunication, and development: power in paradigms', *Journal of Communication*, 40 (3): 84–103.

Sarikakis, Katharine (2000), 'Citizenship and media policy in the semi-periphery: the Greek case', *Cyprus Review* 12 (2): 17–133.

Sarikakis, Katharine (2004a), 'Ideology and policy: notes on the shaping of the Internet', *First Monday*, 9 (8). http://www.firstmonday.org/issues/issue9_8/sarikakis/index.html

Sarikakis, Katharine (2004b), *British Media in a Global Era*, London: Arnold.

Sarikakis, Katharine (2004c), *Powers in Media Policy: The Challenge of the European Parliament*, Oxford, Bern: Peter Lang.

Sarikakis, Katharine (2005), 'Defending communicative spaces: the remits and limits of the European Parliament', *Gazette: The International Journal for Communications Studies*, 67 (2): 155–72.

Sarikakis, Katharine and George Terzis (2000),'Pleonastic exclusion from the European Information Society', *Telematics and Informatics* 17 (1–2): 105–28.

Sassen, Saskia (1999), *Globalization and Its Discontents: Essays on the New Mobility of People and Money*, New York: New Press.

Sassen, Saskia (2001), *The Global City: New York, London and Tokyo*, Princeton, NJ: Princeton University Press.

Sassen, Saskia (2002), 'Global cities and diasporic network: microsites in global civil society', in M. Glasius, M. Kaldor and H. Anheier (eds), *Global Civil Society*, Oxford: Oxford University Press, pp. 217–40.

Saunders, Robert, Jeremy Warford and Björn Wellenius (1994), *Telecommunications and Economic Development*, Baltimore: Johns Hopkins University Press.

Schiller, Dan (1999), *Digital Capitalism: Networking the Global Market System*, Cambridge, MA: MIT Press.

Schiller , Herbert I. (1992), *Mass Communications and American Empire* 2nd edn, Boulder, CO: Westview Press.

Schiller, Herbert I. (1996), *Information Inequality: The Deepening Social Crisis in America*, New York: Routledge.

Schiller, Herbert I. (2000), *Living in the Number One Country: Reflections from a Critic of American Empire*, New York: Seven Stories Press.

Schramm, Wilbur (1964), *Mass Media and National Development: The Role of Information in the Developing Countries*, Palo Alto, CA: Stanford University Press.

Scott, Anne, Lesley Semmens and Lynette Willoughby (1999), 'Women and the Internet: the natural history of a research project', *Information, Communication & Society* 2 (4): 541–65.

Seiter, Ellen (2005), *The Internet Playground: Children's Access, Entertainment and Mis-Education*, New York: Peter Lang.

Selian, Audrey N. and Kenneth Neil Cukier (2003), 'The World vs the Web: the UN's politicization of the Information Society; Geneva, December 2003', *Information Technologies and International Development* 1 (3–4): 133–8.

Sen, Krishan and Maila Stivens (eds)(1998), *Gender and Power in Affluent Asia*, New York: Routledge.

Servaes, Jan (1999), *Communication for Development: One World, Multiple Cultures*, Creskill, NJ: Hampton.

Shade, Leslie (2003), 'Here comes the DOT Force! The new cavalry for equity?', *Gazette: The International Journal for Communications Studies*, 65 (2): 107–20.

Shashikanth, Sangeeta (2005), 'Intellectual property and the WIPO "development agenda"', in Instituto del Tercer Mundo (ITeM), *Information Society for the South: Vision or Hallucination? Briefing Papers towards the World Summit on the Information Society*, Montevideo, Uruguay: ITEM, pp. 165–86.

Shiva, Vandana (1998), *Biopiracy: The Plunder of Nature and Knowledge*, Darlington: Green Books.

Shiva, Vandana (2000), *Stolen Harvest: The Hijacking of the Global Food Supply*, Beacon: South End.

Sinclair Jenny (2002), 'Women push for bigger role in IT', *The Business Review Weekly* 16 July. http://www.theage.com.au/articles/ 2002/07/15/ 1026185154228.html (accessed on 19 July 2002).

Sinclair, John (1999), *Latin American Television: A Global View*, Oxford: Oxford University Press.

Singh, J. P. (1999), *Leapfrogging Development? The Political Economy of Telecommunications Restructuring*, Albany: SUNY Press.

Siochrú, Seán Ó (2003), *Global Governance of Information and Communications Technologies: Implications for Transnational Civil Society Networking*, New York: Social Science Research Council Research Council. http://www.ssrc.org/ programs/itic (accessed on 15 December 2004).

Siochrú, Seán Ó (2004), 'Will the real WSIS please stand up: the historic encounter between the information society and the communciation society', *Gazette: The International Journal of Communication Studies*, 66 (3/4): 203–24.

Siochrú, Seán Ó, Bruce Girard and Amy Mahan (2002), *Global Media Governance: A Beginner's Guide*, Boulder, CO: Rowan & Littlefield.

Smith, Michael Peter (2001), *Transnational Urbanism: Locating Globalization*, London: Blackwell.

Soley, Lawrence (1999), *Free Radio: Electronic Civil Disobedience*, Boulder, CO: Westview Press.

Spender, Dale (1995), *Nattering on the Net: Women, Power and Cyberspace*, Melbourne: Spinifex.

Spigel, Lynn (1992), *Make Room for TV: Television and the Family Ideal in Postwar America*, Chicago: University of Chicago Press.

Splichal, Slavko (1995), 'From state control to commodification: media democratisation in East and Central Europe', in F. Corcorran and P. Preston (eds), *Democracy and Communication in the New Europe: Change and Continuity in East and West*, Creskill, NJ: Hampton Press. pp. 51–65.

Staudt, Kathleen (1998), *Policy, Politics and Gender*, West Hartford, CT: Kumarian Press.

Steinmetz, George (1999), 'Culture and the state', in George Steinmetz (ed.), *State/Culture: State-Formation after the Cultural Turn*, Ithaca, NY: Cornell University Press, pp. 1–50.

Stepulevage, Linda (1999), 'Becoming a technologist: days in a girl's life', *Information, Communication & Society* 2 (4): 399–418.

Stiglitz, Joseph (1998), 'More instruments and broader goals: moving beyond the Washington consensus', UNU World Institute for Development Economics Research (UNU WIDER): http://www.wider.unu.edu/publications/ annual-lectures/annual-lecture-1998.pdf: 34 (accessed on 17 February 2005).

Streeter, Thomas (1996), *Selling the Air: A Critique of the Policy of Commercial Broadcasting in the United States*, Chicago: University of Chicago Press.

Sussman, Gerald (1997), *Communication, Technology, and Politics in the Information Age*, London: Sage.

Sussman, Gerald (2001), 'Telecommunications after NAFTA: Mexico's integration strategy', in Vincent Mosco and Dan Schilled (eds), *Continental Order: Integrating North America for Cybercapitalism*, Boulder, CO: Rowan and Littlefield, pp. 136–62.

Taussig, Michael (1997), *The Magic of the State*, New York: Routledge.

Taylor, Peter (2004), 'The new geography of global civil society: NGOs in the world city network', *Globalizations* 1 (2): 2265–77.

Teivainen, Teivo (2003), 'The world social forum: arena or actor', *Third World Quarterly* 23 (4): 621–32.

Thussu, Daya K. (2000), *International Communication: Continuity and Change*, London: Arnold.

Tigre, Paulo Bastos (1999), *The Political Economy of Latin American Telecommunications: Multilateral Agreements and National Regulatory Systems*, Washington DC: World Bank. http://www1.worldbank.org/wbiep/trade/papers/Telecom.pdf.

Toros, Hilmi (2005), 'Big business shine at Information Society Summit', *Terraviva* 10 December. http://www.ipsterraviva.net/tv/tunis/viewstory.asp?idnews=393

Truong Thanh-Dam (1999), 'Gender and technology policy in Vietnam', *Gender, Technology and Development*, 3 (2): 215–34.

Tunstall, Jeremy (1977), *The Media Are American*, New York: Columbia University Press.

Turner, Eva (2001), 'The case for responsibility of the IT industry to promote equality for women in computing', *Science and Engineering Ethics*, 7: 247–60.

UNDP (1999), Development Report, New York: UNDP.

UNESCO (1980), *Many Voices One World: Communication and Society Today and Tomorrow*, The MacBride Report, Paris: UNESCO.

USA Communication (2000), Council for Trade in Services S/CSS/W/21. http://docsonline.wto.org

Vaidyanathan, Siva (2001), *Copyrights and Copywrongs: The Rise of Intellectual Property and How It Threatens Creativity*, New York: New York University Press.

Vartanova, Elena and Yassen Zassoursky (1995), 'Television in Russia: is the concept of the PSB relevant?', in G. F. Lowe and T. Hujanen (eds), *Broadcasting and Convergence: New Articulations of the Public Service Remit*, Göteborg: NORDICOM, pp. 93–108.

Venkatesh Viswanath and Michael G. Morris (2000), 'Why don't men ever stop to ask for directions? Gender, social influence, and their role in technology acceptance and usage behavior', *Mis Quarterly* 24 (1): 115–39.

Venturelli, S. (2002), 'Inventing e-regulation in the US, EU and East Asia: conflicting social visions of the Information Society', *Telematics and Informatics* 18: 69–90.

Verdery, Katherine (1996), *What Was Socialism, and What Comes Next?*, Princeton, NJ: Princeton University Press.

Vipond, Mary and John Jackson (2002), 'The public/private tension in broadcasting: the Canadian experience with convergence', paper presented at the RIPE Conference 17–19 January, Helsinki.

Virnoche, Mary E. and Matt Lessem (2006), '*The ABCs of Internet negotiation: wiring teachers on the fringes*', in K. Sarikakis and D. K. Thussu, *Ideologies of the Internet*, Cresskill, NJ: Hampton Press (in press).

Voss, Lex Heerma van and Marcel van der Linden (2002), *Class and Other Identities: Gender, Religion, and Ethnicity in the Writing of European Labor History*, New York: Beghahn Books.

Wade, Robert and Frank Veneroso (1998), 'The Asian crisis: high-debt model and the IMF-Wall Street complex', *New Left Review*, March/April: 5–28.

Waisbord, Sylvio and Nancy Morris (eds)(2001), *Media and Globalization: Why the State Matters*, Boulder, CO: Rowan and Littlefield.

Wajcman, Judy (2004), *Technofeminism*, London: Polity Press.

Webster, Frank (2002), *Theories of the Information Society* 2nd edn, London: Routledge.

Webster, Juliet (1999), 'Technological work and women's prospects in the knowledge economy: an agenda for research', *Information, Communication & Society* 2 (2): 201–21.

Wellenius, Bjorn (1997), 'Telecom reform: how to succeed', *Public Policy Journal*, The World Bank. http://rru.worldbank.org/PublicPolicyJournal/Summary.aspx?id=130

Wellenius, Bjorn and Peter Stern (eds)(1994), *Implementing Reforms in the Telecommunications Sector: Lessons from Experience*, Washington DC: The World Bank.

Williams, Mary F. (n.d.), *Access and Merit: A Debate on Encouraging Women in Science and Engineering*. http://www-unix.umbc.edu/~koreman/wnst/links_sci.htm (accessed on 1 November 2002).

Williams, Raymond (1976), *Communications*, 3rd edn, Harmondsworth: Penguin.

Wing, Susanna D. (2002), 'Women activists in Mali: the global discourse on human rights', in Nancy Naples and Manisha Desai (eds), *Women's Activism and Globalization: Linking Local Struggles and Transnational Politics*, New York: Routledge, pp. 172–88.

Winseck, Dwayne (1995), 'Power shift?: Towards a political economy of Canadian telecommunications regulation', *Canadian Journal of Communications* 20 (1): http://info.wlu.ca/~wwwpress/jrls/cjc/BackIssues/20.1/winseck.html (accessed on 14 November 2003).

Winseck, Dwayne (1997), 'Power shift?: Towards a political economy of Canadian telecommunications and regulation', *Canadian Journal of Communication [Online]* 20 (2). http://info.wlu.ca/~wwwpress/jrls/cjc/BackIssues/20.1/winseck.html

Winseck, Dwayne (1998), *Reconvergence: A Political Economy of Telecommunications in Canada*, Creskill, NJ: Hampton Press.

Winseck, Dwayne (2002), 'The WTO, emerging policy regimes and the political economy of transnational communications', in Marc Raboy (ed.), *Global*

Media Policy in the New Millennium, Luton: University of Luton Press, pp. 19–38.

World Summit on the Information Society (WSIS)(2002a), *Extract of the Report of the First Session of the Inter-Agency Network on Women and Gender Equality*, document WSIS/PC-1?CONTR/13-E. www.itu.int/dms_pub/itu-s/md/02/wsispc1/c/S02-WSISPC1-C-0013!!MSW-E.doc (accessed on 30 August 2005).

World Summit on the Information Society (WSIS)(2002b), *Proposed Themes for the Summit and Possible Outcomes*, document WSIS/PC-1/DOC/4-E 31 May 2002. www.itu.int/dms_pub/itu-s/md/ 02/wsispc1/doc/S02-WSISPC1-DOC-0004!!MSW-E.doc (accessed on 3 June 2004).

World Summit on the Information Society (WSIS)(2002c), *Reflections of the European Union*, document WSIS/PC-1CONTR/3-E. http://www.itu.int/wsis/

World Summit on the Information Society (WSIS)(2002d), *United States of America*, document WSIS/PC-1/CONTR/9-E. http://www.itu.int/wsis/

World Summit on the Information Society (WSIS)(2003), *Declaration of Principles: Building the Information Society: A Global Challenge in the New Millennium ITU*. http://www.itu.int/wsis/docs/geneva/official/dop.html

WSIS Civil Society (2003), 'Civil Society priorities document (15 July 2003)', presented to the Intersessional Meeting, Paris 15–18 July 2003. http://www.wsis-si.org/intersession-DOCS/WSIS-CS-CT-Paris-071503.html

WSIS Gender Caucus (2002), Key Recommendations of the WSIS Gender Caucus, 'The African regional preparatory meeting for the Word Summit on the Information Society WSIS, Bamako, Mali 25–30 May 2002 at http://www.wougnet.org/WSIS/wsisgrecommendations.html

Wunsch-Vincent, Sasha (2003), 'The digital trade agenda of the U.S.', *Aussenwirtschaft*, 58, Jahrgang (I): 7–46.

Young, Iris (2000), *Inclusion and Democracy*, Oxford: Oxford University Press.

Zauchner, Sabine, C. Korunka, A. Weiss and A. Kafka-Lutzow (2000), 'Gender-related effects of information technology implementation', *Gender and Information Technology*, 7 (2): 119–32.

Zernetskaya, O. V. (1996), 'Ukraine: public broadcasting between state and market', in M. Raboy (ed.), *Public Broadcasting for the 21st Century*, Luton: John Libbey Media/University of Luton Press, pp. 195–211.

Zhao, Yuezhi (2004), 'Between a world summit and a Chinese movie: visions of the "Information Society" ', *Gazette* 66: 275–80.

Zhao, Yuezhi (2005), 'China and global capital: the cultural dimension', in Leo Panitch and Colin Leys (eds), *The Socialist Register: The Empire Reloaded*, London: Merlin Press 197–217.

Zhao, Yuezhi and Dan Schiller (2001), 'Dances with wolves: China's integration into digital capitalism', *Info*, 3 (2): 135–50.

Index